Back to the Source

The Spiritual Principles Of Jesus

Dr. Mic Hunter

ISBN-10: 1453803696
EAN-13 9781453803691

Disclaimer
The author makes reference to, and quotes from, materials produced by various Twelve Step-based fellowships including Alcoholics Anonymous. The opinions and ideas expressed here are completely those of the author and do not reflect the position of A.A. or any other fellowship based on the Twelve Steps. None of these fellowships endorse or oppose any cause including the contents of this book.

Dedication

To Jesus-who got it right,

And to my mother Norma-

Who was more interested in developing her spirituality

Than following social convention,

And who supported me in finding my own path to God

Acknowledgements

My thanks to Stephen Parker, Ph.D., of Northland Therapy, Mark Umbreit, Ph.D., from the University of Minnesota's Center for Restorative Justice and Peacemaking, Father John Clay of Saint Stanislaus Catholic Church, Reverend Rob Eller-Isaacs of Unity Unitarian Church, and Kate An Hunter, D.V.M., for their thoughtful reading of my first draft and their helpful comments, and to Norma Hunter for her repeated proof reading. This is a better book because of them.

Table Of Contents

Section III-Living Life According To The Principles Taught By Jesus

Foreword

During the many years I have practiced as a psychotherapist I have seen hundreds of people eager to develop spiritually. Some arrive with little or no experience with spirituality, while others come with a long cherished relationship with their religious tradition. Still others have rejected not only religion but God as well, because members of the clergy sexually abused them. I have also witnessed people who had long thought of themselves as Christians move from having a superficial understanding of the life of Jesus to a deep respect for what he taught and an equally strong desire to live a life based on these principles. Regardless of their histories, all of these people benefited from examining their spiritual beliefs and learning how to apply them to enhance their lives. It has been a fascinating and moving experience to be a part of their journey; it is something that has changed me as much as it changed them. Spirituality is an individual's personal connection with a power greater than oneself, usually called God. Spirituality is the reason religions developed. Religion is an expression of one's spirituality in a prescribed manner as agreed upon by fellow believers, which usually involves specific rituals. The focus of this book is the spirituality of Jesus rather than the religion of Christianity. One needn't be a Christian to benefit from it, and those who are practicing Christians will gain a deeper understanding of Jesus. According to *The Book Of Matthew* (7:28) the people who actually heard Jesus were, "astonished at his teaching." Nearly two thousand years later what he taught is still astonishing people. In Emmet Fox's book, *The Sermon On The Mount,* he claimed; "Wisdom is the perfect blending of intelligence and love."[1] Intelligence without love is cold and unfeeling, while love without intelligence for guidance leads to unintended harm despite good intentions. If you don't already think that the principles Jesus taught were the right mixture of intelligence and love by the time you finish this book you will.

In 2009 *Newsweek* published a cover story titled, "The Decline and Fall of Christian America." The author, Jon Meacham, pointed out that from 1990 to 2009 the number of Americans who claimed no religious affiliation nearly doubled (8% to 15%), and that the percentage of American who identified themselves as Christians dropped (86% to 76%). During this same time there was a steady increase in the number of Americans, sometimes referred to as "the seculars," who weren't connected to a particular religious institution, but still had a relationship with God that they cherished. Although many people are able to express their spirituality in Christian churches, there are a significant number who don't because they find the importance many congregations place on the miraculous aspect of the stories in the Bible troubling rather than comforting. However, they are still very much attracted to the teachings of Jesus. One such person, Anne Graham Lotz, the daughter of evangelist Billy Graham described herself as, "a believer in exile" as she wandered from church to church looking for, "a home." As a result of her search she came to believe as long as one has a personal relationship with Jesus one's denomination really doesn't matter. In fact, she went so far as to say that some religions have become so focused on creeds, ritual, and dogma that it becomes, "an impediment to knowing God."[2]

More and more people are shifting their attention from the stories of miracles to the simple yet profound teachings of Jesus. They aren't interested in endlessly debating the details of the stories in the Bible or attempting to prove them. For the most part they forgo attempts to convert others to their faith, instead putting their energy into truly living in accordance with the principles that Jesus taught.

In other words, this second coming is appearing in the form of people, and I count myself among them, getting back to the original teaching of Jesus.

Columnist E. J. Dionne Jr. has watched the changes in how the teachings of Jesus are understood. He isn't worried that the central message of Jesus' teaching will be lost because of, "the adaptability of its core message." Mr. Dionne celebrated the fact that, "conservative Christians themselves are rediscovering the Church's mission to the poor, the sick, the strangers and outcasts. This [indicates] new life, not decay." He concluded, "Grace is never cheap, and a Christianity that is struggling with itself is on the path of rediscovering its true calling."[3]

Of course, I have been on my own personal journey to find God. As a child I was raised in a family that attended a Christian church on a regular basis. My father said grace at the beginning of meals and my mother prayed with us at bedtime. She sang in the choir and taught Sunday school. I was enrolled in confirmation courses, and sincerely believed what I was being taught. I was an eager student and wanted to know all I could about any subject I was studying, so I asked a lot of questions. I expected that my teachers would be delighted with a genuinely curious student, so I was shocked when they told me to stop asking questions because it showed I had a lack of faith. I began to wonder what kind of a religion is afraid of the questions of a little boy, but I still believed in God and Jesus. However, over time I eventually decided not only was Jesus not my personal savior, but also that God didn't exist. I turned my life over to drugs, sex, and rock and roll (not necessarily in order of importance). Fortunately after some years when I joined a group of spiritually minded people I rekindled my belief in the existence of God. Then I returned to my long neglected study of religion and Jesus; this book is the result of those efforts.

As we examine the principles Jesus taught his original followers, I will frequently illustrate them using examples from Twelve Step-based mutual-help programs such as Alcoholics Anonymous. I will use examples from these groups, not merely because of my general respect for them, but primarily because I think they are excellent examples of how the teachings of Jesus can be applied in today's world. In my many years as a psychotherapist, I have been impressed by how these groups that consist of people from all ethnic backgrounds, income levels, and religions manage to function together without any leaders who impose beliefs or enforce behaviors. In these groups, anyone is free to declare him or herself a member and to agree or disagree with any of the principles of the Twelve Steps. Since A.A. was created, people from around the world have successfully adapted Twelve Step principles to cope with all types of afflictions. Members of these groups are some of the most kind, generous, and spiritual people I have ever met. I have no doubt that Jesus would approve of them regardless of whether they considered themselves to be Christians or not. Given that Jesus was described in the New Testament as a glutton and a drunkard (*Matthew* 11:19; *Luke* 7:34), if he were around today, he might even be attending Twelve Step meetings. One of the men who would go on to help found A.A., Bill W., was fond of telling a story about when an old drinking buddy, Ebby, showed up and told him he had quit drinking and added, "I've got religion!" Bill thought he was hearing, "The ranting of an alcoholic crackpot."[4] Not only Bill, but many of the early members of A.A. had troubled relationships with religion, particularly those religions they viewed as "churchy," those that constantly reminded alcoholics they were sinners and self-righteously looked down on them. Over time most of the early A.A. members overcame their resentments about religion and were able to benefit from the teachings of Jesus. Some of the earliest members of what was to become A.A. thought *The Book of James* was so useful to their recovery they considered calling their fellowship the "James Club."[5] The two men most credited with starting A.A., Bill W. and Dr. Bob, both said that Jesus' Sermon on the Mount was the foundation of the philosophy of the Twelve Steps. Just as the founders of A.A. learned important lessons by following the example of Jesus, we can learn valuable lessons from the wisdom of the Twelve Step program on applying the teachings of Jesus to our lives.

Theology is a very personal thing, and there is much disagreement between religions and even within religions. This has been true since the beginning of religion itself. Disagreements about the teachings of Jesus were raging even in Biblical times. In the fourth chapter of his letter to the Philippians, Paul referred to a disagreement between two members of the early church and encouraged them, "to come to a mutual understanding in the Lord." I have no doubt that some people will find some aspect of what I have written unsettling; but as you read please keep in mind that truth fears no questions. Thomas Kuhn once observed, "The answers you get depend upon the questions you ask." David Bayles and Ted Orland expressed a similar sentiment when they wrote, "Over the long run, the people with the interesting answers are those who ask the interesting questions."[6] I hope the questions I raise in this book assist you in better understanding the Bible, your relationship with Jesus, and yourself as a spiritual person. In 2005, in Georgia, a federal judge was asked to rule on whether public school textbooks ought to have a warning label that read, "This textbook contains material on evolution. This material should be approached with an open mind, studied carefully, and critically considered."[7] Maybe this book you are now reading ought to have such a label; "This book contains material on religion. This material should be approached with an open mind, studied carefully, and critically considered." Or better yet a sticker that quotes the Reverend Billy Graham; "What we all need to do is return to the Bible afresh-not going to it to prove a point, but seeing what it says as the Holy Spirit opens our eyes."[8] I sincerely hope you will take his counsel, and that what I have written will help you to better apply the teachings of Jesus to your own life.

Mic Hunter

"To insure a long existence to religious sects or republics, it is necessary frequently to bring them back to their original principles."

Machiavelli (1469-1527 A.D.)

Questions To Help In Personal Reflection Or Group Discussion

What first motivated you to consider reading this book?

What do you hope to gain by reading this book? (Once you have finished reading the text and answering the questions I have provided throughout the book come back to this question and see if you got what you had hoped for or something else.)

Section I

What Jesus Taught

The Principles Taught By Jesus

When people say, "The Bible says..." that covers a lot of text, but if we limit ourselves to what Jesus said, then the amount of words we have to work with becomes quite small. Although the Bible contains many verses about Jesus, the actual number of words attributed to him is relatively small, approximately 2000, depending on the version of the Bible one is consulting. Just the foreword to this book contains about 1800 words! Since Jesus' teaching methods included metaphors and parables the lessons he sought to convey aren't always obvious, and therefore require thoughtful study. Jesus wasn't purposely being difficult or speaking in some form of code so that only those in the know could understand; he had to resort to symbolism because ordinary language was inadequate to fully convey what he was attempting to explain to people.

Long before me, others have tried to summarize of the teachings of Jesus. Christian theologian and founder of the Evangelical Methodist movement John Wesley (1703 – 1791 A.C.E) provided this simple summary:

Do all the good you can,
By all the means you can,
In all the ways you can,
In all the places you can,
At all the times you can,
To all the people you can,
As long as you can.

More recently Monika Hellwig, a Georgetown University theologian, head of the Association of Catholic Colleges and Universities, and author of many books, wrote of Jesus:

> His message was to look not to self-defense but to the needs of the other; to be most concerned about those in greatest need; not to ask what people deserve but what they need; not to defend one's rights by violence but by a simple challenge to conscience, to be concerned at all times with seeing that the will of God is accomplished in the society, trusting that all other needs will be met; to judge people by what they do and not by the words and banners in which they declare their loyalties; to take no revenge but to de-escalate violence and evil by initiating a different style of life and pattern of relationships; to live simply and avoid grabbing and hoarding and enriching oneself because it does not increase happiness but only makes barriers against others and adds anxiety; not to be worried about saving one's life but always ready to give it.[9]

Although these are excellent summaries of the teachings of Jesus in order to put his teachings fully into practice, a deeper understanding of them is required. Therefore we will examine the principles that underlie all of Jesus' teaching. These principles can be applied to the thoughts and actions related to one's relationships with God, oneself, and with other people. The principles Jesus taught combined to form a coherent philosophy in which none of the principles contradicted one another, and many of them overlap so that what is true about one principle is equally true for another. This is one reason they have continued to be studied for two thousand years.

The Principles Taught By Jesus

Your Relationship With God

-Remember everyday is judgment day-so behave as if you will be meeting with God tonight not in the distant future

-Believe God is not only great, God is also good

-Focus your prayers on requests for sustenance, forgiveness, for assistance in forgiving others, and being strong in the face of temptation and evil

Your Relationships With Others

-Treat people the way you want God to treat you

-Treat everyone the way you want to be treated by other people

-Remember the wellbeing of others is more important than following rules

-Stop judging other people

-Focus on your behavior rather than on the behavior of others

-Be compassionate

-Be forgiving

-Love

-Remember we are all one people

-Serve others

-Remember everyone is worthy of our loving attention

-Remember to love your enemy
-Wage peace and use non-violent resistance to fight injustice

Your Relationship With Yourself
-Be humble and focus on interpersonal relationships rather than rank or status
-Remember faith isn't sufficient, so act on your beliefs
-Live fully today

Questions To Help In Personal Reflection Or Group Discussion

What do you think of John Wesley's summary of the teachings of Jesus?

What parts of Monika Hellwig's summary of the teachings of Jesus do you agree with and with which don't you agree?

In reviewing the principles listed in The Principles Taught By Jesus are there any of them you don't think fit with the teachings of Jesus? Are there any principles that ought to be included, but aren't?

Q: What Day Is Today?

A: Judgment Day

"What will I do when God confronts me?
What will I answer when called to account?"

Job 31:14

No doubt Jesus would have approved of Ralph Waldo Emerson's journal entry; "No man has learned anything until he knows that every day is the Judgment Day." Unlike many people in our time, Jesus didn't think judgment day would occur in the far off distant future or that a Second Coming was required. When he said, "Now is the judgment of this world" (*John* 12:31), and, "We are judged at every encounter with our neighbor," (*Matthew* 25:40) he was pointing out that judgment day occurs each and every day. Alcoholics, drug addicts, and people with similar afflictions know all too well that each day is judgment day for them. Any relapse could be the one that is fatal. I have heard more than one patient declare, "I know I have another relapse in me, but I don't know if I have another recovery left." They know the harsh result of addiction can be incarceration or death. Those who forget this fact pay for their lack of vigilance. I know many people who decided to get high, "just one last time" the night before going to check into a drug treatment program. Unfortunately for some of them it was indeed their, "last time," because that was the occasion they died of an overdose.

When I tell people my job involves working with addicts they often respond, "That must be depressing." In fact, most of the time it is exactly the opposite, it is invigorating. People who know they have to pay attention to their spiritual fitness on a daily basis in order to remain sober take their spirituality much more seriously than those people who think of death and judgment day as an event in the distant future that can be ignored or merely given lip service. Imagine your reaction if on a regular basis the clergy at your place of worship announced that another member of your congregation had been sent to prison, committed suicide, or had died because of not being diligent in their spiritual practice. No doubt it would get your attention and cause you to take stock of your own spiritual condition. This is exactly what members of Alcoholic Anonymous, Narcotics Anonymous, and other Twelve Step fellowships experience; their spirituality can't afford to be something that only exists in theory or is practiced superficially. This level of commitment is what leads some members to describe themselves as, "grateful recovering addicts," because their affliction put them in a situation in which they had to make a decision to take spirituality seriously thereby growing emotionally, psychologically, and spiritually in ways they had never imagined. Such a person was Reverend Jo [sic] Campe.[10] In 1999 he was assigned to the United Methodist Church in Minneapolis where eleven people attended the first service he officiated. He hung in and eventually he oversaw the creation of two churches in two cities with eight hundred members. Given that some mega-churches boast of having thousands of members this may not seem like that much of an accomplishment, but these two little churches specialized in ministering to addicts, practicing and sober, and their loved ones. Reverend Campe was no beginner when he began the first Recovery Church. He had already earned a master's degree in divinity from United Seminary and a doctorate from Princeton Theological Seminary, spoken at some of the largest Methodist congregations, and could debate the fine points of theological issues with the best of them. But Reverend Campe knew that theory was of little use to practicing addicts; "I've spoken on a podium with a choir behind me, and it was a great style for those churches. But this church is filled with people who understand life differently. They know if they don't change the way they are living, they are going to die." Given the makeup of his congregation Reverend Campe frequently officiated at the funerals of young people; "I'm standing in front of a casket of a 19-year-old girl who died of an overdose, and I'm supposed to say something to her parents, try to explain to them this crazy disease" [addiction]. He also had a more difficult time keeping track of the whereabouts of his congregation; it wasn't uncommon for someone to attend every service for months and then suddenly disappear. He never knew if they left town, were incarcerated, relapsed, or had died. Despite all these challenges, Reverend Campe remained hopeful; "So many lives have been saved because of what the people do here and how much they care...If there's a place anyone should be accepted, it's in church." Reverend Campe knew all too well that A.A. co-founder Bill W. was correct when he said, "A dying man is open to suggestion." Reverend Campe's message was simple; "Alcohol is not the problem; life is the problem. There is a power that heals you by giving you a different way of life... We stress how things can turn around, how Christianity can work." Of course one needn't be an addict in order to make one's spirituality an important focus of one's daily living; we are all going to die someday, and none of us knows exactly when. Saint Francis of Assisi, (1182-1226 A.C.E.) who is usually shown surrounded by cute woodland creatures, was portrayed in 1639 (A.C.E.) by painter Francisco de Zurbaranin in *Saint Francis In Meditation* with a human skull because when Francis signed his letters he drew a little skull by his name. He did this to remind his readers they will die and can never know when.

Why does the Almighty not set times for judgment?"

Job 24:1

Jesus taught that today is the day to live according to spiritual principles. This was never more obvious to me then when I worked in a hospice with terminally ill patients and their families; I saw on a daily basis how the awareness of the imminence of death can motivate people to focus on their relationships with their loved ones and God instead of material concerns. One day I returned to the hospice after being away for several days to find that several patients had died while I was gone. I felt sad and a little guilty I hadn't said goodbye to them when I left to go on my trip. I vowed that every day before leaving the hospice I would say goodbye to every patient. That evening I went from one room to another letting them know I was leaving for the day and saying goodbye. When I said goodbye to one man he asked, "Why are you saying goodbye?" I responded, "Well, because you might not be here when I get back." With a smile he said, "What makes you think you'll be coming back? I'm sick, but you're going out in the world where you could get hit by a car, tumble down some stairs, fall in the shower, or be killed in some other accident. I'm not at risk for any of that in here!" We both laughed because he was right. I had assumed that since he had an incurable illness that he would die before me, but in fact who really knew which of us would be alive tomorrow? I thanked him for his wisdom and went home. The next day I was leaving for work in a rush because I had hit the snooze button once too often. I had neglected to kiss my wife goodbye because she was in the shower and I was afraid I was going to be late for work. As I got into my car I promised myself I would give her two kisses when I got home that evening. Then I imagined the man in the hospice saying, "What makes you think you'll ever be coming back to your house, or that your wife will be there if you do come home?" I quickly got out of the car, ran into the house, kissed my wife, and told her that I loved her.

Nearly everyday in my work as a psychotherapist, I see people who postpone living a life according to the principles Jesus taught because they believe they have years yet to live. Once I was working with a middle-aged couple who were fighting about how to spend their weekends. He wanted to spend many of them at a lake cabin that had been in his family for generations where he had enjoyed many happy times. She didn't like the cabin because it had belonged to in-laws whom she didn't like when they were alive. Once in a great while she would reluctantly go to the cabin, but then would spend the entire time complaining and trying to make her husband's weekend miserable. The wife wasn't opposed to cabins in general, just the one that her in-laws had owned. She said she would be glad to go to a different cabin with her husband, if only he would sell the family's cabin and buy a different one. The husband was in a bind because it seemed like he had to choose spending time at his favorite place or spending time with his favorite person somewhere else, but that he couldn't have both. In one session I asked the woman, "What would you do if you knew for a fact that your husband was ill and had only a short time to live?" Without hesitation she responded, "I would take him up to the cabin and take care of him until he died." Then I asked, "Would you be willing to go the cabin this weekend and treat him like the two of you didn't have much more time to be together?" She refused, insisting that it was a silly request since he wasn't ill and he certainly had many more years to live. Jesus didn't teach us to be kind and loving only towards dying people; he taught us to kind and loving to all people everyday. People know if you love them by the way you treat them today and everyday. In America we spend five times more dollars on medical expenses during the very last year of a person's life than are spent for any other year of life.[11] Whether there is a good reason for that is debatable, but what is clear is that there is no reason to give people five times more love and kindness in the last year of their lives when we can love them fully everyday regardless of their health.

Q: What Day Is Today?
A: The Sabbath Day

"Behold now is the day of salvation."
Jesus (2 *Corinthians* 6:1-2)

"We should live our lives as though [Jesus] were coming this afternoon."
U.S. President Jimmy Carter

The corollary to, "each day is judgment day" is, "every day is the Sabbath." According to *Exodus* God told Moses 1400 years before the birth of Jesus, that we were to remember the Sabbath and keep it holy. The word *holy* has several relevant definitions:

Relating to, belonging to, or coming from a divine being or power
Devoted to the service of God
Morally and spiritually perfect and of a devoutly religious character
Dedicated or set apart for religious purposes
Of a unique character, evoking reverence
Something sanctified or venerated.[12]

As an indication that they were keeping the Sabbath holy the Jews in Jesus' time performed no work on that day of the week. However, the Bible tells of Jesus violating God's commandment by performing work on the Sabbath. Jesus insisted the Sabbath was created for people, rather than people having been created for the Sabbath. Jesus did everything, whether he was engaged in work, rest, or play, with spiritual principles in mind, thereby making everyday holy. This point is illustrated in this story of a minister and a farmer. On his way home from Sunday services a minister came upon a member of his congregation plowing a field preparing it for planting. The minister approached the farmer and scolded the farmer; "I noticed you didn't attend either service today, and what's more now I find you performing work on the Sabbath." "Well," replied the farmer as he wiped sweat from his brow, "I figured God would rather have me out here plowing and thinking about spiritual matters than sitting in church thinking about plowing."

"Remember the weekday, to keep it holy."

Elbert Hubbard [13]

Questions To Help In Personal Reflection Or Group Discussion

Do you believe that after death, people face judgment before God?

If so, are you prepared today to face that judgment?

If not, what would you want to do to prepare to meet God?

How does the idea that judgment day is today and every day affect your view of how you live your life?

If you knew for a fact that you had only a few months or weeks to live, how would that information affect the way you treat your loved ones today?
Is there somebody in your life you have caused harm to whom you would make amends?

Is there somebody you would forgive for harming you?

The farmer claimed, "God would rather have me out here plowing and thinking about spiritual matters than sitting in church thinking about plowing." Do you agree or disagree? List the rules and principles you used to decide whether he was correct or not.

Given the definitions of *holy*, how holy are you treating today?

God Is Not Merely Great, God Is Good

"None of us can be as great as God,
but any of us can be as good."

Mark Twain[14]

More than once I have heard someone complimented or eulogized as, "a God fearing person." I find myself wondering why God fearing? Why not God loving? To me developing a relationship with God based on mutual love is more admirable than one based on fear. One reason for this focus on God fearing is that much of the Hebrew Bible or Old Testament focused on the greatness of God- the ability to perform incredible feats such as the parting of the sea or bringing down fire from the sky: "Be exalted, O LORD, in thy strength! We will sing and praise thy power (*Psalms* 21:13), and; "Come, behold the works of the LORD, how he has wrought desolations in the earth" (*Psalms* 46:8). In the New Testament Jesus focused his attention, not so much on the greatness of God, but more on God's goodness-God's remarkable ability to love. People who focus more heavily on the greatness of God tend to be those who admire power, value justice over forgiveness, and live in fear of God's wrath. Those people who focus more on the goodness of God are in awe of God's ability to forgive and love. Therefore they seek to please God, not out of fear, but out of affection and gratitude. Jesus' focus on the goodness of God is particularly significant considering the numerous Old Testament verses that directed people to fear God. The authors of the Hebrew Bible/Old Testament feared God because they viewed God as jealous, angry, and dangerous: "The LORD your God in the midst of you is a jealous God; lest the anger of the LORD your God be kindled against you, and he destroy you from the face of the earth" (*Deuteronomy* 6:14).

Old Testament Verses on Fearing God

"You shall **fear** your God."

Leviticus 19:14

"You shall **fear** your God."

Leviticus 19:32

"You shall **fear** your God."

Leviticus 25:17

"**Fear** your God."

Leviticus 25:36

"**Fear** your God."

Leviticus 25:43

"You shall **fear** the LORD your God."

Deuteronomy 6:13

"You shall **fear** the LORD your God."

Deuteronomy 10:20

"You shall walk after the LORD your God and **fear** him."

Deuteronomy 13:4

"He may learn to **fear** the LORD our God."

Deuteronomy 17:19

"Assemble the people, men, women, and little ones, and the [visitors] to your towns, that they may hear and learn to **fear** the LORD your God."

Deuteronomy 31:12

"You may **fear** the LORD your God forever."

Joshua 4:24

"Ought you not walk in the **fear** of God?"

Nehemiah 5:9

"You shall not fear other gods, you shall **fear** the LORD God."

Second Kings 17:39

"And he said to them, 'I am a Hebrew, and I **fear** the LORD."

John: 1:9

"I know that it will be well with those who **fear** God."

Ecclesiastes 8:12

Fear God, and keep his commandments."

Ecclesiastes 12:13

"You will understand the **fear** of the LORD."

Proverbs 2:5

"Come and hear, all you who **fear** God."

Psalms 66:16

"God has blessed us; let all the ends of the earth **fear** him!"

Psalms 67:7

"If you will **fear** the LORD and serve him."

First Samuel 12:14

"Do you not **fear** me? Says the LORD."

Jeremiah 5:22

""'Let us **fear** the LORD our God."

Jeremiah 5:24

"Now then, let the **fear** of the LORD be upon you."

Second Chronicles 19:7

"The grandeur and majesty of God do not come to expression in the display of ultimate sovereignty and power, but rather in rendering righteousness and mercy."

Abraham Joshua Meschel[15]

Jesus focused not on fearing God, but on loving God. He said we ought to love God with all our heart, soul, and mind (*Matthew* 22:35-39). According to Jesus, God is generous, welcoming and kind: "Ask and it will be given to you; seek, and you will find; knock, and it will be opened to you. For every one who asks, receives, and he who seeks finds, and to him who knocks, it will be opened" (*Matthew* 7:7-8 & *Luke* 11:10). With his parable about the laborers in the vineyard, he taught that God is kind and generous (*Matthew*, 20:1-16). The laborers that worked only a very short time were paid exactly the same as those who had toiled all day. Anyone who thinks the moral of the story is the vineyard owner's payment schedule wasn't fair missed the point. The lesson of the story is that one can't work to gain more of God's favor than is given to others. God's grace is given freely and equally to all, and because it is a gift, it isn't earned. But many people continue to believe they must pay a great price to obtain God's love. In one of her songs Lucinda Williams, described what she was willing to do in order to, "get right with God," including; kissing a poisonous snake, burning the soles of her feet and the palms of her hands, and sleeping on a bed of nails until her back is torn and bleeding.[16] Jesus never indicated that God required anything like that. Self-injury was never something Jesus preached was necessary in order to be close to God. Quite the opposite, Jesus indicated that we are to love God, our neighbors, our enemies, and ourselves, not inflict injury.

Jesus used the parable commonly known as the prodigal son to illustrate that God is a loving and accepting even when we are foolish, wasteful, and sinful (*Luke* 15: 11-32).

In this story a man had a son who left home, squandered his inheritance, violated Jewish law by taking a job tending pigs, and then returned home. When the father recognized his son in the distance he rushed to him, and greeted him with hugs and kisses. The father then put on a great feast to celebrate the return of his son. He did all of this without insisting that his son beg for forgiveness or even admit he had done wrong. Nor did the father ever tell the son he was forgiven. The way this parent behaved is a model of the God in which Jesus believed; a God that joyfully rushes to the sinful, doesn't demand penance, and doesn't even need to forgive. Forgiveness from God isn't necessary because God doesn't take offense at our mistakes and foolish choices.

Over and over Jesus referred to God as being like a parent. Not only that but the Aramaic word *abba* he used when speaking to God is most accurately translated as *daddy*, which is a more affectionate term than the formal *father* (*Mark* 14:36). Like any devoted Earthly parent, God loves us not because we are happy and grateful, but in order to facilitate our becoming happy and grateful. A devoted parent patiently loves a child even when that child misbehaves, is stubborn, ungrateful, and crabby. Jesus focused, not on judgment and punishment by God, but on love and acceptance from God.

In Twelve Step groups, new comers are offered the assistance of a "sponsor," an experienced member who, much like a good parent serves as a source of support and guidance.[1] The sponsor assists the sponsee in working the Twelve Steps and, just as importantly, is a steady source of acceptance and emotional support. The sponsor accepts the sponsee in the good times of sobriety and in the bad times of relapse. I remember a patient who

---

1 In *The 12 Steps & Shame* (available through Hazelden Educational Materials) I explained in detail how the Twelve Steps are a shame reduction program.

told me how amazed he was at the level of support and acceptance his sponsor offered him; "He said I could call him any time of the night or day. He said I could call before I relapse, after I relapse, or even while I'm in the middle of a relapse. He told me, 'Now that you are in the program you never again have to face anything alone.' He's almost got me thinking I'm worthwhile person!" The sponsor accepts and treats the sponsee with loving-kindness even when the sponsee doesn't believe he is worthy of it until the sponsee can accept and develop self-love. Members of Twelve Step programs don't get acceptance and support because they are sober; they get and stay sober because of the acceptance and support they receive. Since many members of Twelve Step fellowships experienced neglect or abuse as children, their relationships with their sponsors may be the first time they have experienced unconditional acceptance. Once they have this experience with a sponsor they can more easily imagine having a similar relationship with God.

Just as a young child often doesn't understand the reasons behind her parents' behavior we often don't understand God. This lack of understanding may lead to anger. When Archbishop Desmond Tutu was asked if he ever doubted his faith he responded: "Doubts? No. Anger with God? Yes. Plenty of that. I've remonstrated [argued with] God quite frequently and said, 'What the heck are you up to? Why are you letting these oppressors get away with this injustice?' But doubting that God is good? That God is love? No."[17]

But not everyone agrees that God is loving and forgiving. The members of the Westboro Baptist Church in Topeka, Kansas insist that the belief that God loves everyone is, "Straight from Satan and the Most Damning Concept Known to Man." Furthermore they maintain the idea of a loving God is, "straight from the mind of Satan and his ministers that serve him."[18] It seems to me that these people have not grasped the primary message of the New Testament that is God isn't to be feared, but to love and be loved by. Whether this was due to God changing over the centuries between when the books of the Old Testament were written and the time of Jesus, or because our understanding of God matured, isn't important. What is important is the fact that the God portrayed in the New Testament is very different than the God described in the Old Testament. The Old Testament is filled with judgments that lead to punishment and death. Contrast this with the New Testament story of the adulterous woman (*John* 8: 1-11).

> The teachers of the law and the Pharisees brought in a woman caught in adultery. They made her stand before the group and said to Jesus, "Teacher, this woman was caught in the act of adultery. In the Law Moses commanded us to stone such women. Now what do you say?" They were using this question as a trap, in order to have a basis for accusing him. But Jesus bent down and started to write on the ground with his finger. When they kept on questioning him, he straightened up and said to them, "If any one of you is without sin, let him be the first to throw a stone at her." At this, those who heard began to go away one at a time, the older ones first, until only Jesus was left, with the woman still standing there. Jesus straightened up and asked her, "Woman, where are they? Has no one condemned you?" "No one, sir," she said. "Then neither do I condemn you," Jesus declared. "Go now and leave your life of sin."

Even though the woman had violated Old Testament law by the end of the story nobody condemned the woman, not the authority figures, not Jesus, and not even the woman herself. Is the moral of the story, do whatever you want, even if it violates religious or secular law, because your actions don't matter since everybody has done something wrong? No, Jesus made it clear he didn't approve of adulterous behavior, calling it a sin, but he refused to condemn the woman. Jesus behaved this way because he believed in a God that refuses to condemn.

As brother John Jacob Raub noted, some of the early followers of Jesus also had a difficult time grasping and believing in the God described by Jesus:

> Matthew is the most Old Testament of all the gospels, and we would expect to find a heavy emphasis on judgment and punishment[2] It is Matthew who repeatedly uses the phrase "weeping and gnashing of teeth" which is used nowhere else in the New Testament except once in Luke. In a similar vein, Matthew used the word "hell" about a dozen times, Mark and Luke three times each, and John and Paul who comprise the largest part of the New Testament, never mention it (p. 109).

Questions To Help In Personal Reflection Or Group Discussion

Which aspect of God gets more of your attention, greatness or goodness?

---

2 This is because *Matthew* was originally written to appeal to Jews who were used to an angry punitive God from reading the books of the Old Testament.

How does that affect your relationship with God and other people?

What do you think of Jesus' claim that God is kind and generous?

Is God's grace as a gift to be received or something to be earned?

Are you are worthy of God's grace?

If not, what would you have to do to be worthy?

Do you have someone that you can rely on to accept and support you in both the good times and the bad?

To whom have you offered that level of acceptance?

When have you been angry with God? What did you do about it? Do you think it is safe to express anger towards God or will you be punished?

Focus Your Prayers

"PRAY, v. To ask that the laws of the universe be annulled in behalf of a single petitioner confessedly unworthy."

Ambrose Bierce, *The Devil's Dictionary*

A Lot Of People Pray-A Lot

If the results of numerous surveys can be believed, then prayer is a popular and frequent activity in America. Less than one in ten Americans surveyed reported they never prayed, while two thirds of people said they prayed at least once a day, and almost a third reported praying several times a day.[19] People pray alone, with others, and on the telephone. On the Internet there are websites where people post requests for others to pray for a cause. Using technology in the service of prayer has been around since at least 1890 when the Unity church began offering prayers-by-mail. Anyone could write requesting that members of the church pray for him or her. In 1907 the church members started a telephone service that still exists as 1-800-Now-Pray, and later they added a prayer service to their web site. By 2008 they were receiving 200,000 prayer requests from the Internet, 500,000 by mail, and 1.3 million by telephone. In 2009 Joel Gross, age 25, founded the Internet site Prayer Helpers. For $9.99 Prayer Helpers would pray for you. This service was designed for people who had some private issues and weren't comfortable asking friends or family to pray for them. Mr. Gross, an agnostic was not the person praying; instead his longtime friend, who had studied religion and was a Christian, did the actual praying. Prayer Helpers offered a free prayer to customers who wanted to try the service without risking any money. Mr. Gross explained; "We are so confident in the power of our Prayer Helpers to petition God on your behalf, in a fashion that leaves you totally satisfied, that we are offering an absolutely free prayer trial. We know that after you try our free prayer service, you will come back to us for every important issue that you need the help of God to resolve." Not long after came an Internet subscription service, Information Age Prayer, which used a computer with text-to-speech capability to incant prayers for people who were too busy to do it themselves: "The service gives you the satisfaction of knowing that your prayers will always be said even if you wake up late, or forget. We use state of the art text to speech synthesizers to voice each prayer at a volume and speed equivalent to typical person praying. Each prayer is voiced individually, with the name of the subscriber displayed on screen." Subscribers could choose prayers from six categories-Jewish, Muslim, Catholic, Protestant, "other religions," and "unaffiliated." The cost varied, depending on your denomination and what prayer service was desired. A Catholic could get the Lord's Prayer for $3.95 a month, or the computer could recite a Hail Mary in the customer's name for seven cents.[20] As an incentive to try the service, a free prayer "for luck" was offered. In the Company of Prayer was specifically aimed at entrepreneurs and executives aiming to, "provide a quick, daily prayer specifically to businessmen and women, who, like us, find prayer to be an inspirational tool in the management of our professional lives." In 2010 a group of Catholics working for the French telephone-company AABAS set up the Line of the Lord so that other Catholics could confess without having to go to church and meet with a priest. Callers are offered an, "atmosphere of piety and reflection," in which they can listen to church music, get advice on confessing, make a confession, or even listen to other people's confessions.

The Conference of French Bishops disapproved of the service, but in the first week it received 300 calls.

And You Pray For…?

"If only God would give me some clear sign!
Like making a large deposit in my name in a Swiss bank."
Woody Allen, American comedian

Minnesota storyteller, Kevin Kling, looked back over his life and found that his prayers had changed over time. When he was a child his prayers consisted exclusively of asking God to give him things. One Christmas he prayed to Jesus to tell Santa to give him the spider monkey he had seen advertised in the back of a comic book. By the time he was a teenager, his prayers had changed; now he was begging God to get him out of dangerous situations in which he had put himself. Something to the effect of, "God if you just get me out of this, I promise I'll never do anything so stupid ever again. And this time, I really mean it!" Having survived adolescence and young adulthood mostly intact, his prayers again changed. He no longer was asking God for something, instead his prayers consisted of expressing gratitude to God (however, he still coveted a spider monkey).

Anne McCaffrey, a physician at the Harvard Medical School, used the results of a national telephone survey of 2,055 people to determine how people used prayer and found that about thirty-five percent of them asked for help with their health. Of those who prayed seventy-five percent prayed to stay healthy and twenty-two percent prayed for relief from all types of illness including allergies, depression, headaches, back pain, cancer, and heart problems.[21] A quick glance at sites such as Prayabout.com and Ourprayer.org shows that some people pray for very specific outcomes. For example, one woman asked that people pray for her husband to listen to his psychiatrist and that the psychiatrist would see that her husband had, "major issues that need to be worked on ASAP."[22] We have no evidence that Jesus ever prayed for God to intercede in politics or sporting events; but that hasn't stopped many people from encouraging God to intervene on behalf of their favorite team or political party. During the 2008 presidential election Reverend Arnold Conrad was worried if the candidate he supported didn't win God's reputation would be damaged: "There are millions of people around the world praying to their god –whether it's Hindu, Buddha, Allah-that his opponent wins, for a variety of reasons. And Lord, I pray that you would guard your own reputation because they're going to think that their god is bigger than you if that happens."[23] During the 1966 World Cup between England and Argentina player Diego Maradona made a controversial, and game winning, goal. After the soccer game he claimed the goal was due in part to his skill, and in part to, "the hand of God." In 2007 when the Colorado Rockies baseball team qualified for the World's Series, the management and players credited God for their victories. "You look at some of the moves we made and didn't make. You look at some of the games we're winning. Those aren't just a coincidence. God has definitely had a hand in this," declared general manager and born again Christian, Dan O'Dowd.[24] In 2003 Christian broadcaster Pat Robertson urged his television audience to pray for God to remove three justices from the Supreme Court, so that they could be replaced by people more to Mr. Robertson's liking; "We ask for miracles in regard to the Supreme Court," Mr. Robertson announced on the Christian Broadcasting Network program *The 700 Club*. He then launched a twenty-one day, "prayer offensive" directed at the Supreme Court Justices. In a letter to supporters, he wrote; "One justice is 83-years-old, another has cancer and another has a heart condition. Would it not be possible for God to put it in the minds of these three judges that the time has come to retire?"[25] Pastor Rodney McGill went even farther than praying for those with whom he disagreed to retire. Prior to being sentenced to twenty years in prison for real-estate fraud he prayed aloud in the court room: "Jesus, Jesus, Jesus, for every witness called against me, I pray cancer in their lives, lupus, brain tumor, pancreatic cancer."[26]

"God answers all our prayers.
Sometimes the answer is yes.
Sometimes the answer is no.
Sometimes the answer is,
You've got to be kidding."

President Jimmy Carter, 1997

Jesus And Prayer

Jesus provided guidance on what were appropriate requests to make during prayer. According to the books of *Matthew* and *Luke,* Jesus taught his earliest disciples a prayer that focused on a very few aspects of life. Although the authors of the books of *Matthew* and *Luke* never claimed that Jesus had a name for the prayer he taught them, it eventually became known as "The Lord's Prayer." The first known written reference to it by that name wasn't until the third-century in a document by Cyprian of Carthage.[27] Saint Thomas Aquinas believed the Lord's Prayer was perfect because it was what Jesus taught his disciples when they asked how to pray. However perfect the prayer itself, the wording of it isn't identical in the two books that include it (The italics indicate the sections that appear in *Matthew*, but not in *Luke*.):

Our Father *who art in heaven*
Hallowed be thy name

Thy kingdom come
Thy will be done
On Earth as it is in heaven
Give us this day our daily bread
And forgive us our trespasses
As we forgive those who trespass against us
And lead us not into temptation
But deliver us from evil

If we were to precisely adhere to the prayer Jesus taught we wouldn't pray for a better job, a bigger house, a new car, to win the lottery, or for our candidate to prevail in an election. Jesus' prayer indicated that it was appropriate to ask for nourishment, forgiveness for oneself, for assistance in forgiving others, and for being strong in the face of temptation and evil. Other than that, we ought to be careful what requests we make as illustrated by the story of the clergyman and the bear.

The Clergyman And The Bear

Although it is the Sabbath a minister wants to go hunting, so he pretends to be sick and cancels the church service where he is supposed to officiate. After skipping out on his responsibilities he makes his way into the nearby wilderness. He is trudging up a steep mountain trail when suddenly encounters a huge bear. As the bear lunges at him the minister attempts a shot. The recoil of the powerful rifle knocks the minister off balance causing him to fall backward tumbling down the mountainside. During the descent he loses his rifle. Unarmed, dazed, and seeing the snarling bear advancing on him the minister calls out, "God, I repent for all my sins, and ask that you make this beast a Christian." Suddenly, the bear stops charging the minister, falls to its knees, clasps its paws together, and says, "God, I give thanks for the food I am about to receive from your generous bounty."

Thy Kingdom Come

According to Neil Douglas-Klotz, a man who could speak both Greek and Aramaic (the language Jesus spoke), the phrase usually translated from Greek to English as, "Thy kingdom come," is more accurately, "Create your reign of unity now through our fiery hearts and willing hands."[28] I prefer that translation because it indicates that merely wishing, hoping, or praying that the Kingdom of Heaven comes to Earth isn't enough to make it happen. Instead we are expected to fervently work for it to occur; in effect, we will be co-creators with God. So instead of in effect praying, "I sure hope God's will is eventually done on Earth," one prays, "Fill me with the knowledge of your will and the power to make it happen." Mr. Douglas-Klotz also pointed out that the Aramaic word for *will* (*tzevyanach*) doesn't mean *willpower*, (the mental might to get things done), it is better understood as a state in which one has so embraced the values and priorities of God, that they have become second nature. If one is to earnestly practice the principles contained in the Lord's Prayer, then before any action one ought to ask, "If I take this course of action will I be increasing or decreasing the probability that the Kingdom of Heaven will be manifest on Earth?"

Who's Will?

In *Alcoholics Anonymous,* the active alcoholic was described as, "self will run riot;" in recovery, members are encouraged by the third Step to turn their, "will and lives over to the care of God." In order to accomplish this, they constantly remind themselves they are, "no longer running the show," and "humbly saying to ourselves many times each day 'Thy [God's] will be done.' "[29] Similar to the Lord's Prayer, the Twelve Steps suggests that prayer be focused; the seventh Step encourages members to humbly ask God to remove their shortcomings, while the eleventh Step suggests prayer and meditation be used to gain knowledge of God's will and the power to carry that out. This guidance is in line with the teachings of Jesus on prayer, as one is asking for knowledge of what God wants, rather than asking God for what one wants for oneself. It is an offer to serve God rather than asking God to serve one's own desires. This principle is summed up in the statement, "Thy will, not mine, be done."

Man Shall Not Live By Bread Alone

> Give us today our daily bread.
>
> Jesus *Matthew* 6:11

If one reads the Bible literally, Jesus was instructing his followers to pray for a loaf of bread. But I think he was referring to more than the combination of grain and water baked to a crunchy crust. Take note of the phrase "daily bread," Jesus was encouraging us to focus on the present and trusting we will have enough of what we need. Members of Twelve Step-based fellowships are likewise encouraged to develop this attitude; hence the slogans, "One day at a time," and "Just do the next right thing."

Does God Tempt Us?

For many people the portion of The Lord's Prayer, "And lead us not into temptation," is confusing, even disturbing. If one is asking God not to lead one into temptation, doesn't that imply that, at least on some occasions, God does lead people into temptation? Some people understand this to mean that God does in fact direct people into situations that will tempt them to commit wrong acts, but God is only doing it to test them. However the God of my understanding doesn't lead me into temptation, probably figuring there are plenty of naturally occurring opportunities to do wrong; I don't need any additional ones put in my way. When law enforcement personnel purposely try to convince someone to commit a crime so they can then make an arrest, it is called entrapment, and is grounds for the charge to be dropped. As a psychotherapist I work with many people who have addictive disorders. I would never put a bottle of liquor or a rich pastry in my waiting room to test my clients who are recovering alcoholics or compulsive overeaters. I figure there were plenty of saloons and bakeries on the way to my office they don't need me to add one more temptation in their lives. To do so seems cruel, and I can't imagine my God being cruel. Do any verses in the New Testament support my view of God? I think *The Book of James* makes it perfectly clear: "Let no one say when he is tempted, 'I am tempted by God'; for God cannot be tempted with evil and he himself tempts no one; but each person is tempted with evil when he is lured and enticed by his own desires" (1:13-14). The wording of the phrase, "And lead us not into temptation, but deliver us from evil," is the result of translating Greek into English. Neil Douglas-Klotz translated the Aramaic into English as, "don't let us be tempted (or diverted) by that which is false." The prayer is a way of asking God for help to avoid those things that distract from doing what is right.[30]

Questions To Help In Personal Reflection Or Group Discussion

Do you use the Lord's Prayer? How, when, and why? Do you use the version in *Matthew* or the one in *Luke*? Are the differences between these two prayers significant?

What is the role of prayer in your life?

Do you think we ought to limit the focus of prayer?

For what things do you pray?

For what things do you think it is inappropriate to pray?

Do you think if you ask in prayer God will intercede in sporting events or politics?

If you think God intercedes in the outcome of sporting events what is God's rationale in doing so?

How would your behaviors change if before taking action you asked yourself: "If I take this course of action will I be increasing or decreasing the probability that the Kingdom of Heaven will be manifest on Earth?"

What percentage of the time during your own prayer are you asking God to do your will and what percentage are you asking for knowledge of God's will for you?

If you were to follow the guidelines provided by the author how would that change the role of prayer in your life?

In thinking back over your past is there anything for which you prayed and now on reflection you are grateful didn't come to pass?

Do you think God tempts us? If so, how and to what purpose?

Treat Other People The Way You Want God To Treat You

With the parable of the unforgiving man, Jesus encouraged his disciples to think about how they wanted to be treated by God as well as how they behaved towards other people (*Matthew* 18:23-24). In this story a peasant was in debt to his king, who not only threatened to take all the peasant's possessions but also to sell him and his family as slaves. The peasant begged for the king's pity, and in an act of kindness and generosity, the king completely forgave the debt. Immediately after leaving the king the peasant came upon someone who owed him money, whom he seized by the throat and demanded immediate payment. The debtor accepted responsibility for the debt but asked for additional time to pay. Instead of treating his debtor with kindness and generosity, the way he had been treated by the king, the peasant had his debtor thrown in prison. The king heard of this and summoned the peasant and berated him; "You wicked servant! I forgave you all that debt and shouldn't you have mercy on your fellow servant as I had mercy on you?" (18: 35). Jesus was pointing out that although we all desire mercy from God most of us don't offer much compassion to those around us. In the Lord's Prayer we very much like the idea of, "forgive us our debts" (or trespasses), but have much less enthusiasm for the section that says, "As we forgive our debtors" (or those who trespass against us). Many people view the words "debts" and "debtors" in literal terms as if the principle applies only in financial matters. Likewise, using the term "trespass" invokes images of people wandering where they don't belong. A deeper understanding of the prayer indicates there are two principles being addressed. First, all of us are in a position of owing and being owed. We all have been violated in some manner by someone and also have violated others either accidentally or intentionally. None of us are exclusively victims, or only perpetrators. The second principle involved in this prayer is the importance of forgiveness. We ask God to forgive us for the harm we have done to others, and in turn we promise to forgive those who have injured us.

Okay, On Three Let's Forgive. 1…2…3!

According to the book of *Mark* Jesus said, "But if you do not forgive men their trespasses, neither will your Father forgive your trespasses" (6:15). Many people understand this verse and the phrase in the Lord's Prayer, "as we forgive," to mean God's forgiveness is conditional on our willingness, ability, and timing when forgiving others:

> "I cannot call myself a Christian and refuse to forgive others or hope to have my sins forgiven."[31]

> "Jesus says in the plainest possible language that if we forgive others, God will forgive us; but if we refuse to forgive others, God will refuse to forgive us...If we say, "I will never forgive what so-and-so did to me," and then go and take this petition on our lips, we are quite deliberately asking God not to forgive us...No one is fit to pray the Lord's prayer so long as the unforgiving spirit holds sway within his heart."[32]

I don't believe God withholds forgiveness from us because the God described by Jesus is generous, forgiving, and loving. Therefore in my understanding, the phase, "as we forgive" doesn't mean we forgive in the exact same manner as God, nor does it mean we will only forgive others after God has forgiven us. What it means is that even as God is forgiving us, we are in the process of forgiving others. These two processes are occurring simultaneously, because God is forgiving us for what we have done wrong we are more able and willing to forgive others.

Questions To Help In Personal Reflection Or Group Discussion

If God treated you the way you treat others, would that be good news or bad news for you?

Can God forgive you for all your various trespasses? Is there anything you have done, or neglected to do, that in your eyes cannot be forgiven by God?

To whom are you in debt, whether it is financial, emotional, or spiritual?

Who is in debt to you? What prevents you from forgiving this debt?

Do you believe God withholds forgiveness for you until you have forgiven others?

Who do you have more difficulty with forgiving, your enemies, your friends, your family, or yourself?

Treat Everyone The Way You Want To Be Treated

"The great principle of morality, 'To do as one would be done to,' is more commended than practiced."

John Locke

An Essay Concerning Human Understanding, 1690 A.C.E.

How Many Times Do We Have To Hear This Before We Get It?

Jesus said; "So whatever you wish that men would do to you, do so to them; for this is the law and the prophets" (*Matthew* 7:12). One might think this directive would be unnecessary since Jesus had already instructed us to treat one another as we want God to treat us. Perhaps Jesus knew that those people who view God as punitive and punishing would use the first teaching to justify treating others that way, so Jesus thought to add this additional lesson. Ask yourself when your behavior falls short of ideal do you want others to shame you, judge you, banish you, and label you with some nasty term? I think it's safe to say you don't. So as a follower of Jesus, don't do that when others aren't perfect. God must really want us to get the message on how to treat others because master teachers throughout the ages, even before Jesus, have been saying effectively the same thing.

"One should never do that to another
which one regards as injurious to one's own self.
This, in brief, is the rule of dharma. Other
behavior is due to selfish desires."

Brihaspati, Hindu teacher from the
8th Century before Jesus

"Do not that to thy neighbor that thou wouldst not suffer from him."

Pittacus of Lesbos,
One of the seven sages of ancient Greece
(650-570 B.C.E.)

"What you do not want done to yourself, do not do to others."

Confucius, Chinese philosopher (551-479 B.C.E.)

"Do to others as I would they should do to me."

Plato, Athenian philosopher (428-348 B.C.E)

"Try your best to treat others as you wish to be treated yourself, and you will find that this is the shortest way to benevolence."

Mencius (371-289 B.C.E.)

Anonymous: "How should we behave to friends?"
Aristotle: "As we should wish them to behave to us."

Aristotle, Greek philosopher (384-322 B.C.E.)

"So whatever you wish that men would do to you, do so to them; for this is the law and the prophets."

Jesus (*Matthew* 7:12)

"What is hateful to you don't do to another.
This is the whole Torah [religious law];
the rest is commentary."
Rabbi Hellel (first century A.C.E.)

"To do unto all men as you would wish to have
done unto you, and to reject for others
what you would reject for yourself."
Prophet Muhammad (570-632 A.C.E.)

Faith Based Politics

When it comes to politics, regardless of party affiliation, few people follow the teachings of Jesus. In the presidential election of 2004 George W. Bush defeated John Kerry with 50.7% of the popular vote.[33] Regardless of how you voted, this meant that about half of your fellow Americans didn't agree with you on who ought to lead our country. How did you regard the approximately 61,147,000 voters that disagreed with you? Did you speak of them as stupid or unpatriotic? Is that the way you would want to be treated by the other half? How can a person claim to love America while pronouncing half of its citizens insufferable? How does one claim to be a follower of Jesus and yet view half of the country with distain? Take for example the memo titled, "Language: A Key Mechanism of Control" sent in 1990 by Newt Gingrich to other members of his political party. The goal of the memo was to, "clearly define the policies and record of your opponent and the Democratic party." It contained a list of words to use to describe an, "opponent, their record, proposals and their party." The list of recommended words and phrases included:

anti- (flag, family, child, jobs)
betray
bizarre
corrupt, corruption
cynicism
decay
destroy, destructive
disgrace
endanger
excuses
failure (fail)
greed
hypocrisy
incompetent
insecure
insensitive
intolerant
obsolete
pathetic
self-serving
selfish
shallow
shame
sick
traitors[34]

As a Baptist since graduate school, and then after 2009 a Catholic, Mr. Gingrich was no doubt familiar with the teachings of Jesus, yet apparently he did not see these principles as applying to politics. As a licensed marriage and family therapist I can guarantee that if a person referred to the their spouse as a, "Bizarre, selfish, sick, incompetent, pathetic, excuse for a person," that the marriage wouldn't last, or if they decided to remain married they both would be miserable. For a politician to view his opponent as a bad person unworthy of respect, rather merely as well-meaning person with flawed ideas does more than demonize the opponent, it also casts those that voted for that representative as equally worthless. In America, that usually means approximately half of the voting population. But perhaps the most disturbing thing about this style of politics is that the American people accepted it then, and continues to accept, even welcome, it now.

Newsman Walter Cronkite was, according to one poll taken when he was the anchor of the *CBS Evening News*, the most trusted man in America. In his decades as a war correspondent both in World War II and Vietnam he had witnessed a lot. In 1973 in an interview he disclosed how disturbed he was with how his fellow Americans treated one another:

> I just don't understand hard-shell, doctrinaire, knee-jerk positions. I don't understand people not seeing both sides, not seeing the justice of other people's causes. I have a very difficult time penetrating what motivates such people. I'm speaking now of the particularly militant left as well as the particularly militant right. But I'm also speaking of people in that great center, whom I sometimes despair of when they accept so glibly the condemnation of other factions within our society-whether it's welfare people or the rich.[35]

"[We must] not try to conceal the thinking of
our own people.
They are part of America."

U.S. President Dwight Eisenhower
Commencement address, 1953[36]

What If It's Not "Just A Theory?"

Jesus said, "Judge not, that ye be not judged" In the traditions of Hinduism and Buddhism the concept underlying this statement is called karma. It has also been called the Law of Retribution.[37] Our modern equivalents are, "what goes around comes around," and "the people you step on when you are on your way up are the same people you meet on the way back down." When was the most recent time you woke up and decided to test the theory of gravity by throwing yourself off the roof just to see what would happen? I think it is safe to say not recently, if ever. Why don't you test the theory of gravity every morning to make sure it still exists? It is because you believe in gravity; you have faith that gravity is going to exist and function the same way every day. You might even insist gravity is a fact or a law of nature. So what about what the Law of Retribution; is it more than just a theory; is it a law of nature? How would you treat others if you believed with all your heart that one way or the other, sooner or later, the things you did today to another person would be done to you, if not by that specific person, by somebody?

Would You Do That To *Jesus?*

`The book of *Matthew* (25:31-46) contains the often cited account of Jesus telling his disciples that people are judged by that which they do, or fail to do, for "the lowliest of my brothers," and "the least of my brothers." Jesus even went so far as to tell his disciples he viewed whatever they did, for good or for ill, to the hungry, thirsty, naked, sick, imprisoned, and homeless, was being done to him also. Bestselling Catholic author Garry Wills explained the lesson:

> What exactly does that mean? "Whenever you did these things to the lowliest of my brothers, you were doing it to me." It means that priests who sexually molest boys are molesting Jesus. Televangelists who cheat old women of their savings are cheating Jesus. Those killing members of other religions because of their religion are killing Jesus. Those who despise the poor are despising Jesus. Those neglecting the homeless are neglecting Jesus. Those persecuting gays are persecuting Jesus.[38]

Up to this point, we have already examined two methods for determining the appropriateness of one's actions. Before taking an action one can consider the questions:

Is this the way I want God to treat me?

Is this the way I want to be treated by other people?

The story in *Matthew* provides a third tool for deciding the correctness of one's actions -Would I treat Jesus this way? If the answer is no, to even one of these three questions, then one ought not take the action, or if taking the action, at least acknowledge that it is in violation of the principles Jesus taught.

Questions To Help In Personal Reflection Or Group Discussion

In your experience, how does your life go better when you treat someone the way you want to be treated by other people?

When was the most recent time you treated someone with whom you disagreed on some significant issue in the manner you would want to be treated?

When your political candidate or sports team wins, how do you view and treat those who were rooting for the side that lost?

How would you treat others if you believed with all your heart that one way or the other, sooner or later, the things you did today to another person will be done to you, if not by that specific person, by somebody?

How could you make use of these three questions to assess your actions?

Is this the way I want God to treat me?
Is this the way I want to be treated by other people?
Would I treat Jesus this way?

What is something you did to another person that you wouldn't have done if you knew for a fact that it was Jesus on the receiving end of your act?

Be More Concerned With The Well-being Of People Than With Rigidly Following Rules

During the time of Jesus, observant Jews were told by their religious leaders that in order to be right with God they needed to follow approximately six hundred rules each day.[39] As in Biblical times, some people continue to live according to strict interpretations of the scriptures. For example, recently there was a debate among Biblical scholars as to whether drinking tap water that had gone through a filter before entering a drinking cup violated the prohibition against doing work on the Sabbath.[40] Jesus was never preoccupied with rigidly following religious rules and traditions. He ignored or violated the rules set down by Pharisees and Scribes, and even those written in the Hebrew Bible/Old Testament. Throughout the gospels Jesus violated religious laws when he thought they were too rigid and interfered with being loving towards others. He opposed ritual purification, sacrifice, public prayer, fasting, eating taboos, and not working on the Sabbath. He went about teaching his radical theology without any authority from religious leaders. Furthermore, Jesus spoke out against legalism, the tendency for regulations to become an end in themselves rather than a means to an end. Brennan Manning explained it this way; "Jesus resolutely insisted that law was the expression of the love of God and neighbor and that piety that stands in the way of love stands in the way of God himself."[41] Jesus was more interested in teaching a set of principles that individuals could use to guide day-to-day behavior, than he was in providing a set of rules to be blindly followed. These principles focused on right thinking rather than specific behaviors. Jesus knew that if a person's beliefs, attitudes and general thinking are spiritually tuned, then proper behavior consistently occurs. Jesus indicated that one's responsibility to other people supercedes one's responsibility to follow religious practices; "So then, if you are bringing your offering to the altar and there remember that your brother has something against you, leave your offering there before the altar, go and be reconciled with your brother first, and then come back and present your offering" (*Matthew* 5:23-24). Unfortunately too many people were, and are, more interested in doing it right (rigidly following the rules) than doing right (behaving like Jesus).

"When man appears before the Throne of Judgment,
the first question he is asked is not: 'Have you
believed in God?' or
'Have you prayed and observed the ritual?'
He is asked: 'Have you dealt honorably and faithfully
in all your dealings with your fellow man?'"

Talmud (Rabbinical reflections)

Members of Twelve Step fellowships aren't provided with a set of rules that they are expected to follow. When the founders of A.A. laid out the Twelve Step program they didn't insist that newcomers or old timers believe anything specific, nor did they require any certain behaviors. Instead they merely described what they had done that proved helpful to them; "Our stories disclose in a general way what we were like, what happened, and what we are like now."[42] The sentence that introduced the Twelve

Steps to the world began, not with a directive but, with a suggestion; "Here are the steps we took, which are suggested as a program of recovery…"[43] Old timers are more interested in seeing that newcomers get the help they need rather than trying to impose any beliefs on them or demanding that they follow any rules. Likewise Jesus made it clear that the principles he taught were what was important, not religious rules or rites: "Woe to you, teachers of the law and Pharisees, you hypocrites! You give a tenth of your spices—mint, dill and cumin. But you have neglected the more important matters of the law—justice, mercy and faithfulness. You should have practiced the latter, without neglecting the former" (*Matthew* 23:23). He again made this point, as well as a lesson on humility, in his story of the Pharisee and the tax collector. The Pharisee was portrayed as a man who meticulously followed all religious rules, but with a holier than thou attitude. The tax collector performed a job that made him very unpopular, even despised, because the tax money went to fund the cruel Roman occupational army: "Two men went up to the temple to pray, one a Pharisee and the other a tax collector. The Pharisee stood up and prayed about himself: 'God, I thank you that I am not like other men—robbers, evildoers, adulterers—or even like this tax collector. I fast twice a week and give a tenth of all I get.' But the tax collector stood at a distance. He would not even look up to heaven, but beat his breast and said, 'God, have mercy on me, a sinner.' I tell you that this man, rather than the other, went home justified before God. For everyone who exalts himself will be humbled, and he who humbles himself will be exalted" (*Luke* 18:10-14). The Pharisee was arrogant, he thought himself better than other people because he strictly followed religious rules. But Jesus taught that of the two men, the humble tax collector was the more devout and we ought to follow his example.

Hypocrisy

"It is in our lives, and not from our words,
that our religion must be read."
U.S. President Thomas Jefferson

In 1868 Andrew Carnegie wrote, "The amassing of wealth is one of the worst species of idolatry, no idol is more debasing." However, only few years after that, he founded the Carnegie Steel Company, which by the 1890s, was the largest and most profitable industrial enterprise in the world and made him the second-richest man in all of recorded history. Given his 1868 statement, in later years did Mr. Carnegie consider himself to be the second-worst idolater in all of recorded history? Not that he ever mentioned in public. As now, in Jesus' time there are hypocrites, those who claimed to be moral and upright, yet behave in ways that consistently violate their stated principles, such as the marriage therapist that preaches kindness and understand to his clients, but is mean to his family when he gets home. Jesus was not the first, nor the last, to complain of hypocrisy:

"You talk one way, you live another."
Seneca The Younger (5 B.C.-65 A.C.E.)

"They play one tune and dance to another."
John Clarke (1639 A.C.E.)

"The words of an Angel, the deeds of a Devil."
James Howell (1659 A.C.E.)

"A Pharisee is a man who prays publicly
and preys privately."
Don Marquis (1878-1937 A.C.E.)

"The hypocrite's crime is that he bears false
witness against himself."
Hannah Arendt (1963 A.C.E.)

"Why do grown-ups always say, 'Don't hit,'
and then the go and start a big war?"
Benjamin Rottman, in a letter to the *L.A. Times*
(1991 A.C.E.)

Unfortunately, just as in Jesus' time, within every gathering of humans, including churches, political parties, and psychotherapy centers, hypocrisy can be found. Of course in Twelve Step meetings, there are hypocrites-people who, "talk the talk, but don't walk the walk." When it is time to discuss the Steps they have plenty to say and may even be able to quote the fellowship's main text, citing the page on which the sentence is printed. However, when it comes to actually living in accordance with the underlying principle they fall flat. There is also the phenomenon of "two Steppers;" these are people who admit they have a problem such as alcoholism (Step 1), and then immediately attempt to carry the message of recovery to others (Step 12). Two Steppers can't be bothered with the other ten Steps that involve rigorous personal examination and demanding personal change. The "Big Book" of Alcoholics Anonymous warned such people, "Some of us have tried to hold on to our old ideas and the result was nil [nothing] until we let go absolutely."[44] Similarly in every church there are those who hear the teaching of Jesus and then think they are ready to spread the good news.

These people can't be bothered with the difficult task of actually applying the principles taught by Jesus to their own lives. They believe as long as they profess their belief in Jesus and accept him as their personal savior that the heavy lifting is over and done with, rather than grasping that it has only just begun.

More troubling than the man who doesn't grasp the fact that his behavior is hypocritical is the man who knows he is behaving in a hypocritical way and doesn't care. Jesus taught that hypocrisy was dangerous to both the person engaged in it as well as to others: "Woe to you, scribes and Pharisees, hypocrites! Because you shut the kingdom of heaven against men; for you neither enter yourselves, nor allow those who would enter to go in" (*Matthew* 24:13).

Examples Of Modern Day Hypocrisy

What Part Of "Thou Shall Not Bear False Witness" Don't You Understand?

In the case of Kitzmiller v. Dover School District that involved the teaching of "intelligent design" in a public school one of the defendants claimed under oath ("So help me God") not to know the source of funds for the sixty copies of a book on Intelligent Design that appeared in the school library. Court authorities considered charging him with perjury after his canceled personal check that had paid for the books was entered into evidence.[45]

Doesn't That Violate "Thou Shall Not Steal"?

Robert Beale was a successful businessman. After he graduated from the Massachusetts institute of Technology he started a computer technology company with revenues of fifteen million dollars a year that supported seventy employees. He owned fine homes in Minnesota and in Florida. He was active in politics as a delegate to his party's national convention and contributed more than ten thousand dollars to his party's candidates. He founded the Minnesota Christian Coalition, which was affiliated with the Christian Coalition of America. One of his sons wrote Christian fantasy novels. Another of his sons worked beside him in the family business and insisted that, "Robert Beale is a good man." Although Robert Beale may have been a good man, according to the U.S. attorney's office he did bad things. Over a four-year period Mr. Beale allegedly declined to pay income tax on his income of $5,696,574. He not only didn't file tax returns he set up a shell company to hide his income and ordered his employees not to file normal payroll documents for him. When Mr. Beale didn't appear for his trial in federal court his son explained his father's absence, "His philosophy on particular issues with taxes has taken him and his family...a little farther down the road than he would like to be."[46]

Exactly Which Of Your Marriages Needs Defending From The Gays?

In 1996, Congress adopted the federal Defense of Marriage Act (DOMA). Supporters claimed it was necessary because a recent court decision had indicated there was a right to same-sex "marriage" contained in the Hawaii Constitution. Some people viewed this as a part of an "assault on marriage, " that they claimed had already been waged for decades. The DOMA had two sections. The first defined "marriage" for purposes of federal law as a legal union between one man and one woman, and that the terms "husband," wife," and "spouse" only applied to heterosexual couples. The second section reaffirmed the power of the states to make their own decisions about marriage: "No State, territory, or possession of the United States, or Indian tribe, shall be required to give effect to any public act, record, or judicial proceeding of any other State, territory, possession, or tribe respecting a relationship between persons of the same sex that is treated as a marriage under the laws of such other State, territory, possession, or tribe, or a right or claim arising from such relationship." Supporters, including Speaker of the House Newt Gingrich, warned that permitting same-sex marriage would violate the sanctity of marriage as an institution, and somehow endanger existing heterosexual marriages. He warned, "I think that it [homosexuality] is a very dangerous threat to anybody who believes in traditional religion."[47] Mr. Gingrich had been a practicing Baptist until he became a Catholic when he married. He made it clear that his faith was the basis of his politics. He ran for office on a "family values" platform. When asked, "How does your faith impact your policies?" he answered, "If you truly try to understand what God wants, and truly try to do what God wants, that has to impact how you behave."[48] However, in one year alone there were five ethics complains filed against him with the House ethics committee.

Like every other American Mr. Gingrich was within his legal rights to express whatever opinion he choose on the issue of same-sex marriage. However, unlike every other American, he had an unusual marital history. Mr. Gingrich was married three times and divorced twice. When decided to divorce his first wife he informed her of his decision while she was in a hospital bed recovering from major surgery. His third wife was his mistress while he was married to his second wife, who had been his mistress during his first marriage.[49] Nor did he limit his extra-marital sex acts to only one mistress at a time; it was common knowledge that at any given time he had sexual relationships with several women. While proceeding with impeachment charges against President Bill Clinton for lying about his sexual relationship with Monica Lewinsky, Mr. Gingrich himself was engaged in an extra-marital affair.

Expectations

When I claim Jesus believed that the well-being of people was more important than rules, some folks think I am only referring to laws or written rules, but I am also including unspoken expectations, such as thinking, "If I do something for you, then you should respond the way I want you to." In the film *Harold & Maude,* there is a scene in which the two main characters are standing by the ocean. As sign of his affection for Maude, Harold gives her a gift. She is delighted with the present, exclaiming; "Ohhhhh! This is the nicest present I've received in years." She kisses it and joyfully tosses it into the ocean. Harold's face registers shock, hurt, and disbelief. Just as his mouth is forming the word "why?" she turns and happily explains, "So I'll always know where it is." Harold is learning the lesson that by giving a gift to Maude it becomes her property and she is free to do with it what ever suits her, even if it doesn't meet his expectations.

Many of us engage in an act of supposed generosity, but then expect something in return. Similar to the way Maude taught Harold an elderly woman helped me to learn about my expectations of others when I found a wallet in the street. After I examined the contents I discovered that, in addition to numerous credit cards, it contained several hundred dollars. A diver's license provided me with the owner's address, and on the way to her home I pondered how much of a reward I was entitled to receive. I expected since I was returning, not only the credit cards, but also a large amount of cash, I had a significant reward coming my way since I could have easily kept the cash for myself and the owner would have thought somebody else took it before I found the wallet, and would still have admired me for seeing that her credit cards arrived back in her possession. I practiced my acceptance speech for when she gratefully handed me some money because I wanted to make sure it sounded appropriately humble-something to the effect of, "Oh, that's not really necessary, but if you insist." Imagine my surprise after I handed her the wallet and she said, "Thank you young man," then she shut the door! When I recovered from my shock and disappointment, I realized that even though I told myself I was doing what was right, I still expected to be paid for my honesty, as if doing what was right wasn't reward enough.

Conditional Acts

A common form of expectations is when one person offers to assist another person only if the person being helped agrees to certain conditions. In these cases the act isn't one of kindness, generosity, or love-it is a trade. In none of the stories of Jesus' healing was there any mention of him doing so conditionally. He didn't require, or even request, that anyone pay him or do something in return for his actions. The closest he ever came was when he asked that those he had healed not tell others what he did. Conditional acts are not charitable. The word *charity* has several definitions. It can refer to an organization whose mission it is to help others. But more importantly the word *charity* applies to individuals:

The voluntary provision of money, materials, or help to people in need;

The willingness to judge people in a tolerant or favorable way;

The impartial love of other people.[50]

None of these definitions mentions the acts being conditional. In addition, charity is voluntary-one can't be forced to be charitable-it is done willingly. Finally authentic charity is impartial-no individual, or group of people, are more or less worthy of loving-kindness.

What's The Catch?

I once heard a man speak of being on the receiving end of a long series of unconditional acts of kindness.

He was giving me a ride to the airport from the drug treatment center where I had given a presentation. I asked him how he came to be employed by the treatment center:

> I was a drunk and a junkie living on the streets. I heard that there was this treatment center where I might get a handout, but I didn't want drug treatment. One night I was mighty hungry so I went to the center, knocked on the door, and when one of the night staff opened the door I asked, "What would I have to do to get something to eat? I was shocked when she said, "Nothing." 'Course I didn't believe her since the center is sponsored by the church so I figured she would immediately start trying to save my soul, but I was so hungry I decided I could tolerate that. She let me in and gave me a sandwich and some juice. She asked me about my life, commented on how hard and lonely it sounded, but she never tried to convert me to her religion or tell me I should stop drinking and shooting dope. I thanked her and got out before she changed her mind and started lecturing me. A few weeks later I went back and asked what I would have to do to get a shower. Again she let me in and showed me where I could clean up. When I finished she gave me some clean socks that had been left behind by someone. I was sure this time she'd start in on saving me, but she just smiled and wished me well. About two months later I showed up again. I think I surprised her when she asked me, "How can I help you?" and I said, "Would you tell me what happens in rehab?" She explained the program to me in a way I could understand. When she finished

> I expected her to tell me I should check myself in for treatment. But she didn't, all she said was, "Anything else I can do for you?" I told her I was getting by, and said maybe I'd come back another time. She smiled and gently shut the door. The very next night I went back. This time I asked her, "If I agreed to start treatment would I be locked up?" "Nope, you can leave any time you want," she assured me. "Well, how much does it cost?" I wondered aloud. "How much have you got?" she responded. "Nothing," I admitted. "Then it's a good thing for you that the center is supported by donations," she said with a grin. That was five years ago. I've been clean and sober ever since that night when I decided to stay. Once I completed the program I applied for a job at the center. I was a janitor for a time, and then I got this job. I get to drive people from the treatment center to their new job or new apartment. I get to hear their stories. Just like "The Big Book" says; "Our stories disclose in a general way what we used to be like, what happened, and how we are now." I get to see miracles all the time. Don't you know every time when I stop by at the treatment center and I see that nurse that was so kind to me I give her a big hug. She knew if she had tried to talk me into getting sober I'd still be on the street or more likely dead by now. I consider my own recovery a miracle, so I've made it a habit to get down on my knees every morning and night and thank God for people like her.

It was the most inspiring ride I'd ever taken. I felt sad when we arrived at the airport and we had to part.

Questions To Help In Personal Reflection Or Group Discussion

In the past how has your desire to follow the rules interfered with your ability to act in a loving manner towards yourself or others?

What are the expectations you have for others when you help them?

When have you been conditional with your kindness?

What role does charity play in your life?

Think of an example where someone ignored a rule in order to act in a loving way towards you.

When have you ignored a rule in order to be more loving towards another person?

What is your reaction to Doesn't That Violate The Commandment, "Thou Shall Not Steal?"

What is your reaction to What Part Of "Thou Shall Not Bear False Witness" Don't You Understand?

Why didn't Jesus put conditions on giving assistance to others?

Do you think the nurse should have required the stranger to accept Jesus in exchange for help because the treatment center was religiously based?

The nurse helped the stranger four times without apparent expectations. How many times should she have helped him before putting some conditions on her assistance?

Stop Judging Others

"Mercy triumphs over judgment"

The Epistle of James 2:13

When U.S. Supreme Court Judge Oliver Wendell Holmes, Jr. was asked, "What great principle has guided your judicial decisions?" he responded, "I have spent seventy years finding out that I am not God."[51] Jesus didn't think it was the place of any person to pass judgment on others; "Judge not, that you be not judged" (*Matthew* 7:1). In fact he even though it wasn't his place to judge others; "I judge no one" (*John* 8:16). By both his words and deeds he showed he was adamant that any judging would be the responsibility of God and not any of us. If we are to be authentic followers of Jesus, it isn't our role to judge others. But what if those around us are, in our opinion, "doing it wrong?" Surely Jesus would want us to insist that wrong doers behave the way they "should." More likely Jesus would have agreed with Robert Frost when he declared in 1935; "I hold it to be the inalienable right of anybody to go to hell in his own way." As the often-cited story of Jesus and an adulterous woman makes clear, one can disagree with another's behavior without passing judgment on that person. Although Jewish law called for the woman to be stoned to death Jesus didn't condemn her, even though he clearly believed what she had done was sinful because he bid her to, "go and sin no more" (*John* 8:11). Jesus was demonstrating there is a big difference between telling someone, "You did something of which I don't approve, therefore you are evil and hated by God," and thinking,

"That behavior doesn't fit in my value system, therefore I refuse to engage in it. But it is not my role to judge others who do behave that way." In their book, *Loving What Is*, Byron Katie and Stephen Mitchell proposed a method for reducing the tendency to judge others that involved asking oneself some simple questions:

1. Is what I thinking about another person true?
2. Can I absolutely know that what I am thinking is true?
3. How do I feel having this belief about another person?
4. Who would I be if I didn't have this belief?
5. What happens if I use this belief to assess my own behavior?

"God, please save me from your followers."

Prayer on a bumper sticker

Once we stop looking at others through judgmental eyes we begin to see similarities between those who we have been judging and ourselves. Such insight is bad for maintaining arrogance but great for developing humility. Thomas Merton put it this way, "A man becomes a saint not by conviction that he is better than sinners but by the realization that he is one of them, and that all together need the mercy of God!"[52]

In Twelve Step groups members are taught two seemingly contradictory slogans, "Stick with the winners," and, "There but for the grace of God go I," The first acknowledges that there are members who won't or can't consistently practice the principles of the Steps, so they are at greater risk for relapse. Obviously in order to stick with "the winners," one has to determine who are the winners.

But the second slogan, "There but for the grace of God, go I," curbs the tendency to judge others, encourages members to develop tolerance and compassion for those with whom they disagree, and to look for similarities between all members rather than focusing on insignificant differences.

Is there any way to influence the behavior of others and still be true to the teaching of Jesus? We could learn from Tradition eleven of Alcoholics Anonymous that states; "Our public relations policy is based on attraction rather than promotion."[53] Members of Twelve Step fellowships are taught that they have a responsibility to assist those seeking help, but aren't expected to go out and recruit new members. A religious version of Tradition eleven is the saying; "You may be the only copy of the Bible someone ever sees." In both cases, the lesson is the same; focus on being the best person you can be, and those who are interested in that kind of life will naturally be attracted to you and want to learn from your example. Then if they ask how it is you have managed to obtain this level of honesty, compassion, and serenity you can share, as they say in Twelve Step groups, your "experience, strength, and hope." There are those who find the policy of attraction, rather than promotion, inadequate. Take for example fifteen-year old Emily Sapp who was sent home from school along with a few of her fellow students for wearing shirts bearing the statement ISLAM IS OF THE DEVIL. A lawyer for the Alachua Country, Florida school system acknowledged that students have a right to free speech, but that the school has the responsibility to ban clothing that may "disrupt the learning process." For her part Emily claimed that Muslim people are, "fine," and, "They can be saved like anyone else." Personally, I don't understand how denouncing another religion as unholy, would attract converts to Christianity.[54]

"Christ has no visible body other than Christians,
And no other love to be seen but theirs."
Father Louis Evely[55]

Questions To Help In Personal Reflection Or Group Discussion

How do you react to being judged by others?

Thinking about today, who have you judged?

What motivates you to judge others?

What have you done that might lead someone to think; "If that's how followers of Jesus behave I <u>don't</u> see any reason to be one of them"?

What have you done to be an attractive example of a follower of Jesus?

~

Focus On Your Own Behavior

"CHRISTIAN, n. One who believes that the New Testament is a divinely inspired book admirably suited to the spiritual needs of his neighbor. One who follows the teachings of Christ so far as they are not inconsistent with a life of sin."

The Devil's Dictionary by Ambrose Bierce

One of the most well known stories in the New Testament concerns a crowd bringing before Jesus a woman accused of adultery. According to Old Testament law the act of adultery condemned her to a slow painful death by stoning. Despite the fact that Biblical law was clear on the matter, Jesus challenged those in the mob to look at their own behavior with the famous verse, "He who is without sin among you, let him cast the first stone." Of course, back then, as today, no one was without sin. Another Biblical story with the same message is the person who was able to see something as small as a "speck" in someone else's eye, yet seemed completely oblivious to the fact that his own eye contained something as obvious as, depending on the version of the Bible, a plank, beam, or log. This principle was important enough to the teachings of Jesus that it was included in the books of *Matthew* and *Luke,* as well as in the *Gospel Of Thomas.* In the tenth Step of the Twelve Step program, members are encouraged to focus on their own behavior rather than that of others, [we] "Continued to take personal inventory, and when we were wrong promptly admitted it." Nowhere in the Twelve Step program is there any Step that promotes judging the behavior of others; all of the Steps focus only on transforming one's own behavior.

Give Me That Old Time Religion

Not everyone agrees with the way Jesus handled the adulterous woman. After the 1979 (A.C.E.) revolution when Iran went from a secular state to a religious state a new criminal code was implemented that included stoning. Sine then, at least one hundred people have been legally killed by stoning, of these at least six took place between 2006 and 2008. In 2010 seven women and three men were imprisoned awaiting deaths by stoning. Although the Qur'an (the holy book of Islam) doesn't prescribe stoning it continues to be a legal form of capital punishment in a number of Muslim countries including Iran, Nigeria, Pakistan, Saudi Arabia, Somalia, and Sudan.

Like most forms of capital punishment carried out by governments an official stoning involves a carefully prescribed formal procedure. Convicted persons are to have their hands tied behind their backs and their bodies bound in cloth to reduce struggling. Then they are to be buried in sand in a standing position, men to their waists and women to the point where their breasts are covered so they can't attempt to run away. The stones used are to be larger than pebbles, but not large enough that death will occur after only a few are thrown. If the conviction was made with a confession of adultery then the judge who tried the case must throw the first stone. In case where the guilty verdict is the result of testimony by witnesses one of those who testified against the defendant must cast the first stone.

The stoning of adulterous women has a long history; first to serve as a warning to others, and second to insure that illegitimate child aren't born thereby complicating blood lines and inheritance. Since males don't give birth they have rarely been put to death for having sex outside of marriage even in the strictest societies. Unless of course they were convicted of having sex with another man, in which case they were often put to death by having a brick wall collapsed onto them.[56]

Questions To Help In Personal Reflection Or Group Discussion

In the past week what percentage of your time did you spend focusing on your behavior and what percent was spent focused on the behavior of others?

How do you react when someone tells you how you should think and behave when that person isn't behaving that way?

What did you think and feel while reading the section on stoning? For what crimes do you think stoning would be an appropriate punishment? Would you be willing to witness a stoning? Would you be willing to take part in a stoning of a legally convicted person? Would you be willing to cast the first stone?

How many people do you know (including yourself if appropriate) who have committed adultery? Which of these people deserve to be stoned to death?

The law that prescribed that a woman be put to death for adultery didn't require that only people who were without sin take part in a stoning. How do you think Jesus justified not putting the adulterous woman to death as prescribed by religious tradition and law?

Be Compassionate

"If you want others to be happy, practice compassion.
If you want to be happy, practice compassion."
Tenzin Guatso, The Dalai Lama

Jesus directed, "Be compassionate as your heavenly Father is compassionate" (*Luke* 6:36). Compassion is more than mere empathy. Empathy merely means understanding how another person feels. Compassion goes beyond just knowing how another feels, to caring about the reason the person feels that way and taking some meaningful action to assist.

Have I not wept for those in trouble?
Has not my soul grieved for the poor?
Job 30:25

Brennan Manning stressed the importance of action in accordance with the teachings of Jesus, "Copious Christian tears shed for the dehydrated babies in Juarez is heartfelt emotion; when combined with giving them a cup of water, it is compassion."[57] The word compassion comes from two Latin words, *cum* and *patior* meaning, "to suffer with." If God is indeed compassionate then God suffers when we suffer; therefore when we suffer along with those less fortunate we are behaving in a God-like manner. Suffering along with another doesn't mean having the same problem, but it does mean taking action that will cause us to be out of our usual comfort zone. I once heard a story that illustrates this point. As a part of the Twelve Step program Sex Addicts Anonymous, a man was working on Step nine in which he was expected to make amends to those he had harmed.[3] Before getting into a recovery program he had regularly hired prostitutes. He determined he would give a certain amount of money to a charity whose purpose was to assist prostitutes to get off the streets and stop selling their bodies. When he informed his sponsor, (the person assisting him in working the Step) of his plan the sponsor asked; "Are you comfortable giving away this amount of money? Will it have a negative effect on your lifestyle?" "No, it won't have any effect on my financial life," reassured the first man. "Well, then," said the sponsor, "maybe you aren't giving enough."

Attribution

"But go and learn what this means:
'I desire compassion, and not sacrifice,'
for I did not come to call the righteous, but sinners"
Jesus (*Matthew* 9:13)

There is a tendency for humans to automatically engage in what psychologists call the fundamental attribution error. Harold Nicolson described this as an inclination, "to judge ourselves by our ideals, others by their acts."[58] This means when we assess the appropriateness of our behavior, we tend to cut ourselves a great deal of slack; "Well, it was the best I could do, <u>given the circumstances</u>." We excuse our less than ideal behavior by claiming it was the result of the situation in which it occurred.

3 "Made direct amends to those we had harmed, except when to do so would injure them or others."

However, most of us are far less understanding when it comes to explaining other people's behavior; we tend to underestimate the influence of the situational factors on and overestimate the impact of their personality traits. If we don't like someone's behavior we blame the person, not the situation; "Well, that's just the sort of person she is. That's the way that type of person acts." Attribution error shows up in the language we choose when retelling events. When describing our own behavior we use verbs; "In situations like that I get annoyed so that's why I did what I did." However, when detailing the acts of others we use words that categorize them as people; "He's just an impatient crab-that's why he acted like that." The attribution error interferes with the development of empathy and compassion because it causes us to think we are different than others; we do bad things because of the situations we are in, whereas others do bad things because they are bad people. Therefore we think of them as unworthy of our empathy and compassion. Spiritually advanced people are willing and able to have compassion for others, understand the impact of situations on their choices, and not judge them as bad people. Empathy and compassion make it possible for us to overcome the attribution error. Jesus could witness people doing bad things, and yet not see them as bad people. In the life of Jesus, the most powerful example of this was his willingness to forgive those who took part in his execution. He understood that the Roman soldiers were probably ignorant of his teachings, and more importantly, were in a situation where if they had refused to carry out their orders they would have been put to death for insubordination.

Members of Twelve Step groups are encouraged to, "act as if," and "fake it till ya make it." These slogans are based on the belief that it is more effective to act one's way into a new way of thinking and feeling, than it is to think one's way into new behaviors. This lesson can be applied to the teaching of Jesus. If we begin to treat others with kindness and respect in time we will develop empathy and compassion for them. Even though originally we may have acted with kindness merely because it seemed like the right thing to do, it doesn't take long before we find we are behaving like Jesus because we want to, not because we think we should.

There, But For The Grace Of God, Go I

My favorite example of compassion leading to forgiveness is a story from the Twelve Step fellowship Sex Addicts Anonymous. At the start of the meeting a basket was passed for donations to pay for the rent on the meeting space and other expenses. Most members put in a dollar or two before passing it on. Once the basket had traveled around the circle the person acting as the "trusted servant" asked the member serving as the group's treasurer for a status report on the group's funds. Immediately the treasurer burst into tears as he confessed that not only had he not paid the rent for several months he had stolen the group's money and used it to buy pornography. For a moment there was silence; then without a word being spoken the basket was again passed and this time most members put in ten or twenty dollars in order to replenish the missing funds. Once the basket had gone around again the trusted servant handed it and all the newly collected money to the still crying treasurer, and asked, "Is there any more business to discuss before we focus on the Step of the week?" These men understood that shame is the fuel that drives addictive behavior, and they knew the treasurer was at great risk for continued self-destructive behavior. They knew as addicts themselves they too were capable of doing all kinds of hurtful things including stealing to support their habit. They didn't judge the treasurer because they were humble enough to know, "there but for the grace of God go I." They not only felt compassion for a suffering addict, they demonstrated their compassion by immediately forgiving him and giving him a chance to redeem himself by paying the rent.

> "Be compassionate and you will become a saint."
>
> Vincent DePaul, 17th century mystic[59]

Questions To Help In Personal Reflection Or Group Discussion

How do you usually behave when you see someone suffering?

When was the most recent time you gave so much to a charity that you couldn't afford some luxury for yourself?

How much do you spend on alcohol, tobacco, or coffee per month? How would it affect the quality of your life if instead of spending that money on yourself you donated half of it to a charity that improved the lives of others while not improving your situation?

Donating money to your church positively affects the quality of your life; how might you benefit if you donated that money to a financially struggling church, synagogue or mosque that you don't attend?

Think back on your most recent misbehavior, and write a description of it.

Now write a description of the misbehavior of someone else.

Look over the two descriptions you wrote to see if you engaged in the attribution error. Did you view your own behavior as the result of situation factors but the other person's misbehavior as an indication of their personality?

What did you think of the story about the treasurer who stole the group's funds?

~

Forgive

"To err is human, to forgive divine."
English poet Alexander Pope
An Essay on Criticism, 1711 A.C.E.

An Eye For An Eye

"Where would Christianity be if
Jesus got eight to fifteen years,
with time off for good behavior?"
New York Senator James H. Donovan
during a speech in support of capital punishment[60]

When discussing forgiveness with others I often hear people cite the Old Testament verse, "eye for eye, tooth for tooth" (*Deuteronomy* 19:21) as justification for punishing others before forgiving them. Usually people who like this verse place more emphasis on settling the score by making sure offenders get what they have coming than on compassion and forgiveness. I frequently find that these same people are not so zealous about this verse when they themselves offend; at that point they become enthusiastic supporters of immediate kindness and mercy and of omitting punishment. Most people who cite this verse interpret it to mean-if someone knocks out your tooth then you are permitted, perhaps even required, to bash out one of their teeth. It is this interpretation of, "eye for eye," that in 2010 lead a Saudi judge to rule that a man who had been convicted of damaging the spine of a man with whom he was in a knife fight ought to have his spine damaged so that he too was paralyzed.[61]

"Eye for eye," wasn't so much a requirement as it was the maximum limit of punishment. The purpose of this ancient Jewish law wasn't to compel a certain punishment but rather to ensure that the punishment fit the crime. In order to put a stop to constant violent feuding and honor killings between families, the law was part of creating a formal process to resolve conflict; "If a malicious witness rises against any man to accuse him of wrongdoing, then both parties shall appear before the priests and judges who are in office in those days" (19:16-17). If the officials found someone guilty of a crime they relied on the laws to determine the appropriate punishment. The purpose of the law was to put an end to on-going cycles of revenge and violence by the society putting limits on what individuals were allowed to do. Prior to the law it was customary for someone to be attacked, even killed, over what we would now consider a minor offense such as insulting another person; the response was out of proportion. The law sought to limit revenge rather than endorse it. Imagine a society in which people were free to inflict whatever punishment they thought was appropriate on whomever they wanted to, whenever they felt like it. That is the type of society that existed prior to the introduction of the laws found in *Deuteronomy*.

Jesus And Forgiveness

Those who are engrossed with ensuring that others get punished are ignoring the teachings of Jesus. They are more enthralled with the Old Testament verse about an eye for an eye than they are with the New Testament verses, "Let him who is without sin among you be the first to throw a stone at her" (*John* 8:7), and "Father, forgive them" (*Luke* 23:34). If we are all a part of one great family and want to live in peace then we need to forgive those who hurt us and be forgiven by those we harm. In Biblical times, Jews were taught that when someone did harm, the injured person wasn't expected to forgive the offender until after the offender had publicly repented. Jesus taught a new radical level of forgiveness, one that promoted forgiving people before they had repented and even before an admission of wrongdoing. Forgiveness was to be universal; no one was to be excluded from forgiveness, not sinners, not criminals, not the outcasts of society, not even one's enemies. Forgiveness was to be continuous. There was to be no limit to the number of times a person is to be forgiven; in the words of Jesus, "seventy times seven" (*Matthew* 18:22). According to the book of *Luke* even as Jesus was dying he sought forgiveness for those who were killing him, "Father, forgive them" (*Luke* 23:34). Jesus preached that offenders were not only to be forgiven but also to be shown mercy, compassion, and even love. It was then, and is now, a tall order.

Examples Of The Power Of Forgiveness

Brryan [sic] Jackson was much like many eighteen year-old Americans; he liked to flirt, was learning to play the guitar, and working towards high school graduation. In others ways he was different; he gave public speeches in support of Upward Bound Ministries and Camp Kindle, a summer camp for children ill from serious diseases. He helped found Hope Is Vital, an organization that sought to educate the general public about AIDS and the power of faith and forgiveness. Despite all his good works, he was not invited to other teen's parties, and parents forbade their daughters to date him. He was treated this way because he had AIDS. You might think, "Well that is what he deserves for getting infected," thinking that the virus must have entered his body from a needle during illegal drug use or during sex with another male. But if there ever were someone with AIDS who was totally innocent of any wrongdoing, it would have to be Brryan. He became infected at the tender age of eleven months when Brian Stewart, who had previously denied being his father until paternity tests proved otherwise, purposely injected him with HIV-tainted blood. Mr. Stewart was able to obtain the blood because he worked in a hospital drawing blood from patients. His goal was to kill his son so he wouldn't have to pay child support. He might have gotten away with it, but physicians became suspicious because of all the illnesses Brryan suffered over the next six years. Eventually Mr. Stewart was convicted of first-degree assault and given the maximum sentence, life in prison. When Judge Ellsworth Cundiff passed sentence, he said Mr. Stewart was in the same category as, "the worst war criminal," and declared, "I believe when God finally calls you, you are going to burn in hell from here to eternity." As of age eighteen Brryan had never visited his father in prison, but that is not to say he hadn't forgiven the man who tried to kill him. Kendra Sontag, a friend of Brryan, observed, "He could be mad forever but he chooses to forgive, because that's what God would do." Brryan agreed; "God wants us to forgive people. Am I going to make myself as low as he [his father] is? I've got to be the better person."[62]

Many of my psychotherapy clients were physically or sexually abused by people whose whereabouts are unknown or who are dead so that the perpetrator can't apologize and ask for forgiveness. Does this mean the victim can't forgive? Fortunately no, the victim can forgive with or without the cooperation of the perpetrator. I was privileged to be a participant in a ritual of reconciliation with one of my patients who I will call Carl. As a child, the clergyman of his church had repeatedly sexually abused Carl. As one might predict, this made it difficult for him to attend that church, even when the offending clergyman was no longer there. Not only did Carl leave that particular church, he rejected all religion because he blamed God for allowing the abuse to take place. By the time Carl was a young man, he was an active drug addict. Fortunately he was able enter to a rehab program where he was introduced to the Twelve Step program. After being discharged, he became an active member of Narcotics Anonymous, even though he balked at the spiritual aspects of the Twelve Steps. In order to deal with the effects of the sexual abuse, he entered psychotherapy where he realized that prior to the abuse his relationship with God and his church had been a very important aspect of his life. Now as a young man he wanted to enter a church but every time he tried he was filled with resentment. He was angry that the abusive clergyperson had damaged his relationship with God and his church. He considered suing the church in civil court, but didn't want to go through the long, emotionally painful process that would be involved. We discussed how if he forgave those involved in the abuse it didn't mean what had occurred was acceptable, but only that it was too emotionally and spiritually costly to continue holding on to resentments about the abuse. I pointed out that if he wanted to reconcile with God and his religion, he would have to forgive first. He agreed and went about designing his own ritual of reconciliation. It consisted of him taking a clergyperson he still trusted, his mother, and myself on a tour of the church where the abuse had taken place. He tearfully described what had occurred there. Following the tour we all stood at the altar where the clergyperson read an apology from the church that asked Carl to forgive those who had not protected him from the abuse. Then his mother read a similar statement she had written, and I read A Document on the Witnessing of Reconciliation. Finally Carl proclaimed his desire to forgive everyone involved, including the offending clergyman and God, and his wish to reconcile with his religion and God. It was a moving event for all of us, and had a profound effect on Carl's life.

A Document on the Witnessing of Reconciliation

Let it be know to all gathered here within and to all others with interest in this matter that I, Mic Hunter, have been privileged to the most personal aspects of Carl's life for a significant number of months. During this time I have found him to be a worthwhile young man who has suffered under the burden of shame and other emotional distress. A major source of Carl's pain was the misuse of authority by a trusted representative of his religious community. This mistreatment caused Carl to reject the teachings of his church and the support of those within any religion, and that lead to him leading a lonely existence. This same abuse resulted in Carl's relationship with his creator being severely damaged to the point of becoming spirituality isolated.

Let it also be known to all who share an interest in this matter that Carl has chosen to reach out in the spirit of justice and forgiveness to those who represent the one who harmed him. He has chosen to believe that there are some crimes which are better handled by the laws of God and morality than by the laws of human courts.

I, Mic Hunter, by the authority invested in me by the Minnesota Board of Psychology, Minnesota Board of Marriage and Family Therapy, and the Institute for Chemical Dependency Professionals do hereby publicly declare that Carl is sane and honest. Therefore, any reasonable person ought to accept what Carl has disclosed concerning the events that he has described to us as true and accurate.

As a member of the human family it is my sincere desire that Carl be at last freed of his painful burden by whatever psychological and spiritual means necessary. On this date I pray that any and all blocks that prevent Carl from obtaining and maintaining a joyous, intimate relationship with the God of his understanding be removed. May his soul, sexuality and mind, be healed so that he lives a long life filled with serenity. May this be so from this day forward until the last minute of the last hour of the last day of his life.

**Forgiving My Enemies Is One Thing,
But Forgiving My *Family*?**

"We read that we ought to forgive our enemies;
but we do not read that we ought to forgive our friends."

Cosimo De Medici 1389-1464 A.C.E.

Some people understand that holding on to resentment reduces their own quality of life because it leads to chronic negative thinking and self-pity. A.A. members know that resentment is dangerous because it often leads to relapse. For them holding on to a resentment is like drinking poison and expecting some else to die. As a psychotherapist, I have often seen people who have had an easier time forgiving their enemies and strangers who have harmed them than they did forgiving their friends and family. These people are willing, even enthusiastic, to forgive strangers and enemies, and yet insist on maintaining resentments towards family and friends. People who had successfully forgiven a non-family member for an outrageous offense, still stubbornly clung on to resentment towards a family member over some slight transgression. Over and over I have seen family members who haven't spoken to one another in years because of some perceived slight.

What Can We Learn About Forgiveness From The Twelve Steps?

Despite the fact that the word *forgiveness* doesn't appear in any of the Twelve Steps, the concept of forgiveness is a vital aspect of recovery. Steps one through seven concentrate on improving one's relationship with the God, and forgiving oneself for mistakes made and harms committed. Steps eight and nine involve making a list of people one has harmed and making direct amends to them unless to do so would further harm them or others. Making amends doesn't require that one ask to be forgiven; rather it involves taking responsibility for one's misbehavior and making meaningful efforts to reduce the likelihood that similar inappropriate behavior occurs. Members are expected to make amends to those they have harmed regardless of whether the other person thinks any harm was done. Furthermore members are expected to make amends to whomever they have harmed, regardless of whether the other person has caused harm to them. "That person hurt me more than I hurt him. I'll make amends to that person only after he has made amends to me" isn't considered an acceptable excuse. As I have watched people prepare to make amends I have noticed two things occur. First, even as they get ready to make amends they are already beginning to forgive themselves for having harmed others. Secondly, by accepting responsibility for their actions they begin to see those who have harmed them in a different way; the people who have hurt them no longer seem to be as wicked as they once did, and their offenses seem less severe. In other words, accepting responsibility for their wrongs and forgiving themselves has the added benefit of freeing them from the burden of resentment towards others.

But What If I Don't Want To Forgive Others?

Certainly nobody can force anyone forgive. But the members of A.A. are warned of the dangers of resentment:

> Resentment is the "number one" offender. It destroys more alcoholics than anything else. From it stems all forms of spiritual disease, for we have been not only mentally and physically ill, we have been spiritually sick. When the spiritual malady is overcome, we straighten out mentally and physically... It is plain that a life which includes deep resentment leads only to futility and unhappiness. To the precise extent that we permit these, do we squander the hours that might have been worthwhile. But with the alcoholic, whose hope is the maintenance and growth of a spiritual experience, this business of resentment is infinitely grave. We found it is fatal. For when harboring such feelings we shut ourselves off from the sunlight of the Spirit...[Resentments] may be the dubious luxury of normal men, but for alcoholics these things are poison.[63]

In my experience, resentments are dangerous not only for alcoholics and other addicts, but also for everyone else. They are indeed a "dubious luxury." I have yet to meet a person who can afford such a luxury. I have witnessed many a person who seems willing to sacrifice time, peace of mind, relationships, and contentment in order to cling to a cherished resentment. So what does A.A.

suggest alcoholics do to be freed of hazardous resentments? Members are encouraged to see those for whom they have resentments as, "spiritually sick." In addition recovering alcoholics are encouraged to ask God to help them develop, "the same tolerance, pity, and patience" they would, "cheerfully grant a sick friend," towards those they have resented.[64]

Questions To Help In Personal Reflection Or Group Discussion

Make a list of your top five resentments.

How is resentment a "dubious luxury" you can't really afford?

What are you willing to do to be free on one of your resentments?

How did you react to the story of the ritual of reconciliation?

If you were to create a ritual to forgive those who have injured you, who would be invited to take part?

All You Need Is Love

"We have just enough religion to make us hate,
But not enough to make us love one another."

Jonathan Swift 1667-1745 A.C.E.

As we have seen compassion and forgiveness was important to Jesus, but he went even further and asked that we love. If the teachings of Jesus were to be summarized in a single word it would have to be *love*. It is written in *John* (4:8), "He who does not love does not know God; for God is love." While love is mentioned in all of the Gospels, *The Book Of John* contains nearly twice the number of terms related to love than the other three Gospels combined.[65] Jesus directed us to love God, the outcasts, and even our enemies. Then there is a thorny instruction to love our neighbor as ourselves. It must be an important concept in the teachings of Jesus since it appeared in the New Testament repeatedly; the book of *Matthew* even mentioned it twice.

"You shall love your neighbor as yourself." *Mark* 12:31

"You shall love your neighbor as yourself." *Matthew* 19:19 & 22:39

"You shall love the Lord your God with all your heart, with all your soul, with all your strength, and with all your mind, and your neighbor as yourself." *Luke* 10:27

"If you really fulfill the royal law according to the Scriptures, you shall love your neighbor as yourself." *James* 2:8

If You Love Your Neighbor As Yourself, Is That Good News Or Bad News For Your Neighbor?

"Do unto yourself as you would have others do unto you."
Sam Keen[66]

"The correlative to loving our neighbors as ourselves is hating ourselves as we hate our neighbors."
Oliver Wendell Holmes, Sr.[67]

When I ask people what is meant by loving one's neighbor as one loves oneself most tell me something along the lines of, "You ought to be as nice to other people as you are to yourself." In some cases that is good news for the neighbors, but in others cases it is bad news. If you love yourself and treat yourself with kindness, respect, and forgiveness, then by all means treat your neighbor that way. However many of my clients suffer from massive amounts of shame, even to the point of self-hatred. They mistreat their bodies by consuming huge amounts of nicotine, caffeine, alcohol and other drugs, as well as unhealthy foods. They think of themselves as unworthy, unlovable, unredeemable, and their deeds as unforgivable. These people are generally polite, even kind, to others, but not so to themselves; they love others, but not themselves. They would never think of seeing a neighbor walking by and yelling out, "Hey, you're fat and stupid, and you'll never amount to anything. You should just kill yourself!" Yet only minutes before that was exactly what they were thinking as they looked at themselves in the mirror. Nowhere was it written that Jesus said, "Love your enemy, but hate yourself," but it was written he said, "You shall love the Lord, your God, with all your heart, with all your being, with all your strength, and with all your mind, and your neighbor as yourself (*Luke* 10:27). How is one to understand this directive? Are we expected to go to great efforts to love God, but only love our neighbors to the degree that we love ourselves, or are we being told to strive to love God, other people, and ourselves to the fullest? Jesus taught that one ought neither be selfish (loving only oneself) nor selfless (loving only others). Other than the directive to love one's enemy, this is perhaps the most difficult teaching of Jesus to follow.

There is an old prayer, "O God, if there be a God, save my soul, if I have a soul." The wording of it implies one doesn't need faith in order to begin praying; instead start praying and faith with develop. As I mentioned earlier, members to Twelve Step groups are encouraged to, "Fake it till you make it." This technique can be applied to many aspects of life- including learning to love. If we treat others in a loving manner we will learn to love them. Likewise, if we treat ourselves in a loving way we will learn to love ourselves, and that makes it easier to more deeply love others. Notice I wrote "treat" because merely loving others or oneself without acting on that love doesn't benefit anyone. If someone is drowning throw a rope, don't just yell out, "I love you!" Unless you make an obvious attempt to actually save her it is unlikely her last thought as she goes down for the final time will be, "At least I can die knowing someone loved me." C.S. Lewis had a similar viewpoint:

> Do not waste time bothering whether you "love" your neighbor; act as if you did. As soon as we do this we find one of the great secrets. When you are behaving as if you loved someone, you will presently come to love him. If you injure someone you dislike you will find yourself disliking him more. If you do him a good turn, you will find yourself disliking him less.[68]

So how does one act as if one loves another? We could use *Corinthians* (13: 4-7), one of the most frequently quoted Bible passage: "Love is patient and kind; love is not jealous or boastful; it is not arrogant or rude. Love does not insist on its own way; it is not irritable or resentful; it does not rejoice at wrong, but rejoices in the right." When you read the checklist notice it doesn't say, "I am being PERFECTLY patient." This list is provided as a guideline to assist in self-reflection with the goal of improvement, not as a method for keeping track of imperfection with the goal of self-indictment. If you tend to suffer from all or nothing thinking where you think about the one time in the day you were impatient instead of all the times you were patient then maybe you ought to pencil in the word *reasonably* into each of the statements (e.g. I am being reasonably patient) or assign a percentage to each statement (e.g. I was patient 65% of the day). Keep in mind the slogan heard at Twelve Step meetings, "We claim progress, not perfection."

Checklist For Being Loving Today

Check All The Apply
___. I was patient.
___. I was kind.
___. I was trusting.
___. I was humble.
___. I was polite.
___. I was cooperative and compromising.
___. I was tolerant.
___. I was calm.
___. I was forgiving.
___. I was saddened when wrong was done.
___. I celebrated when right was done.

Let Me Help You, I'm Working On Being More Selfish

Members of Twelve Step fellowships are encouraged to carry the message of recovery to those with a similar affliction. The obvious reason to do so is to assist those who still suffer- the "love thy neighbor" portion of Jesus' directive. The, "as thy self," segment comes in the form of being helped by being of service to others. Members are told that the Twelve Step program involves a paradox; it is a selfish program that one has to give away to keep. Over the years many people balked at the use of the phrase "selfish program." One of the co-founders, Bill W., eventually explained the meaning of the term:

> The word "selfish" ordinarily implies that one is acquisitive, demanding, and thoughtless of the welfare of others. Of course, the A.A. way of life does not at all imply such undesirable traits. What do these speakers mean? Well, any theologian will tell you that the salvation of his own soul is the highest vocation that a man can have. Without salvation - however we may define this - he will have little or nothing. For us in A.A. there is even more urgency. If we cannot or will not achieve sobriety, then we become truly lost, right in the here and now. We are of no value to anyone, including ourselves, until we find salvation from alcohol. Therefore, our own recovery and spiritual growth have to come first - a right and necessary kind of self-concern.[69]

The flight attendants' directive, "Put your own mask on before attempting to assist others," summarizes the same philosophy; in order to be of service to others one first must be able to function. Only after one changes from being an <u>active</u> alcoholic to becoming a <u>recovering</u> alcoholic can one be of aid to others and reap the benefits that are described in *Alcoholics Anonymous*:

> Near you, alcoholics are dying helplessly like people in a sinking ship. If you live in a large place, there are hundreds. High and low, rich and poor, these are future fellows of Alcoholics Anonymous. Among them you will make lifelong friends. You will be bound to them with new and wonderful ties, for you will escape disaster together and you will commence shoulder to shoulder your common journey. Then you will know what it means to give of yourself that others may survive and rediscover life. You will learn the full meaning of "Love thy neighbor as thyself." The age of miracles is still with us. Our own recovery proves that! [70]

Blessed Are The Consistent (Perfection Not Required)

It was written that Jesus said; "Blessed are the pure of heart, for they shall see God" (*Matthew* 5:8). Many people read the word *pure* and think of definitions such as, "clean and free from impurities" or "virtuous and chaste."[71] They think since they don't meet those high standards they can't see God. However, in Aramaic, the language Jesus spoke, the word *dadkeyn,* which has usually been translated as *pure*, is more accurately translated as *consistent*. To be consistent is to be, "able to maintain a particular standard or repeat a particular task with minimal variation."[72] For most folks consistency is a much more attainable standard than purity since "minimal variation" leaves room for the existence of at least some deviation, therefore perfection isn't expected. The expectation is to be perfectly human rather than a human who is perfect.

Like Jesus, the framers of the Twelve Steps recognized that no matter how diligently people strive to do what is right at some point we all fall short. This is the reason the tenth Step suggests one continue to take a personal inventory and *when* wrong promptly admit it; the use of the word *when* wrong rather than *if* wrong indicates that mistakes will be made.

The twelfth Step of Alcoholics Anonymous suggests that members practice the principles found in the Steps in all aspects of their lives. They are encouraged to be open and honest with all people, not just other alcoholics or members of A.A. In other words they are practicing being consistent. A.A. co-founder Bill W. knew that most alcoholics have a streak of perfectionism in them so immediately following the section where the Twelve Steps appear in *Alcoholics Anonymous* he wrote this caution:

> Many of us exclaimed, "What an order! I can't go through with it." Do not be discouraged. No one among us has been able to maintain anything like perfect adherence to these principles. We are not saints. The point is, that we are willing to grow along spiritual lines. We claim spiritual progress rather than spiritual perfection.[73]

Neil Douglas-Klotz, translated Jesus' words, "Blessed are the pure of heart, for they shall see God," as, "Blessed are the consistent in heart; they shall see God everywhere."[74] I think his translation from Aramaic to English is more accessible and profound than is the English version that was translated from Greek. More accessible because consistency is more attainable than purity, and more profound because it indicates that Jesus was saying we don't have to wait for an afterlife to see God. If we love consistently we will begin to see God all around us, right here.

But you might ask, didn't Jesus say, "be you perfect" (*Matthew*, 5:48)? Well, it depends. When going from Greek to English that is how the phrase is usually translated, but when going from Aramaic to English the translation is, "be you all-embracing."[75] Now I'm not saying being all-embracing is easy, but it is surely a more attainable goal than being perfect. The Jesus of my understanding wouldn't set up his followers for certain failure by asking us to do something impossible like be perfect. Another example of Jesus having reasonable expectations can be found in the Lord's Prayer. In Aramaic the phrase usually translated from Greek into English as, "And forgive us our debts/trespasses, as we forgive our debtors/those who trespass against us," is more accurately read as *failures* or *mistakes*. Who among us hasn't failed at something or made mistakes? This same attitude of having realistic expectations of oneself and of fellow humans can be found in the Twelve Steps. As a part of the repair and transformation in Step Six members become, "entirely ready to have God remove" their "defects of character," while in the next Step they humbly ask God to remove their "shortcomings."

"Love is described as an energy by virtue
of its capacity to produce effects;
it is subtle, not because its effects are subtle,
but because it has been ineffable to science."

Judith Green, 2000 A.C.E.

Questions To Help In Personal Reflection Or Group Discussion

In the past week how have you been less than perfect when it came to being loving?

What is a recent example of you acting loving towards others?

Is your tendency to, "love your neighbor as yourself," good news or bad news for your neighbor?

If you treat yourself better than others, or treat others better than yourself, how do you account for this double standard?

For the next thirty days to use this checklist on loving each night prior to going to bed to review how you have treated at least one person.

___. I am being patient.
___. I am being kind.
___. I am trusting.
___. I am being humble.
___. I am being polite.
___. I am being cooperative and compromising.
___. I am being tolerant.
___. I am being calm.
___. I am being forgiving.
___. I am saddened when wrong is done.
___. I am celebrating when right is done.

All In The Family:
We Are All One People

"Born here a woman, born here a man,
Came to this country to become what I am,
And there isn't a history that isn't my own.
I am Muslim, I am Christian, I am Jewish to the bone.
I am Hindu, I am Buddhist, I'm a skeptic to the bone.
Young and old, gay and straight, every color and hue,
I am you, I am one, I am you."

I Am You
Anne Hills & Michael Smith[76]

Jesus taught his followers to pray beginning with the phrase, "Our father..." Using the term "father" in reference to God does more than characterize our relationship with God, it also describes our relationship with one another-we are all siblings-brothers and sisters. In the book of *John* it is written, "If any one says, 'I love God,' but hates his brother, he is a liar; for whoever does not love a brother whom he has seen cannot love God whom he has not seen" (4:20). Unless one believes by using the term "brother" Jesus was referring literally to one's biological brother, then Jesus was teaching us that we are all part of God's family. He didn't begin the prayer with, "The God of Abraham," indicating only Jews were part of the family; there were no exceptions made because to Jesus everyone was a member of God's family. Proposing that we are all members of a family of humankind was a radical stand in Biblical times, and remains so to this day. For centuries Hebrews had been taught the importance of keeping themselves separate from other groups in order to remain religiously pure. The Jewish people considered themselves to be God's chosen people, therefore all others groups were judged to be inferior, even evil. This was one of the themes in the Old Testament books of *Ezra* (10:12, 15) and *Nehemiah* (13:1-3). Further evidence of Jesus' focus on all of humanity is found in the wording of "The Lord's Prayer." In the version in the book of *Matthew,* from the first word, the focus isn't on the individual, but on the group-"Our father" and the group focus is further confirmed with, "give us our daily bread." We are directed to pray for more than our own needs; it is a community prayer, not a self-centered prayer.

Like Jesus the founders of Alcoholic Anonymous understood the importance of treating everyone as members of the human family. A.A. has a statement of responsibility; "I am responsible. When anyone, anywhere, reaches out for help, I want the hand of A.A. always to be there. And for that: I am responsible." This is quite a pledge because it doesn't limit one's responsibility to only alcoholics who are of a certain race, political party, sexual orientation, or social class. It says simply, "anyone." I once had the opportunity to witness this pledge in action. I was waiting in a busy airport terminal when I noticed a man pacing back and forth in front of a tavern. He looked like he was struggling to keep from entering the place. I guessed he was a recovering alcoholic who was liable to relapse if he didn't get some support soon. Not being a recovering alcoholic myself, and thinking what he needed was to speak with someone who knew about his craving from personal experience I went to the courtesy phone and asked the person who answered if she would make an announcement over the public address system.

Seconds after I hung up I heard my request fulfilled as a voice boomed from the speakers throughout the airport, "Any friends of Bill W. please meet immediately at [name of the tavern]." I knew from working with alcoholics over the years that this statement would be understood by recovering alcoholics as a cry for help. Suddenly from all over the airport the sound of running feet could be heard. From every area men and women appeared. Some were in the uniforms of pilots and flight attendants. Others wore clothing that indicated they worked behind the scenes loading suitcases on carts or pumping fuel. In no time at all they recognized which man was in need of help and gathered around him guiding him to sit with them as they put on a spontaneous A.A. meeting. It was a touching act of caring without regard to class, race, sex, or age. Here was a fellow alcoholic who needed assistance; therefore it was their responsibility to try to help him without any conditions. The man, who only minutes before was about to have the drink that likely would lead to him getting drunk, missing his flight, and who knows what consequences in terms of business and family, was smiling. When the meeting ended a couple of people walked with him to the gate where he made his flight. As for me, I had the privilege of witnessing a group of strangers gather together to gladly offer unconditional love to someone they considered a brother in God's family.

Questions To Help In Personal Reflection Or Group Discussion

How do you understand Jesus' use of the word "brother?" Did he literally mean one's biological brother or that all men are brothers in God's family?

Since Jesus used the word "brother" were women excluded?

What was your reaction to the story about the alcoholics in the airport?

Serve Others

"Preach the gospel always.
Use words if necessary."

Francis of Assisi

Since Jesus taught that we are all members of God's family, it makes sense that we ought to look out for one another and be of service to those less fortunate than ourselves. The book of *John* (21: 15-17) contains the story of Jesus asking Peter three times if Peter loves him. Each time Peter insists that he does love Jesus and furthermore Jesus already knows this. Every time Peter professes his love, Jesus directs him to care for his "sheep." Despite the repetition Peter seems to have to missed the point; if you claim to love Jesus you will show it by being of service to others. This lesson also appears in the description of the last supper found in the book of *John* when Jesus sought to wash the feet of his disciples. When they protested he insisted that if they couldn't understand his desire to serve rather than to be served, they didn't understand his teachings. Jesus' attitude and practice of being of service to others is no more popular now than it was when he attempted to teach it to his early disciples. Rather than asking, "How can I be of service to others?" most people ask, "What have YOU done for me lately?" and "What's in it for me?" Not so in Twelve Step fellowships. Many people mistakenly refer to Twelve Step fellowships as <u>self-</u>help groups; more accurately they are <u>mutual</u>-help groups because when one member assists another member both of them benefit. The twelfth Step in the program includes the responsibility of carrying the message to others and Tradition five states the primary purpose of each group is to carry the message to those who still suffer.[77] However, members are reminded they can only try to carry the message, and that it is inappropriate to try to force anyone, no matter how unmanageable his life might be; "We cannot be helpful to all people, but at least God will show us how to take a kindly and tolerant view of each and every one."[78]

Make A Wish

John Halgrim was a normal fourteen-year-old middle-class American boy. He enjoyed fishing with his brother, was a better than average soccer player, attended church most Sundays, and he had recently developed his first crush on a girl. But by the time John turned fifteen his life was changed dramatically. The change came in the form of an inoperable malignant brain tumor that stubbornly refused to stop growing even though physicians treated it with radiation. One day Sue Fenger, a volunteer from the Make-A-Wish Foundation, came to visit John. "Think of me as your fairy godmother," she told him, and then told him that the purpose of the Foundation was to see to it that terminally ill children had a chance to have one of their dreams come true. She asked him what dream he wanted, and expected to hear one of the usual responses such as wanting to meet a famous sports figure or movie star, to ride in a racecar, or swim with dolphins. Sue was taken aback when she heard John's wish; "I want to open an orphanage in Africa." Word got out about John's unusual wish and a minister from a local church came and made a video of John to be shown to congregations in order to raise the funds necessary to build an orphanage. In it John talked about his wish, and said that when he got cancer his view of life changed; "I learned I needed to live my life through God's eyes and not my own. I learned I had been asking him for so much more than I had been giving him." The video helped raise enough money that shortly after John died an orphanage large enough to house sixty children was completed.[79]

Questions To Help In Personal Reflection Or Group Discussion

When Jesus directed Peter to tend for his "sheep" do you think he literally meant a flock of animals, or do you think he was using a metaphor?

Can you imagine the president of the United States of America offering to shine the shoes of his or her cabinet members? How do you think the media of America and the rest of the world would react if it became known this actually took place?

If you are in a position of authority or status such as a teacher, physician, supervisor, employer or minister, how would you feel offering to wash the feet of your students, patients, supervisees, employees or members of your congregation?

How would react if your teacher, physician, supervisor, employer or minister offered to perform a lowly act of service for you?

John Halgrim said: "I learned I needed to live my life through God's eyes and not my own. I learned I had been asking him for so much more than I had been giving him." What do you think of that?

Everyone Is Worthy Of Our Loving Attention

"Divinity is always shared.
It is never exclusive."

Paul Ferrine[80]

Jesus was born into a Jewish society that taught that non-Jews were to be avoided. Jesus refused to abide by such limitations; he sought to accept everyone regardless of religion, ethnicity, national origin, sex, or physical condition. Against tradition he accepted gentiles, prostitutes, adulterers, thieves, and lepers. One of his early disciples, Matthew, had even worked as a tax collector for the oppressive Roman government. Jesus accepted not only those who worked for the occupiers, but even the occupiers themselves. The most outstanding example of this was when Jesus declared a Roman centurion (officer) had more faith than anyone he had ever met-including his own disciples (*Luke* 7:9). That is equivalent to a Frenchman praising the faith of a German officer during the Nazi occupation of Paris. When Jesus was challenged for violating religious laws by eating with tax collectors and sinners he responded, "I came not to call on the righteous, but sinners" (*Mark* 2:17). This acceptance of all people was so central to the teaching of Jesus that father Louis Evely declared, "If you can be resigned to the damnation of a single creature, then you aren't a Christian."[81] More recently Neil Young in his song "When God Made Me" asked if anyone is exempt from the acceptance of God.

When God Made Me

By Neil Young

When God made me
Was He thinking about my country
Or the color of my skin
Was he thinking about my religion
And the way I worshiped him?
Did He create just me in His image or
every living thing?
Was He planning only for believers
Or for those who just had faith?
Did he think there was only one way
to be close to Him?
Did He give us the gift of love
To say who we could choose?
Did he give me the gift of voice
So some could silence me?
Did he give me the gift of vision
Not knowing what I might see?
Did He give me the gift of compassion
To help my fellow man?[82]

Does That Mean I Can Get By Doing Whatever I Want To Do?

Some people worry that Jesus' willingness to spend time with the outcasts of his society will be interpreted as an indication he condoned their inappropriate behavior:

> Here's how this subtle argument goes-Jesus "hung out" with sinners including prostitutes, drunks, tax collectors, people with disabilities, awful sinners and those which the Pharisees and Sadducees disapproved of…so, therefore

> it is perfectly acceptable to live and be like these sinners since Jesus approved of them and accepted them and forgave them all-without exception.[83]

But Jesus' ability to accept (love) people who did bad things ought not be confused with him accepting (condoning) their bad behavior. The best-known example of this is probably the story of Jesus and the adulterous woman (*John* 7:53-8:11). Although at the time the punishment for adultery was death by stoning, when Jesus was asked what he thought should be done he made it clear that no one is without sin and therefore is not in a position to judge others. Jesus refused to "condemn" her, but still directed her to, "sin no more." The moral of this story is love the sinner, but not the sin.

Exceptions To The Rule?

There is a story of a man who went to visit W.C. Fields, the vaudeville and early movie star, when he was hospitalized for a fatal illness. Mr. Fields was notorious for his less than righteous style of living, so his visitor was surprised to see him reading the Bible. When the visitor inquired as to the reason Mr. Field was reading that particular book the cynical old man answered, "I'm looking for loopholes." Unfortunately, or fortunately, depending on your outlook, from what we know Jesus didn't leave any loopholes (Maybe Jesus Left Some Loopholes). It was written in the books of *Matthew* (7:7-8), and *Luke* (11:9-10) that Jesus said, "Ask, and it will be given you; seek, and you will find; knock, and it will be opened to you. For every one who asks receives, and he who seeks finds, and to him who knocks it will be opened." He stated, "every one who asks receives," that seems all-inclusive to me. As far as we know Jesus didn't say, "knock and it will be opened to you, unless you are ________."

Maybe Jesus Left Some Loopholes But They Forgot To Mention Them When Writing The Bible

And there upon the crest of the hill Jesus spoke to those gathered to hear his teaching. And among them were the Twelve, his mother, scribes, lepers, and those who suffered from evil spirits. All had come from far and near that they might be enlightened and know the path to righteousness. And on that day Jesus spoke forth saying: "But I say to you, love your enemies, bless those who curse you, do good to those who hate you, and pray for those who spitefully use you and persecute you." He paused for breath and continued: "Unless of course they are fat. Face it nobody likes gluttons. And don't get me started on drunks, but I don't have to remind you to hate them. And heretics, it only makes sense to hate them. Oh and infidels, those guys you can hate all you want, don't let me stop you there. As for fat drunk gay heretic infidels, well I think that goes without saying, who could blame you for hating *them*? I mean come on, you're only human!" And the people were amazed at his wisdom. Then they cheered making a sound louder than the horn of Gabriel; "Certain are we that this is the will of the Lord!" They went forth from that place with their hearts filled with hatred for those who deserved it. They took his words throughout the land, and instructed many to hate as they had been taught, and smote those who in their rejection of God's word refused to hate as they had been commanded. And all was as it had been before, and still they hated, because to do less was too much to ask.

Questions To Help In Personal Reflection Or Group Discussion

Do you think Jesus really meant "every one" as recorded in the books of *Matthew* and *Luke* or did he intend there to be exceptions?

How did you react to the lyrics to *When God Made Me*?

How did you react to Maybe Jesus Left Some Loopholes But They Just Forgot To Write About Them In The Bible?

What categories of people are unworthy of your loving attention?

What one individual is unworthy of your loving attention?

What did that person do, or not do to make him/her unworthy?

~

We Are All One People + Forgive Others=Love Your Enemy

"Hate is not conquered by hate;
hate is conquered by love.
This is a law eternal."
The Dhammapada: The Path Of Perfection (100 B.C.E.)

In 1563 the Roman Catholic Church proclaimed in *Canon Law Decree xiii*, "God does not ask the impossible." Despite this claim most people find loving one's enemy nearly impossible. In 1930 Dr. Sigmund Freud, the developer of psychoanalysis, wrote:

> If this grandiose commandment [love thy neighbor as thyself] had run, "Love thy neighbor as they neighbor loves thee," I should not take exception to it. And there is a second commandment, which seems to me even more incomprehensible and arouses still stronger opposition in me. It is, "Love thine enemies."[84]

Most people want either to ignore this love your enemy portion of Jesus' teaching all together, minimize its importance, or rationalize how it doesn't apply to them. Something to this effect: How about if I don't hate my enemy any more, I'll just dislike him. No hatred, but just a little hostility. But don't ask me to love him. That might be okay for Jesus back in Biblical times, but here in the 21st century our enemies, particularly mine, are TOTALLY bad. Sure I know everyone thinks their enemies are bad, but mine REALLY

ARE BAD. It's not my imagination; they are just pure evil. I don't see how even Jesus could love them!

There are many of reasons to hate one's enemy. Tradition is a common one; one group will hate another group long after the original offense between them has been forgotten. Another reason people want to continue to hate their enemies is because it makes it easier not to look too closely at the similarities between themselves and their enemies. I recall when I caught myself doing this very thing. I was angry with a particular politician; "Who does this guy think he is? He is so arrogant. He thinks he knows how everyone should live. I bet he sits around thinking, 'if only they would all do as I say, the world would be perfect.' And now he's trying to impose his will on the rest of us! I know one thing for sure, if I was in charge, he wouldn't get by with that. I'd make sure he and his kind wouldn't be able to spoil things for the rest of us. I'd see to it that he had to do what was right because I know exactly how...oops. Oh no! I sound exactly like him!" Although I disliked realizing that I was so much like the person I was bad mouthing it did teach me an important lesson about arrogance, humility and compassion. I was able to apply this lesson when I taught a course for elementary school teachers who were studying for their master's degree. The course focused on issues related to the sexual abuse of children by adults. On the first day we were discussing their impressions of people who had committed sex offenses against children. I heard the usual statements about sex offenders being monsters that should be castrated or killed. Then I gave them their first assignment: "Tomorrow when you go back to your class room I want you to determine which one of your students would be the safest one for someone to abuse. Then I want you to write a paper on the reasons you choose that child over all the others." The room erupted with objections; "I can't think like that! I can't even imagine such a thing!" Despite all the protests I insisted that it was a requirement of the course and would be counted towards their grade. The next week every single student turned in a paper. When I asked them what they had learned they all agreed the assignment was disturbingly easy once they got started. As I knew they would, they all choose a pupil who came from a troubled family background, had few friends, and was starved for adult attention, and so much the better if he or she already had been in trouble with the law. It didn't take long for them to imagine how they would further isolate the pupil, slowly introduce inappropriate touch, and how to blame the child if they got caught. They were surprised to learn how nearly effortless it was to choose the most vulnerable pupils. They reported their compassion for abused students increased, as they could now understand what easy prey they were to abusive adults. More surprising to them was the level of compassion they experienced for sex offenders: "I guess I'm not completely different from them like I thought. Until now I could never have imagined that I could have anything in common with them. Maybe they are not the monsters I imagined them to be. Now it is easier to see them as deeply troubled humans. I never thought of them even as people before."

What Would Jesus Want Us To Do In This Situation?

Like many men in 2009 Raymond Guay was released from prison after spending many years behind bars. To be exact, Mr. Guay had been imprisoned for thirty-five years. As a result of a prison outreach program Mr. Guay had met Reverend David Pinckney, the pastor of River of Grace Church in Concord, New Hampshire, who invited him to move into his house until he found a job and a place to live. Reverend Pinckney, his wife and four of his children, ages 13 to 18, claimed they were comfortable with Mr. Guay living in their house. Mr. Guay had his own room in the house and never left the house without adult supervision.

The story might have ended there as an example of love, compassion, and forgiveness, but when the other citizens found out that Mr. Guay was in their town, more than two-hundred of them demanded that Mr. Guay be banished from their town. The source of their anger and fear was the fact that Mr. Guay had been incarcerated for all those many years after pleading guilty to killing a twelve-year-old boy. After Mr. Guay's presence became public knowledge Reverend Pinckney reported hearing gunshots outside his house, and claimed one neighbor threatened to burn down the Reverend's house. The town council unanimously voted to have Mr. Guay removed even though they had no legal authority to enforce their will. The town's residents got no comfort from Mr. Guay's offer to wear an electronic monitoring device so that criminal justice officials could know his whereabouts twenty-four hours day. Nor were residents reassured by Mr. Guay's claim that during the thirty-five years he had been behind bars he had become a devoted Christian. "People like that don't find Jesus," insisted one resident.

You've Got To Be Carefully Taught

En-e-my *n*

"Somebody who hates and seeks to harm
or cause trouble for somebody else."

Encarta World Dictionary

Given the strong definition of the word *enemy,* I am surprised how often it is used to describe another person or group. Take for example this letter Mr. Nick Jorgenson wrote to the editor of a Minnesota newspaper:

> If Brett Favre ever dons the purple-and-gold, I will boycott the Vikings for the duration

> of his stay. That means no watching games on TV or buying game tickets, and no purchasing of Vikings merchandise.
>
> Not only has Favre been enemy No. 1 of the Vikings for a dozen years, he is washed up at this point. Even were we to win with Favre in place, it would be tainted-the season with the asterisk. And Packers fans would forever be able to hold it over us. If Favre is a Viking this year, it will be The Year that Must Not Be Named, at least for my family.[85]

For those of you who don't understand the importance of this situation Brett Favre was the quarterback for the Green Bay Packers football team for many years. There has been a long bitter rivalry between this Wisconsin team and the Minnesota Vikings football team because the two States border one another. The author of the letter lives in Sioux Falls, South Dakota, a State that doesn't have a professional football team. My guess is that his intense loyalty to the Minnesota team resulted from the fact that Minnesota and South Dakota have a border in common. I can only guess where his loyalty would rest if he resided in Iowa, where the State borders both Minnesota and Wisconsin. Regardless of how his loyalty originated, my point in citing his letter is that he referred to Mr. Favre as his "enemy." He could have just as easily used the terms that don't so clearly imply hatred such as *rival, opponent, competitor, challenger,* or *contender*.

Can an individual or group of people become one's enemy even without first hand experience with that individual or members of the hated group? Unfortunately yes. I would argue that the primary way most of us begin to hate isn't from personal experience, but rather by being taught to hate by the words and actions of family members, religious leaders, and other role models. This very point was made in the Rodgers and Hammerstein Broadway musical *South Pacific* that opened in 1948 and ran until 1954, and was made into a movie four years later. Even though one of the songs was so controversial that a legislator publicly insisted it was, "a threat to the American way of life," the play still won the Pulitzer Prize for Drama in 1950.[86] What was so dangerous about the song's lyrics that it could threaten our very way of life?

You've Got to be Carefully Taught

You've got to be taught to hate and fear.
You've got to be taught from year to year.
It's got to be drummed in your dear little ear.
You've got to be taught to be afraid of people
whose eyes are oddly made,
and people whose skin is a different shade.
You've got to be carefully taught before
it's too late,
before you are 6 or 7 or 8, to hate all the
people your relatives hate.
You've got to be carefully taught.

Questions To Help In Personal Reflection Or Group Discussion

Who do you consider your enemy?

Who do you consider to be so evil that they can't be, or shouldn't be, loved?

What do you think you would do if you found out a person who had killed a child moved into your town? What do you think of the claim, "People like that don't find Jesus?"

Do you think the teachings of Jesus are powerful enough that a person who has killed a child can be redeemed? If not, what other acts cause a person to be beyond hope?

Think of the individuals or groups of people that you hate; is your hatred the result of personal experience or were you taught this hate?

What if those who taught you to hate were well meaning but misguided or wrong?

To whom have you taught hatred (children, relatives, etc.)?

How did you think teaching them hatred would help them?

What words, actions, or lack of actions, have you used to teach hatred?

Be Humble: Focus On The Humanity Of Others Rather Than On Rank Or Status

"Clothe yourselves, all of you, with humility towards one another"

1st Peter 5:5

From the descriptions we have of Jesus, another person's rank, social class, wealth, status or celebrity didn't impress him. Even his enemies noted his lack of interest in status; "We know that you are an honest man, that you are not afraid of anyone, because a man's rank means nothing to you"(*Mark* 12:14). It is clear that Jesus was willing to interact with anyone regardless of his or her station in life. As a young man, I was fortunate to work for a nationally known treatment center where famous people came to deal with their addictions. Due to the laws that govern treatment centers I was forbidden to tell anyone even that I had met any of these celebrities, so I was unable to try to impress my friends by name-dropping. Furthermore I witnessed how these celebrities, no matter how famous, were still just people with many of the same fears, shame, and problems as the rest of us. This experience helped me to see how focusing on a person's humanity rather than his or her rank or status benefited not only the renowned person but me as well.

In *The Book Of Matthew* (5:3-12) there is a very short section that has a great deal of importance since it is basically a summary of the teachings of Jesus. These statements became known as The Beatitudes. The word *beatitude* refers to obtaining an extreme level of happiness and serenity, so it is in our best interest to take note of them. The Beatitudes was Jesus' way of saying, "If you want to be not just happy, but extremely happy, then behave in these nine ways." The very first thing he mentioned was humility. Now you might be thinking, "Just hold on one minute! The word 'humility' doesn't appear in any of the Beatitudes. I've read them and I know that for a fact!" And you'd be right if reading *The King James Version* or some other edition that was based on Latin or Greek. Those translations state the first Beatitude as, "Blessed are the poor in spirit; for theirs is the kingdom of heaven (*Matthew* 5:3). In English being, "poor in spirit," doesn't sound like a very desirable condition, even if it involves the Kingdom of Heaven. However, to a speaker of Aramaic, like Jesus, it simply meant, "being humble."[87]

Welcome To Sin City, Population: Everyone

Norm Greenbaum scored a hit with the song *Spirit In the Sky* that is still played on classic rock radio stations. In this song he predicted that his relationship with Jesus insured he would enter heaven. Of course there have been many songs that predicted the same outcome; what made *Spirit In The Sky* (at least the version by Mr. Greenbaum) unique was his claim of perfection: "Never been a sinner. I never sinned. I got a friend in Jesus, so you know that when I die He's gonna set me up with the spirit in the sky." I have never met Mr. Greenbaum, but I still find it hard to accept his claim that he has never sinned. His declaration of being sin free conflicts with both the Old and New Testaments:

"There is no man who does not sin" (*1st Kings* 8:46);

"Whoever knows what is right to do and fails to do it, for him it is sin"(*James* 4:17);

"If we say we have no sin, we deceive ourselves, and the truth is not in us" (*John* 1:8);

"All have sinned and fall short of the glory of God" (*Romans* 3:23).

If nothing else, it seems that Mr. Greenbaum was familiar with the sin of pride. In any case, I know I have sinned, and I'm pretty sure everyone who reads this book will have sinned as well. Fortunately Jesus had a soft spot in his heart for sinners: "I came not to call the righteous, but sinners" (*Mark* 2:17); "I have not come to call the righteous but sinners to repentance"(*Luke* 5:32).

Jesus And Humility

Jesus wasn't concerned about the prominence of those around him, nor was he interested in emphasizing his accomplishments or enhancing his reputation. Jesus preached, and more impressively practiced, humility. Jesus encouraged his followers not to make a show of their praying and other spiritual acts. He advised those who were fasting not to make it obvious to others. He insisted it was hypocritical to made sure others knew of one's fasting (*Matthew* 6: 16-18). When ones fasts or engages in other acts it ought to be done to advance one's spirituality rather than with the goal of impressing others and gaining prestige. Likewise, Jesus encouraged private prayer: "And when you pray, you must not be like the hypocrites; for they love to stand and pray in the synagogues and at the street corners, that they may be seen by men...But when you pray, go into your room and shut the door and pray to your Father who sees it in secret and will reward you" (*Matthew* 6: 5-6).

***Whose* Power And Glory Forever and Ever?**

Jesus sought to empower his disciples, not intimidate them with his wisdom. He didn't send out his followers to bring back people to hear the news directly from him because he wasn't seeking to be the center of attention.

He wanted his followers to go forth far and wide to spread to all people the good news of God's forgiveness and love. His message was about the importance of God, not about the importance of Jesus. Even in the stories in which Jesus performed miracles, he continued to practice humility. In *Matthew* there is the story where Jesus brings eyesight to two men, and afterwards Jesus directed them not to tell anyone what he had done. Imagine today if some of our well know religious leaders cured blindness; it would likely be repeatedly broadcast on television and used to appeal for donations.

Many people believe members of Twelve Step fellowships remain anonymous because they are ashamed of their addiction or other affliction. Although when first attending meetings newcomers want to keep their identity secret due to shame, anonymity continues long after the shame has dissipated. At that point the purpose of anonymity is humility as members serve others without expecting to get recognition. There are no awards or member of the year contests in Twelve Step fellowships. The co-founders of A.A. worked to remain humble their entire lives. When Dr. Bob knew he was dying he insisted that he be buried, "like other folks." There is no monument at his gravesite, and his gravestone contains no reference to his role in creating A.A. When *Time* magazine wanted to do a story on A.A. and put Bill W.'s photo on the cover, he refused the honor, even when the editors said they would only show the back of his head. Prior to getting sober he had done everything he could to be "a big shot," but after helping to form A.A., he realized the spiritual importance of humility by way of anonymity. Jesus would have approved of an organization such as A.A. that is dedicated to anonymously serving those who still suffer. Jesus told his early followers; "So when you give to the needy, do not announce it with trumpets, as the hypocrites do in the synagogues and on the streets, to be honored by men" (*Matthew* 6:2). Some modern day followers of Jesus have been less enthusiastic about anonymity as evidenced by naming their religious organization after themselves rather than giving it a name that describes its mission.

More than once I have made the recommendation that a patient consider daily doing at least one kind act for someone, preferably a stranger, and it be done anonymously. If the patient is discovered to be the doer of the good deed some other act for which there is no compensation or recognition is to be completed. In most cases those people to whom I make this suggestion assure me that they already do exactly that many times in a day. But at the next session most admit that when they do something nice they expect to get thanked for it, and if not, they are angry: "Traffic was bumper to bumper on the way to work and I let this guy change lanes in front of me and he didn't even give the 'thanks wave.' Can you believe that guy? What a jerk!" Others admit when they did something generous or kind and the other person didn't respond as expected they pointed it out: "Aren't you going to thank me for what I did? Did you even notice?" In these cases, what was supposed to be an action that helped two people feel better turned into something that made both people feel worse.

Thankfully there are success stories related to this assignment as well. One man came to the next session very excited to tell me his tale of anonymous kindness.

> I was at a retreat center attending a workshop and went out to the parking lot early in the morning to get something. Overnight several inches of snow had fallen. As I was cleaning the snow off my car it occurred to me that it

would be a nice gesture if I were to clear the snow off of all the cars in the parking lot. In no time at all I had finished the task and got back to the retreat center before anyone else had gotten out of bed. At breakfast that morning I was sitting with some other participants when someone came up and exclaimed, "The snow has already been removed from all our cars. Now we won't have to stand out in the cold scraping the windows. That was so kind." I was sitting there feeling pretty proud, even a little smug that I wasn't taking credit for the act when the other person added, "The service at this center is so good. I'm so impressed the employees would think to clean off our cars." When I realized someone else was getting the credit for what I had done I was tempted to speak up and inform everyone exactly who had bothered to be so kind, but then I thought about what you had been telling me about being kind AND anonymous, so I kept my mouth shut. When I stopped thinking about how I wasn't getting the credit I so rightly deserved, I was able to see how much pleasure everyone was experiencing from this simple act of snow removal. I found I was glad I had done it, and more importantly that I had done it without getting credit for doing it. I discovered it didn't even matter to my sense of well-being that someone else was getting the credit for what I had done. What could be more anonymous than that? Since then every day I keep my eyes open for opportunities to be kind on the sly. It's like a little game, but a game where everybody wins.

Who Is In Charge Here?

Since Jesus and his earliest followers were Jews it makes sense that some of them referred to him as rabbi:

> And Jesus answered and said to him, "Simon, I have something to say to you." And he said, "Rabbi, what is it?" (*Luke* 7:40)
>
> A lawyer asked him a question to test him: "Rabbi, what is the greatest commandment in the Torah?" (*Matthew* 22:35-36)
>
> And behold, a [rich] man came up to him and said, 'Rabbi, what good thing must I do to have eternal life?" (*Matthew* 19:16)
>
> And someone in the crowd said to him, 'Rabbi, order my brother to divide the inheritance with me." (*Luke* 12:13)
>
> And some of the Pharisees in the crowd said to him, "Rabbi, rebuke your disciples." (*Luke* 19:39)
>
> "Some of the Sadducees came up to him... and they asked him, saying, "Rabbi...." (*Luke* 20:27-28).

Now most of us think of a rabbi as being the leader of a Jewish congregation, but in the time of Jesus a rabbi was a scholarly person who others viewed as qualified to teach and interpret Jewish law. Leo Rosten explained:

> "Rabbi" means "my teacher." The rabbi is not a priest or minister, in the Christian sense. He is not an intermediary between God and man; nor is he a spiritual arbiter; nor does he exercise any formal religious authority over others; nor

> does he enjoy hierarchical status...A rabbi's influence rests on his learning, his character, his personal qualities.[88]

Jesus made it clear he was against hierarchy within a spiritual community: "Do not be called Rabbi (teacher), since you have only one teacher and you are all brothers. And call no one on earth your father, since you have only one Father, the one in heaven. Don't make others call you a leader" (*Matthew* 23:8-10). How could any organization hope to function without leaders with power over others; such a thing can't possibly exist. In fact, there is a spiritual community that functions guided by the belief that their leaders are, "but trusted servants, they do not govern." This organization has functioned for decades throughout most of the countries of the world, and includes members of all races, classes, and religions. I am speaking of course of Twelve Step-based fellowships, of which Alcoholics Anonymous is the best known. Anyone who claims to be a member of these groups is a member and none can be excommunicated for their beliefs. Members can be married, single, divorced, gay, bi-sexual, heterosexual, rich, poor, educated, or ignorant. There are no fees or dues and these organizations survive on the donations of members, and members only, they do not accept money from other organizations or individuals who are not members. Even members are limited in what they can contribute in order to ensure that no one can buy influence. Some groups practice voluntary poverty on a regular basis, meaning that if their expenses, such as rent on the meeting room, are paid and there is a prudent reserve they give the excess money to another group who is less financially stable.

Jesus expected his disciples to behave as ministers and servants instead of kings and masters: "But Jesus called them to him and said, 'You know that the rulers of the Gentiles lord it over them, and their great ones exercise authority over them. It shall not be so among you' " (*Matthew* 20:25-26); Despite the fact that Jesus warned against the danger of seeking power over others, his early followers continued to vie for his favor and to be more influential than his other disciples; "A dispute also arose among them, which of them was to be regarded as the greatest" (*Luke* 22: 24). And so it is today, people claiming to be followers of Jesus even as they strive for status and personal power, as well as seeking to ensure their nation will have power over other countries regardless of the means necessary to obtain and maintain it. I wonder what Jesus would think of some of the churches that were founded in his name which are organized in a strict hierarchy. Researchers who studied a random selection of 523 mainline Christian congregations to determine which factors lead either to a decline or increase in membership, found that churches that empowered laypersons as leaders were twice as likely to attract and retain new members than congregations with clergy that were unwilling to share authority.[89]

"For God resists the proud
but gives grace to the humble."

1st Peter 5:5

I'm More Humble Than You

"Admitting our defects
is an act of humility
and also of honesty."

Emotions Anonymous

Step Eight of the Twelve Step program is, "Humbly asked God to remove our shortcomings." What does it mean to be humble? Humility is somewhere in the middle between humiliation and grandiosity. In Twelve Step fellowships to be humble is to view oneself "right sized"-not less than others and not better than others. In the basic text of A.A., in the chapter "Working With Others," is an example of having enough humility to acknowledge not having all the answers:

> If [the new comer] be agnostic or atheist, make it emphatic that *he does not have to agree with your conception of God.* He can choose any conception he likes, provided it makes sense to him...He should not be pushed or prodded by you, his wife, or his friends. If he is to find God, the desire must come from within. If he thinks he can do the job in some other way, or prefers some other spiritual approach, encourage him to follow his conscience. We have no monopoly on God; we merely have an approach that worked with us.[90]

Zen Buddhists use the term "beginner's mind" to describe how one ought to approach the practice of meditation. Even those who have practiced for decades still attempt to approach meditation as if it is completely new. Along with practicing meditation they are practicing humility with their understanding that no one has ever totally mastered anything. Some Christians also value beginner's mind; C.S. Lewis was such a man. Although he taught at Oxford University, was the author of thirty books, and was asked to speak over BBC radio on the topic of Christianity in order to improve the morale of the British people during World War II, he still described himself as, "an amateur," and, "a beginner."[91] He claimed his personal experience as a former atheist who converted to Christianity was his most important qualification for speaking to the hundreds of thousands of people he spoke to during 1942 though 1944.

How can one approach the wisdom of Jesus with humility and a beginner's mind? It requires being teachable and accepting the **possibility** that someone else **might** have something worthwhile to offer. In 1927 Elbert Hubbard cautioned; "There is no end to education. We are all in the Kindergarten of God."[92] In Section II we will examine how people move through various stages of faith, and how those who reach the more advanced stages are those who have been open to information that at first disturbed them because it didn't fit with their understanding of spirituality. In short, the more humble a person, the better chance of obtaining a higher level of spiritual growth, and those with the highest levels of spiritual growth also remain the most humble among us.

In A.A. the moment when an alcoholic is so, "sick and tired of being sick and tired," that he or she is willing to do anything, even quit drinking is called, "hitting bottom." The alcoholic finally turns to A.A. as a last resort after everything less demanding has been tried and failed to bring lasting relief. Whether alcoholic or not, some people only become truly interested in spiritual growth when they have a personal crisis such as facing serious illness, death, incarceration, or financial ruin, and their normal coping mechanisms are inadequate to handle the stress. Research over many decades has found that the number of Americans attending church increases during financial hard times such as a recession, but then decreases soon after financial conditions rebound. Everybody wants to be in good with God when there is trouble, but once things are looking good, their relationship with God usually becomes less of a priority.

At the beginning of many A.A. meetings a section titled "How It Works" from the book *Alcoholics Anonymous* is passed from member to member to be read aloud in order to set the tone for what is to follow. It includes these words:

> If you have decided you want what we have and are willing to go to any lengths to get it-then you are ready to take certain steps. At some of these we balked. We thought we could find an easier softer way. But we could not. With all the earnestness at our command, we beg of you to be fearless and thorough from the very start. Some of us tried to hold on to our old ideas and the result was nil until we let go absolutely.[93]

Pretty serious stuff, but then again recovery from alcoholism and other addictions is a matter of life and death. Did Jesus propose any less of a commitment to his followers? No, in fact his version of How It Works was quite a bit more graphic:

> And if thy right eye offend thee,[4] pluck it out, and cast it from thee: for it is more profitable for thee that one of thy members should perish, and not that thy whole body should be cast into hell. And if thy right hand offend thee, cut it off, and cast it from thee: for it is profitable for thee that one of thy members should perish, and not that thy whole body should be cast into hell (*Matthew* 5: 30).

What did Jesus mean by this graphic statement? When he wanted to teach an important lesson, he sometimes

4 Some translations use the phrase "cause you to sin" rather than the word "offend."

used exaggeration to get the attention of his students. In this case his point was that whatever stands in the way of one's relationship with God must be removed no matter what the cost. Whether it is greed, resentment, job, relationship, or wealth one must be willing to let it go if doing so facilitates getting closer to God. In *Alcoholics Anonymous* after the Twelve Steps were listed, were written these words; "Many of us exclaimed, 'What an order! I can't go through with it.' "[94] I imagine the earliest followers of Jesus uttered similar objections.

What Could Someone Like That Teach Me?

In the book of *Luke* there is lesson on the topic of humility:

> Two men went to the temple to pray, one a Pharisee, the other a tax collector. The Pharisee, standing tall, prayed thus: "God, I thank you I am unlike the rest of men, thieves, criminals, adulterers, and that I am not like this tax collector here. I fast twice a week, and pay tithes on all I acquire." But the tax collector, standing at a distance, did not try so much as to lift his eyes to heaven, but he beat his breast and said, "God, have mercy on me, a sinner." This man, I tell you, and not the other, went home reconciled to God.

In this account Jesus sought to capture listeners' attention by reversing the normally expected aspects of a situation (The best known example being "The first shall be last"). People who heard Jesus tell the story would have immediately understood that a Pharisee normally would be thought of as a righteous man since he was a member of a sect noted for being very strict in the observance of religious rites and ceremonies. Listeners would also have expected that the tax collector, as a part of the Roman Empire's army of occupation, would be portrayed as the villain of the story. However, Jesus turned what was considered normal and usual upside down; the lowly tax collector was to be admired because he was humble and sought forgiveness from God. On the other hand, the Pharisee, despite his strict adherence to religious rules, was in fact arrogant, grandiose, and prideful. If Jesus were telling the story today these same characters might be a television evangelist and a child molester, or a bishop and a drug addict. Regardless of the roles of the characters the message would be the same; social position and status are irrelevant when it comes to determining if a person is following an authentic spiritual path. I had a personal experience that drove home that very lesson to me. I was attending a gathering in a church to hear an individual speak on spirituality. I arrived well before the event was to start and was standing outside the church enjoying the fine weather. I watched as a beat up pick up truck limped into the parking lot. It was held together with duct tape and wire. One of the mirrors was dangling and clanged on the side of the vehicle. What had once been a muffler made sparks as it dragged on the pavement. I was amazed it ran at all. Out of this heap of junk climbed a man in a worn shirt and jeans. His work boots had clearly not known polish since they left the factory. He walked toward me, and I imagined he was going to ask me for some spare change. He nodded and smiled at me on his way into the church. I noticed he was missing a few teeth; whether he had lost them in a fight, an accident, or to decay wasn't clear. The scheduled time for the gathering was approaching so I too entered the church and sat on one of the chairs that had been arranged in a circle. A number of people were already seated, including the man from the pick up truck. When all the chairs were occupied, a well-groomed man rose and suggested that we begin the event with a prayer. Once we had finished praying together, the same man stated he was glad we had all come and assured us that we would gain much from listening to the guest speaker. As he continued the introduction I scanned the faces of the people sitting around the circle wondering which one was the person who would be speaking. Much to my surprise after a glowing introduction the man from the pick up truck stood and began speaking. My immediate thought was, "What could this guy possibly teach me? After all I have four college degrees." I considered just leaving rather than wasting my time. But for some reason I stayed. The speaker's grammar wasn't correct, and he used quite a few slang terms, even some that had he been speaking on radio, would have been bleeped out. He spoke of his difficult life. He had been raised in a family, if one could call the collection of people that passed through his childhood a family, where alcohol and other drug use was common and extreme, as was violence. He lived in poverty as a child and became an adult who barely got by financially. He had seen the insides of emergency rooms, jails and prisons. The story he told exactly fit the way he looked. It was painful to listen to what he had endured. Then he began to describe the spiritual awakening he had experienced; how it had changed the way he looked at other people as well as the way he thought of himself. How he began to rely more on people and less on alcohol and other drugs. Even though he didn't know if he believed in God he prayed as if there was a God who could care about the likes of him. All this led him to becoming less focused on selfish matters and more on how he might be of service to others. Here was a man who had almost nothing in terms of belongings and no social status, yet he was thinking about the welfare of others. Here was a man who had not completed high school teaching me the theology of Jesus. He described the ways he attempted to imitate Jesus but by being kind, generous, and loving to everyone to whom he came near. He was not bragging; he actually seemed surprised he was capable of living this type of life. Here before me was the tax collector that Jesus had spoken of so long ago, and I was, much to my embarrassment, the Pharisee.

Questions To Help In Personal Reflection Or Group Discussion

In an average week how much time do you spend focusing on celebrities (watching television shows about the antics of stars, reading gossip magazines, going to web sites about famous people, or talking about them with others)?

How do these activities affect the quality of your life?

In an average week how much time do you spend thinking about God (attending services, praying, meditation, reading spiritual materials, or talking about spiritual matters with others)?

How do these activities affect the quality of your life?

What percent of your spiritual activities are done in public and what percent in private?

Do you think it is possible for a successful organization to exist without leaders who have power over other members?

What have you done related to your spirituality to try to impress others?

Faith Without Works Is Dead

"Deeds of kindness are equal in weight to all the commandments."

Talmud (Rabbinical reflections 100-600 A.D.)

The twelfth Step of the Twelve Step program indicates that once members experience, "a spiritual awakening" they ought to practice the principles underlying the Steps in every aspect of their lives. They are expected to behave honestly and to admit when they are wrong, not just in Twelve Step meetings or only during interactions with other members, but with everyone they meet. An identical expectation was laid out in the teachings of Jesus. In *The Book of James* (2:14) appears the question, "What does it profit, my brethren, if someone says he has faith but does not have works? Can faith save him?" In the next few verses he answered that question with another question: "Suppose a brother or sister is without clothes and daily food. If one of you says to him, 'Go, I wish you well; keep warm and well fed,' but does nothing about his physical needs, what good is it?" He then answers his own question: "In the same way, faith by itself, if it is not accompanied by action, is dead...Show me your faith without deeds, and I will show you my faith by what I do" (2:15, 16, 18). Over and over the importance of actions was stressed as more important than mere thoughts or beliefs:

> You see that a person is justified by what he does and not by faith alone (2:24).

> As the body without the spirit is dead, so faith without deeds is dead" (2:26).
>
> Whosoever heareth these sayings of mine, and doeth them, I will liken him unto a wise man who built his home upon a rock...And every one that heareth these sayings of mine and doeth them not, shall be likened unto a foolish man, which built his house upon sand" (*Matthew* 7:).

His point was to stress the importance of not merely hearing, or even memorizing his words, but to put them into action. To further stress the importance of taking action Jesus told the parable of the Samaritan who took action while the priest and the Levite did nothing to help. Jesus then asked his disciples, "Which of these three was neighbor to the man who fell in with the robbers?" The answer of course was, "The one who treated him with compassion." At which point Jesus gave his directive, "Then go and do the same" (*Luke* 10:36-37). He didn't say, "Then go and <u>feel</u> the same; the operative word in the directive was <u>do</u>. The only way to be a disciple of Jesus is to act upon his teaching. This was true in biblical times as well as today. Throughout history followers of Jesus have restated this message; "Do not merely listen to the word; Do what it says" (*James* 1:22). Over a thousand years later Martin Luther wrote; "[People] are saved by faith alone, but if faith is alone, it is not faith." Hundreds of years after that, David Ahl made the same claim; "James is not writing about how to become a Christian, but rather how to act like one. Having all the correct beliefs about God will hardly suffice: even demons believe in God."[95]

Despite all the emphasis Jesus put on taking action there are many people who place greater importance on having the proper beliefs than on one's actions. For example in a flier entitled, "Have You Heard The Good

News?" the reader was informed; "It is a common misconception that by being baptized or doing good works you will be guaranteed a place in Heaven...It is not what we have done but what God has done for us that will secure our salvation...It takes more than just believing there is a God to secure salvation...Salvation comes through believing that Jesus died for our sins, rose again from the dead, and confessing him as Lord."[96]

"Conduct [is] the ultimate test of the worth of a belief."

U.S. President Theodore Roosevelt

Isn't There An Easier Softer Way?

The early followers of Jesus understood he had high expectations of them. They knew there was more to being a disciple than merely not doing wrong; one had to actively do good. They realized the teachings of Jesus went beyond what <u>not</u> to do: "He who has been stealing must steal no longer, but must work, doing something useful with his own hands, that he may have something to share with those in need" (*Ephesians* 4:28). It is not enough to behave according to the principles Jesus taught only when in church or some other religious setting; one must consistently behave in accordance with the principles at all times, in all places, and with all people no matter what the issue. Alcoholics and other addicts learn very quickly that merely reading about the Twelve Steps and agreeing they sound like a great way to live isn't enough to stay clean and sober. Maintaining sobriety requires at least as much effort as one put into maintaining one's addiction. Unfortunately, unless one is willing to <u>work</u> the Steps, meaning taking meaningful action, recovery is merely theoretical.

"God is a verb, not a noun."

Buckminster Fuller

Questions To Help In Personal Reflection Or Group Discussion

What is your answer to the question; what does it profit if someone says he has faith but does not have works? Can faith save him?"

When the author did an Internet search on the phrase, "Faith without works is dead" he got 69,100,000 citations. What is so important about this concept that it is cited so often?

Do you think followers of Jesus ought to be expected to practice the teachings of Jesus in all aspects of life including family, sports, business, education, and politics?
If not, in what area(s) of life is one free to ignore the teachings of Jesus?

In what area of your life is it most difficult to thoroughly practice the teachings of Jesus?

Live Fully

"Men will angle for religion;
write for it;
fight for it;
die for it;
Anything but-live for it."
Charles Caleb Colton, 1829 A.C.E.

Which One Are You?

In recent years I have been asking people, "Are you primarily a body that happens to have a spiritual component or are you primarily a spirit that currently has a body?" In most cases they answer, "Well, I guess I'm a spirit in a body." Then I ask, "Do you think your spirit will continue to exist after your body dies?" Again, in most cases, people respond that they believe their spirit will survive after the body dies. Then I ask a most profound and confusing question; "If you, in the form of a spirit, will at some point in time exist separate from your body, what was God's motivation for giving you a body in the first place?" Usually this is met with stunned silence. What is your answer to these questions? Is there something you and I can do as embodied spirits that we can't do once we leave our bodies? If God gave us bodies as tools in order to experience or accomplish something, it seems like it would be a good idea to figure that out and get to it while we still have a body that functions.

Eat, Drink, And Be Merry

Know Your Saints

Saint Gregory, the Great preached,
"Pleasure can never be without sin."[97]

According to the book of *John,* Jesus said, "I came that they may have life, and have it abundantly" (10:10). Most Christians understand this verse as a reference to life after death. However, it could just as easily be understood as an invitation to live life on earth fully and authentically. My wife used to refer to me as, "the reluctant hedonist" because I was always vigilant to insure I didn't have, "too much fun."[5] I mistakenly thought I couldn't be both spiritual and enjoy material things like eating food and being sexual. But as I matured spiritually, I began to see that spirituality and enjoyment aren't mutually exclusive. I began to imagine how I would answer if God asked, "So what did you do with the gift of life I gave you?" I decided my answer wasn't going to be, "Well I mostly spent it being miserable. I focused on how unworthy I was because I couldn't be perfect. I didn't fully utilize the talents you gave me because I didn't want to be accused of being arrogant. I didn't celebrate my successes because I didn't want to appear prideful. I was careful not to enjoy myself too much because I believed you wanted me to suffer while I was on Earth if I was to be rewarded in heaven." Regardless of whether one believes in an afterlife or not, it seems to me the best way to express gratitude to God for this life is to live it fully starting right now. Episcopal bishop John Shelby also believed Jesus wanted us to live fully in this life: "John quotes Jesus as saying his purpose is that all may have life and have it abundantly. That sort of guides

---

5 A hedonist is a person who devotes his or her life to the pursuit of pleasure.

everything I do. If an activity doesn't give life, if an activity diminishes the life of any human being, then I don't believe that it can possibly be from God."[98]

"The puritan hated bear baiting, not because
it gave pain to the bear,
but because it gave pleasure to the spectators."

Thomas B. Macaulay

Use Your Talents

The Greek philosopher Socrates claimed, "The unexamined life is not worth living." Since Jesus wouldn't be born for another 400 years he couldn't offer any rebuttal, but if he had I think he might have retorted with, "The unlived life is not worth examining." In Jesus' parable of the three servants entrusted with their master's money he told of the servant that buried the money to keep it safe, and the other two who took risks with the money even though it wasn't theirs. When the master returned from his travels he was pleased that two of his servants hadn't played it safe, but used their talents, and it paid off. The servant that didn't take any risk and didn't utilize his talents was scolded.

"When I stand before God at the end of my life,
I would hope that I would not have a single bit of talent
left and could say,
I used everything you gave me."

Erma Bombeck

Risk Being Yourself

Bishop John Shelby Spong wrote of the principle of living fully, "Jesus touched the depth of being, and the

Christ experience is nothing less than our call to be who we are, inside the love of God. I worship this Jesus when I claim my own being and live it out courageously and in the process call others to have the courage to be themselves."[99] Where would the Bishop get such an idea? Perhaps in the version of *Matthew* (5:48) written in Aramaic; "Be complete, develop yourself to the fullest degree."[100] In my work as a therapist, I constantly see people who are too shameful to be open about their authentic self. Nearly everyday I hear people say, "If anyone got to know the real me, they would reject me." So they spend their lives pretending to be the person they think others want them to be, instead of being their authentic self. Nothing good comes of this; whether they are accepted or rejected they still don't know the outcome if they had just been authentic. I tell people I live by the 10-80-10 percent rule which states no matter what I do approximately ten percent of the people who know about my act will reject me because of it, another ten percent will think what I did was great, and eighty percent won't much care. Since the outcome is the same regardless of what I do, I might as well be accepted or rejected for being the authentic me. For example if I went to work wearing a suit and tie about ten percent of my clients would think, "Well, it's about time he dressed properly. As my therapist he ought to show me some respect by wearing the proper clothes." Another ten percent would think, "Who does this guy think he is, some kind of a big shot? Don't try to impress me with your fancy clothes!" The remaining clients either wouldn't care one way or the other, or might not even notice. Likewise, if I dressed very casually the reaction of ten percent would be, "What? I'm not important enough for you dress up a little? For what I pay you the least you could do is put on a dress shirt!" Meanwhile another ten percent would have the opposite reaction, "Well, finally he has loosened up, and stopped trying to act like he is better than me by wearing those dress shirts!" Since the ratios will be the same, I might as well be the authentic me, whether in dress style or other actions. I give the same advice to the troubled couples who come to my office; stop trying to be who you think your spouse wants you to be and just be your authentic self. Be accepted or rejected for being you. Most of them are relieved to find how much easier it is to be authentic instead of being phony in an attempt to please their spouse.

Be In The Now

"The good Lord gave me a brain that works so fast
that in one moment
I can worry as much as it would take others
a whole year to achieve."

Unknown

Part of living fully is to be in the present moment rather than worrying about the past. Jesus asked, "And which of you by being anxious can add one cubit to his span of life?[6] Therefore do not be anxious about tomorrow for tomorrow will be anxious for itself. Let the day's own trouble be sufficient for the day" (*Matthew* 6: 34). It is that wisdom that led to the modern day adage, "If you're going to pray why bother worrying, and if you're going to worry why bother praying?"

One reason newcomers to Twelve Step meetings are encouraged to live, "one day at a time," is because they, like many humans, have a tendency to ruminate about the past with an endless parade of thoughts that begin, "if only," and "I should have." To counter this they are taught the Serenity Prayer because one thing that can't

6 A cubit is an early unit of measurement equivalent to somewhere between 17-22 inches.

be changed is the past.[7] Another aspect of life that can't be changed, at least not yet, is the future. One can't take action in the future; only in the present can something be accomplished. Newcomers usually balk at the advice of living one day at a time thinking it is simplistic and naïve; "How can any one live without planning for the future?" They have difficulty understanding there is a difference between making plans and obsessing about the future with an endless stream of "what ifs." Rather than living fully one day at a time, they dread one day at time. Instead of waking up thinking, "Oh thank God-another morning!" they awaken with the thought, "Oh God-*another* morning!" The Serenity Prayer is useful in helping them determine the difference between making plans and obsessing. The only way to influence the future is to focus on the present and take action.

Years before Jesus was teaching the importance of being in the now, ancient students of Zen Buddhism were already being encouraged to focus their attention on what was occurring in the present. Modern Zen students are still taught that whatever they are doing, they can do it "mindfully," meaning being consciously focused on the task. When washing dishes, rather than thinking about something other than washing dishes, they seek to be aware of washing dishes-feeling the warmth of the water, smelling the scent of the soap, and hearing the sound the water makes as it moves over and off the dishes. Those who consistently practice mindfulness find it is no longer a technique but has become a way of being. Hence the expression, "Before enlightenment, chop wood and carry water. After enlightenment, chop wood and carry water."

Dr. Larry Morris, a psychologist who also guides trips in the Grand Canyon, taught me a lesson on the value of

---

7 "God grant me the serenity to accept the things I cannot change, the courage to change the things I can, and the wisdom to know the difference."

being in the present moment. He was gracious enough to put together a weeklong trip for several of us, all of whom were employed as psychotherapists. As we gathered at the trail head on the edge of the rim of the magnificent canyon he announced, "If any of you have anything you want to say related to your job, say it now before we take another step because I don't want to hear a single word about your jobs for the next week." He knew since all of us were employed in similar settings, it would be easy for us to spend the entire trip talking about our experiences as psychotherapists, thereby not being fully present in the moment. We would be thinking and talking about the past rather than focusing on being in the Canyon. On the morning of the day that marked the half-way point of the trip Larry declared; "I know exactly what you are thinking-the trip is half over. That's true, but being at the halfway point also means we still have fifty percent of the trip left to enjoy. I don't want you spoiling that time complaining about how much you are going to miss being in the Canyon when you get home. If you spend the next few days focusing on the future you will be missing half the trip. So, everyone is forbidden to talk about how they are going to feel when the trip is over. You will have plenty of time to talk about how you feel about the trip being over *when the trip is over*. In the meantime we are physically in the Canyon, let's be emotionally and spiritually in the Canyon as well." It is such wise statements that make Dr. Morris a sought after guide for trips both in the Canyon and in the quest for spiritual growth.

Questions To Help In Personal Reflection Or Group Discussion

Are you a reluctant hedonist? If you are, of what are you afraid?

Do you think spirituality and enjoyment of this life are mutually exclusive?

Is there such a thing as too much fun?

What would be the result of too much fun?

If such a thing as too much fun exists, how would you know when you are having too much fun?

How would you respond if God asked you, "So what did you do with the gift of life I gave you?"

Are you a body that happens to have a spiritual component or are you primarily a spirit that currently has a body?

Do you believe your spirit will continue to exist after your body dies? If you, in the form of a spirit, will at some point in time exist separate from your body what was God's motivation for giving you a body in the first place?

What can you can do as an embodied spirit that you can't do once you leave your body?

Jesus used the parable of the three servants to illustrate the importance of using one's talents. What God given talents do you posse?

Which talents are you suppressing and which are you expressing?

What do you think would happen if you fully expressed all your talents?

Describe the authentic you. What are the odds that, if someone got to know the authentic you you would be rejected?

What do you think of the 10-80-10 percent rule?

How would you live differently if you live according to the 10-80-10 percent rule?

How much of today did you spend worrying about the past?

How did that affect your day?

Make use of The Serenity Prayer:
"God grant me the serenity to accept the things I cannot change" (List the situations & people in your life over which you are powerless).

"The courage to change the things I can" (List the actions you could take today that are likely to lead to meaningful change).

"And the wisdom to know the difference" (If you did the first two sections then you have demonstrated that you already possess the necessary wisdom!).

How much of today did you spend thinking about the future?

How did that affect today?

What is one thing you can realistically do today that is likely to have a positive impact on the future?

If you believe in a life after death does that belief lead you to focus more on the future or more on the present?

Turn The Other Cheek: Use Non-violent Resistance To Fight Injustice

Many people are uncomfortable with the advice Jesus gave when he said turn the other cheek because they view it as a directive to be weak, passive, and even submissive. I see it as just the opposite-a call to be strong, assertive, and defiant. Jesus lived in a country that was being occupied by a hostile army where attempts at armed revolts were quickly and mercilessly crushed. Those rebels who didn't die from Roman spears or swords met their end through crucifixion. Jesus believed that in the long run more could be accomplished through passive resistance, forgiveness, and love than through violence. We have all heard the expression, "two wrongs don't make a right," which is the basis of Jesus' teaching of non-violent resistance. When we seek to overpower someone who has done us wrong we are practicing the very thing we seek to eliminate-the misuse of power and the desire to have power over someone else. The classic example is the parent who repeatedly slaps her child even as she exclaims, "How many times have I told you not to hit your little brother?" When Jesus said turn the other cheek he was saying don't submit to persecution, instead be defiant. When struck don't strike back, but don't cower either, instead boldly show that you will hold on to your ideals despite being threatened.

Examples Of Non-violent Resistance In The Real World

To bring about a peaceful world in the future, we have to practice peaceful acts now. Our means must be consistent with our ends.[101] As radical as is this principle, it was a fundamental teaching of Jesus. Many people reject this lesson as impractical. While in college I attended a party where a drunken Caucasian student accosted another student who was Asian and had earned a black belt in a martial art. The Caucasian student was inches away from the Asian student's face as he yelled; "You gooks think you're so tough with your stupid Kung-Fu! Any real American can out fight a chink. In fact, I'm fixing to kick your butt right now!" The whole room went silent with every eye on the Asian student, waiting to see what he would do after being insulted and threatened. I hoped he would merely teach the other student a lesson by fighting him but not maiming or killing him. Much to my surprise, and I'm guessing to most of everyone else present, the Asian student slowly stood up, looked right past the Caucasian student and said, "Thank you for inviting me to your party. I think I will go now," stepped past the other student and started to leave. The Caucasian student followed him yelling, "You coward! Come back and fight like a man!" Although I fully expected the Asian student to perform a spin kick and knock out the teeth of the other student, and wouldn't have blamed him for doing so, he just kept walking until he was out of the room. The drunken student turned back to the group who had just witnessed his outburst expecting to be congratulated and cheered; instead he was met with disapproving looks and people turning their back on him in silent protest. The look on his face went from one of victory and pride to one of humiliation as he realized he had made a fool of himself. The only one who had acted in an honorable and impressive manner that night was the Asian student, who Christian or not, had behaved consistent with the ways of Jesus.

When it comes to hand-to-hand martial arts there are two basic types. One style involves blocks, punches and kicks; Kung Fu, Karate, and Tae Kwon Do are examples of this style. When facing an opponent, the martial artist can attack or wait to be attacked. Once the struggle begins, one's attention is focused on blocking the incoming blows while simultaneously attempting to strike the opponent. The physical energy of both of the fighters is directed toward one another. The struggle ends when the loser is injured, maimed, or killed. The other style of martial arts, such as Judo and Aikido, primarily involves utilizing the opponent's own energy to defeat him-the motion of the attacker is redirected. This requires little physical energy so a small person can defeat a much larger person even if the attacker has a club or knife. This is where we get the expression the bigger they are the harder they fall. The struggle ends when the attacker retreats realizing that with every attack he has ended up flat on his back with the wind knocked out of him wondering how he got there. Aikido was developed by Morihei Ueshiba with the goal of combining his martial studies, philosophy, and religious beliefs to create a method of self-defense that didn't cause injury to the attacker, a value very much in accordance with the teachings of Jesus.

The War Between The States

Even though those of African decent had fought in the American Revolution, at the onset of the American War Between The States, the military and civilian leaders of the Northern forces refused to enlist "coloreds." However, the war was costly in terms of casualties and eventually all-black regiments were formed, lead by white officers, because black men were considered incapable of leadership.[8] At that time the payment for white soldiers was thirteen dollars a month, however, believing that black soldiers were inferior to whites the War Department paid

8 I use the term "blacks" instead of the more current term, "African-Americans," because in those days people of Africa decent weren't thought of as being true Americans.

black soldiers only ten dollars a month. Naturally, black soldiers were outraged at the message that their efforts and lives were worth less than those of whites. Rather than accepting this insult or deserting, the black members of the 54th Massachusetts Infantry followed Jesus' lesson on non-violent resistance; they continued to serve with distinction in combat and refused any payment unless it was identical to what their white comrades were paid. It was only after the War Department saw that black soldiers were just as brave as white solders, that the payments were made identical.[102]

World War II

During World War II, the Nazis occupying the country of Denmark ordered that all Jewish Danish citizens wear yellow star patches on their sleeves so they could be easily identified. The day after the order was issued, the King of Denmark took a long ride on horseback through the streets of the capital. Although he was not ethnically or religiously Jewish, he prominently displayed on the sleeve of his jacket a yellow Star of David patch. That same day more and more Danish citizens risked punishment, even death, to show solidarity with their fellow Danes and to defy the Nazis by also wearing the Star of David patch. Their message was simple and profound: We are all Danes; what you do to one of us, you do to all of us. With your military power you have occupied our land, but despite all your might you can't defeat our national spirit. Not content with symbolic gestures when the Nazis planned deport Danish Jews to death camps the Danes coordinated a boatlift of 7,200 Jews from Denmark to Sweden. Fishermen set out in the early morning as if they were going about their usual routine, but their holds were loaded with human cargo. Gustav Goldberg was nine years old when he and his family escaped the Nazis; "This was Denmark's way of telling the Germans to go to hell. 'The Danish Jews are Danes and we're going to take care of them,' and that's exactly what they did." Non-Jewish Danes, such as Frode Jakobsen, explained these events in simple terms; "Some Danes helped other Danes who were in danger." They were able to do this because, in the words of Anelise Sawkins, "No one saw anyone as a Jew or not a Jew, we were all Danes."[103]

Mohandas Gandhi

When most Americans think of Gandhi, they recall the famous photograph of a gaunt man with a shaved head wearing glasses sitting by a spinning wheel. Originally educated as a lawyer, he spent his life attempting to improve the lives of everyday Indians utilizing non-violence. He was a practicing Hindu, but saw all religions as acceptable paths to the same goal. He was inspired by the teachings of Jesus, particularly Jesus' emphasis on universal love, even towards one's enemies, and striving for justice for all people. His philosophy was also influenced by the Indian religions of Jainism and Buddhism that advocates *ahimsa*, the "absence of the desire to kill or harm."[104] Gandhi sought to go beyond merely not causing physical harm to his opponents; he wanted to bear them no hatred or ill will. He believed one had to be willing to suffer or die in order that oppressors may be converted to love. He firmly believed that if violence were used, even in a just cause, the result would only be more violence. He was reported to have said; "An eye for an eye makes the whole world blind." He rejected the use of violence on two grounds; first unarmed people had little chance of success against well-armed police and military forces. Secondly he viewed violence as little more than a clumsy weapon that created more problems than it solved, because it caused so much hatred and bitterness genuine reconciliation was almost impossible. "It is my firm conviction," Gandhi declared, "that nothing enduring can be built upon violence."

Horace Alexander described Gandhi's attitude toward his British opponents:

> On your side you have all the mighty forces of the modern State, arms, money, a controlled press, and all the rest. On my side, I have nothing but my conviction of right and truth, the unquenchable spirit of man, who is prepared to die for his convictions rather than submit to your brute force. I have my comrades in armlessness [sic]. Here we stand; and here if need be, we fall." Far from being a craven retreat from difficulty and danger, nonviolent resistance demands courage of a high order, the courage to resist injustice without rancor, to unite the utmost firmness with the utmost gentleness, to invite suffering but not to inflict it, to die but not to kill. [105]

The main tactic Gandhi and his followers used against the British was *Satyagraha*, which meant "Soul-Force" or "The power of truth."[106] In practice this meant standing up for one's ideals without hatred by refusing to cooperate with the oppressive government, not to follow specific laws if they were unjust, and to being willing to face the consequences of these actions. Other tactics included refusing to purchase British products, to work for British employers, to supply British citizens with services, and enroll one's children to British operated schools. Perhaps the best-known act of non-violent protest was in 1930; for years British law restricted the means of obtaining salt in order to tax it. In public defiance of the law Gandhi made a cross-country trek gathering supporters who joined him in harvesting salt from the ocean. Within weeks people all over India were obtaining their salt illegally, which lead to more than 100,000 people being sent to jail. Despite brutality and even killings committed by the police, Gandhi's followers refused to retaliate with violence even to the point of not defending themselves when attacked by the police.[107] The massive non-violent disobedience to British was a vital step toward India gaining independence from Britain. Jesus would have been impressed by the courage and strength of these people in the face of overwhelming odds.

The closer India came to gaining its independence, the more various factions began to compete for power. Gandhi's appeals to the various religions to work together peacefully put his life at risk. In January of 1948 a bomb exploded near a prayer meeting he was leading. Gandhi knew he was likely to be killed for his actions. Days before he was shot to death he said:

> Should I die by the bullet of a madman, I have to do so with a smile. There must be no anger in me. God must be in my heart and on my lips and you must promise me one thing: Should such a thing happen, do not shed a tear. I have done my deeds for humanity not requested by any human and I cannot stop on request of anybody. I am like God wanted me and I do as he advises me to do. Let him do with me as he pleases. If he wants to, he may kill me. I believe that I do as he orders.

"You can beat us with wires.
You can beat us with chains.
But you know you can't outrun the history train."

Peace Like A River by Paul Simon

"We must evolve for all human conflict a method which rejects revenge, aggression, and retaliation."

Dr. Martin Luther King, Jr.

Martin Luther King, Jr. was a Baptist minister in Montgomery, Alabama in the 1950's and 1960's. His nonviolent methods for social change were influenced by the teachings of Jesus and the example of Gandhi. He gained national attention when he helped organize a boycott of the city's bus system, because it was segregated. By law, black citizens were required to sit at the back of the city buses and to give up their seats to whites. This meant that if a white teenage boy coming home from football practice wanted to sit down he could force an 80-year-old black woman to give up her seat and stand for the remainder of her commute. The bus boycott lasted a year and resulted not only in changing the laws and practices in the South, but also inspired hope in Americans, both black and white, that segregation could be made a thing of the past. In addition to calling attention to injustice regarding civil rights, King also protested against the war Americans were fighting in Viet Nam. As a result of his efforts to improve the lives of others using nonviolent means, he was awarded the Nobel Prize for peace in 1964. He was the youngest person ever to be granted that honor. Dr. King was constantly receiving death threats, but defiantly stated, "If physical death is the price I must pay to free my white brothers and sisters from a permanent death of the spirit, then nothing can be more redemptive." Yes, he said, "white," because he viewed racism as damaging to both the victims and the oppressors. On April 4 of 1968 a white man shot him to death. In 1983 a federal holiday was named for King. He is one of only three people to be so honored, and one of them was President George Washington, a white man who owned black slaves.

Everyday Americans

In November 1993, a group of skinheads threw a bottle through the glass door of a Jewish family's home in Billings, Montana. That same week, they heaved a brick through a window of another Jewish household into the room where there was a 5-year-old boy. In response, the local newspaper, *The Billings Gazette* printed a full-page drawing of a menorah[9], and people of all faiths all over town displayed it in their windows. They also held the biggest Martin Luther King Day march in the history of the town. This non-violent resistance led to the skinheads leaving the city.[108] These actions were in accordance with two of the teaching of Jesus- nonviolent resistance and we are all one people regardless of our different religions.[109]

Questions To Help In Personal Reflection Or Group Discussion

What do you think of the author's claim that to turn the other cheek is an act of defiance rather than an act of submission?

Have you ever personally witnessed non-violent resistance? If so, what was the outcome?

9 The eight-branched candleholder used during the Jewish festival of Hanukkah.

Have you ever engaged in non-violent resistance? If so, what was the outcome?

What similarities did you notice between the teachings of Jesus, Gandhi, and King?

What could you do to follow the examples of Jesus, Gandhi, and King?

The Kingdom Of Heaven
Saint Peter & King Henry

We find ourselves at the Pearly Gates of Heaven where Saint Peter is entrusted with the task of determining who shall enter.

Saint Peter: "Next!" An obese man dressed in leather, lace, and velvet steps forward. "Name?"

Henry: "His Most Gracious Majesty, Henry, raised by the right hand of the Almighty to the Throne of the whole Kingdom of Britain, King of the English, and Lord of Ireland."

Saint Peter looks up from his massive ornate book with a look that implies he has already seen and heard such things far too many times.

Saint Peter: "You can stop with the titles already; I just asked for your name, not your resume."

Henry: "Never have I been spoken to in this manner!"

Saint Peter: "Better get used to it Henry; we're all the same up here."

Henry: "I demand to speak to your supervisor!"

Saint Peter: "Henry, think about it for a second, exactly who do you think my supervisor is?"

Henry: (After a pause.) "Oh, yeah, right, sorry." Getting back to business, Saint Peter begins to search through the pages of the huge book before him.

Saint Peter: (Under his breath) "You'd think we would have gone to electronic records by now. I'd love to have all this on a lap top...Okay, which Henry are you?"

Henry: "The VIII."

Saint Peter: "Let's go over this to make sure I've got my facts right. Other than being King and all that, what did you do to help bring about the Kingdom of God on earth?"

Henry: "I wrote the book, *Assertio Septem Sacramentorum Contra M. Lutherum*, in which I declared the Protestant Martin Luther a heretic. God should look favorable on such a great deed!"

Saint Peter: "For your information, God decides who is a heretic and who isn't, and furthermore God doesn't particularly care for the practice of judging other people's religion."

Henry: "But his Holiness Pope Leo X granted me the title of 'Defender of the Faith' after he read my book!"

Saint Peter: "I've met Leo, he used to dress as fancy as you... Back to the matter of this book; you wrote the whole thing?"

Henry: "You doubt the word of His Most Gracious Majesty, Henry, the..."

Saint Peter: (interrupting) "Henry! You can't lie your way into this kingdom."

Henry: All right, so I had help, but the basic outline was all mine. Maybe I should have given credit where credit was due on an acknowledgement page."

Saint Peter: "It says here that Pope Paul III rescinded the title 'Defender of the Faith.' What makes these guys think the faith needs defending in the first place?"

Henry: "That same year I founded a church. Surely such a deed shall make the face of God, the most high, to smile upon me."

Saint Peter: "Hmmmm, yes, The Anglican Church, also known as the Episcopal Church or the Church of England...seventy-seven million members...it's a legitimate church alright, but it wasn't exactly founded for spiritual reasons; you started your own church because the pope wouldn't grant you a divorce from your wife Catherine."

Henry: "She didn't give me the heir I required."

Saint Peter: "What about your daughter Mary?"

Henry: "Women are not fit to lead."

Saint Peter: "Where did you get that idea?"

Henry: "All of our Lord's apostles were men, none were women."

Saint Peter: "I wish I had a shekel for every time I've heard that one. So after you divorced your first wife you married Anne Boleyn..."

Henry: "And she too failed in her duty to give me a male heir."

Saint Peter: "So you accused her of adultery and condemned her to death."

Henry: "Then I took Catherine Howard as my bride."

Saint Peter: "And had her beheaded; does the phrase 'thou shalt not kill' sound at all familiar?"

Henry: "I'll admit beheading is a bit messy perhaps, but easier than going through another divorce, and then I was free to marry Catherine Parr."

Saint Peter: "It says here that when you broke away from the Catholic Church you disbanded all the monasteries in England and took all the land and property. Ever heard the phrase, thou shalt not steal?"

Henry: "If the king does it, then it isn't stealing."

Saint Peter: "What about these wars you waged against France Ireland, and Scotland?"

Henry: "Those were holy wars, waged in the name of God."

Saint Peter: "It's a good thing I've got all of eternity; this is going to take a while..."

What Did Jesus Say About The Kingdom Of Heaven?

According to the writers of the gospels, Jesus went to great length to try to describe the notion of the kingdom of heaven. He didn't describe the kingdom of heaven in literal terms such as, it is a place that has streets paved with gold, but instead relied on metaphors:

> The kingdom of heaven is like a grain of mustard seed which a man took and sowed in his field; it is the smallest of all seeds, but when it has grown it is the greatest of shrubs and becomes a tree, so that the birds of the air come and make nests in its branches (*Matthew* 13: 31)
>
> The kingdom of heaven is like leaven[10] which a woman took and hid in three measures of meal, till it was all leavened (*Matthew* 13: 33)
>
> Again, the kingdom of heaven is like a net which was thrown into the sea and gathered fish of every kind (*Matthew* 13: 47)
>
> Therefore the kingdom of heaven may be compared to a king who wishes to settle accounts with his servants (*Matthew* 18: 23)
>
> The kingdom of heaven is like treasure hidden in a field, which a man found and covered

10 Yeast or some other fermenting agent used to make dough rise.

> up; then in his joy he goes and sells all that he has and buys that field (*Matthew* 13: 44).
>
> Again, the kingdom of heaven is like a merchant in search of fine pearls, who on finding one pearl of great value, went and sold all that he had and bought it (*Matthew* 13: 45).[11]

From all these verses two things become clear; first the Kingdom of Heaven was important to Jesus, or at least his followers, and it must be a complex concept since he was unable to describe it except by comparing it to earthly things. What if the original disciples and the authors of the New Testament weren't spiritually advanced enough to grasp what Jesus was trying to get across? Maybe he used so many metaphors because every time he taught about the Kingdom the listeners looked at him with confusion on their faces. I can imagine such a scene.

Jesus Attempts To Teach On The Kingdom Of Heaven

Jesus is standing among a crowd of his followers. They are eagerly asking him questions concerning his thoughts on various topics. At last one person calls out, "Teacher, tell us of the Kingdom of Heaven!' The crowd goes wild, "Yes, yes, The Kingdom of Heaven! Tell us of the Kingdom!" The original disciples and the rest of the followers squeeze together to be closer to Jesus so as to better hear his words, and silence falls over those gathered under the hot sun. Jesus calls out, "Be seated," and they all drop to the ground. After what seems like an eternity, Jesus holds

11 In these last two stories a person suddenly finds something valuable even when not searching for it, this teaches, not that the Kingdom of Heaven requires the selling of all one's belongings, but that when a person discovers the Kingdom of Heaven he or she will joyfully do what is necessary to be a part of it. In Twelve Step groups this is called, "being willing to go to any lengths."

out his arm and with a smile declares, "The kingdom of heaven is like a grain of mustard seed which a man took and sowed in his field." He looks around expectantly, but is met only with blank bewildered stares. He speaks again, this time more forcefully, "The kingdom of heaven is like leaven which a woman took and hid in three measures of meal, till it was all leavened." He looks around expecting to see knowing smiles and nods of agreement, but all he sees are people looking at one another and whispering, "What is that supposed to mean? Do you get it?" He thinks to himself, "Hmmmm, tough crowd. But my best material is still to come." Once again he looks out over the sea of faces and declares, "Again, the kingdom of heaven is like a net which was thrown into the sea and gathered fish of every kind." He expects to hear expressions of delight as the lesson finally becomes clear to the listeners. But all he hears are murmurs of confusion, frustration, and even anger. Jesus tries one more time, "All right imagine this, the Kingdom of Heaven is like treasure hidden in a field, which a man found and covered up; then in his joy he goes and sells all that he has and buys that field." He pauses of a moment, sighs, shakes his head, and exclaims, "Come on already! Doesn't anybody get it? What is it gonna take?" When no one responses he holds up his hands and says, "Forget everything I said about what the Kingdom of Heaven is like; just pretend I never said it." The speaking slowly he adds, "Now pay attention, shut up and listen, this is important…love God…love others-even your enemies… and love yourself…Okay? I can't make it any simpler than that folks. If you don't understand or remember anything else I've said, just promise me you'll remember that and do it. I don't think that's too much to ask. Trust me, it could make for a really great life for you and everybody else." After a pause, he perks up and adds, "Hey, you're looking a little overwhelmed. Let's break for lunch. I'm famished. Anybody for some fish and bread?"

Which Is It?

Throughout history the Kingdom of Heaven has been understood in one of three ways. One way to understand what Jesus meant is that it is a place away from earth that one can enter only after death and under certain conditions. Another version of the Kingdom of Heaven is the state the world will be in once Jesus comes back; the Kingdom of Heaven will be on earth, but conditions on earth will be extremely different. Both of these versions are popular with modern day Christians; however they both indicate the Kingdom is yet to come. The third method of understanding the Kingdom of Heaven is the least popular one, probably because it is much less dramatic than streets paved with gold or a final cosmic battle between good and evil, and requires difficult choices in this life. This version holds that the Kingdom of Heaven is already here; there is no reason to wait, or go to another place, because the Kingdom is within each and every one of us. It involves rejecting the idea that God is separate from us, and accepting the idea that everyone, including you, is loved and accepted by God right now.[110] This concept is incredible in its simplicity and at the same time the most difficult idea for many people to accept. It requires that one's energy go into loving acts in this life rather than being concerned about the life hereafter. For years, my mother had a cartoon on her refrigerator in which one character says to the other, "I never ask God why He allows hunger, poverty, and injustice to exist on earth." "Why not?" asks the other character. The first character responses, "Because I've afraid He'll ask me the exact same question."

Questions To Help In Personal Reflection Or Group Discussion

Pop Quiz: The Kingdom Of Heaven- Where Do You Draw The Line?
The Kingdom of Heaven is unavailable to (check all that apply):

___.People who have never heard of Jesus.
___.People who have heard of Jesus, but insist on practicing another religion.
___.Agnostics (people who think it is impossible to know for sure if God exists or not).
___.Atheists (people who don't believe in any god).
___.Atheists who are kind, generous, and loving towards their fellow humans.
___.Devoted Christians who aren't kind, nor generous or loving towards their fellow humans.
___.People who haven't been baptized.
___.People of different race than yourself.
___.People who have violated any of the Ten Commandments.
___.People that believe in evolution.
___.People that don't believe the Bible to be the inerrant word of God and therefore isn't to be read literally.
___.People who are unclean (have a gross sickness).
___.People who are to blame for getting the disease that is killing them, such as those with lung cancer from smoking or those who became infected with AIDS as a result of drug use.
___.People that aren't members of the true church, and therefore are not real Christians.
___.People who haven't accepted Jesus as their personal savior.
___.People who have been sexual before marriage.

___.People in inter-racial marriages.
___.People in same-sex marriages.
___.People whom, while driving drunk, killed someone.
___.People who have violently murdered a stranger.
___.People who have violently murdered a family member.
___.Adults who have been sexual with children.

What did you learn about yourself from this quiz on the Kingdom Of Heaven?

How would your life change if you decided to believe everyone, everything, even you, were a part of God?

How do you define the Kingdom of Heaven?

If Saint Peter asked you whether King Henry ought to be permitted into the Kingdom what would you say?

How would you answer if God asked you, "Why do you allow hunger, poverty, and injustice to exist on earth?"

Section II

Factors That Affect Our Understanding Of What Jesus Taught

Attitudes That Affect Our Understanding Of The Teachings Of Jesus

Warning: Thinking Can Be Habit Forming

Over the years, all of us have developed patterns of thinking that have become automatic. We call these mental habits attitudes; they affect how we think about ourselves, other people, and the whole of creation. In most cases, these automatic responses don't cause any problems and are useful in that they make going about the business of everyday life easier. However some people have attitudes that make their lives more difficult because these responses are based on faulty or obsolete information. That's the bad news. The good news is that if one is willing to slow down and pay attention to what one is thinking, these automatic thoughts become identifiable and can be changed. In this section we will examine the internal factors, the psychology, that commonly affects people's understanding of the teachings of Jesus.

It Says So, Right Here In Black & White

Certainly first-hand experience is more compelling than getting information second-hand which is the reason we have the expression, "Seeing is believing." On the other hand there is a tendency for humans to interpret events in a way that confirms what we already believe. This is important to understand because when people read the Bible they tend to notice those verses that confirm what they already believe about God and their relationship with God, and to ignore those sections that contradict what they believe. They look for confirmation of their current beliefs rather than verses that might lead them to think differently.

What Kind Of People Live Here?

An old wise woman is sitting on her porch next to the road that leads to the town in which she has spent her entire life. Off in the distance she sees a stranger approaching. When he gets within speaking distance she invites him over to rest and have a cool drink. After finishing his drink the stranger asks the woman, "Have you lived here long?" "All my life," she responds. "So you must know the people of your town well, " observes the stranger. "Indeed, I do," says the old woman nodding. "Then tell me kind lady, what type of people will I meet in town?" "What type of people live in your home town?" inquires the woman. "Oh I come from a town of kind generous people," says the stranger smiling. "Well, then that is the type of people you will see in this town," assures the woman. Thanking her for her kindness the stranger heads down the road into town. After a few hours the woman sees another stranger approaching. When he gets within shouting distance he yells out, "Old woman, do you know what type of people live in that town?" "Yes, " she replies. "Well then tell me, what type are they?" The woman asks, "What type of people live in your home town?" "Oh, they are unkind and greedy," he says with a frown. "Well then," she said, "I'm sure that's the type of people you'll see in this town as well."

Given the human tendency to seek some form of confirmation for the beliefs one already holds, suppose a man already believed that God is supportive of masturbation; then the verse, "Whatever your hand finds to do, do it with all your might"(*Ecclesiastes* 9:10) would seem to confirm that belief. But that is only one verse; is that enough evidence on which to base an important belief? What if a man believed God was fan of baseball and therefore had seen to it that hidden in the Bible were references to the game of baseball that could lead to personal salvation or at least to winning the World Series. If he found verses that appeared related to his belief, would that necessarily mean that his belief was accurate? Read the actual Bible verses in Who Is God Rooting For In This Game and decide if they give you meaningful direction on how to live your life or even win a ball game.[111]

My point is that with enough effort, anyone can find some verse, even if it means taking the verse out of context, to "prove" that the Bible supports or rejects nearly anything. Bishop John Shelby Spong once observed that many preachers write a sermon to make their point and once it is complete, "as a matter of second importance" they look for Biblical verses to justify their stand.[112]

Who Is God Rooting For In This Game?

Let the young men...arise and play before us (2nd *Samuel* 2:14).
They stood every man in his place (*Judges* 7:21).
Rebekah came forth with her pitcher (*Genesis* 24: 45).
Who shall go up for us first (*Judges* 20:18).
Seek out a man who is a skillful player (2nd *Samuel* 16:16).
And Moses went out (*Numbers* 11:24).
And none came in (*Joshua* 6:1).
And there was not a man left (*Joshua* 8:17).
And Miriam was shut out (*Numbers* 12:15.
And the men of Israel and of Judah arose, and shouted (*1st Samuel* 17:52).

Q: Was Jesus A Conservative Or A Liberal?
A: That's A Stupid Question; Of Course Jesus Viewed Everything The Way I Do

Although one wouldn't know it by listening to talk radio and watching cable news shows, conservatives and liberals actually have an identical set of moral principles underlying their world-views.

Harm And Care

This principle holds that it is generally better to care for people and relieve their suffering than it is to neglect or harm people.

Fairness And Reciprocity

According to this principle justice and fairness are good and conversely the opposites are bad. Likewise people have certain rights that ought to be upheld in economic, social and political circumstances.

Group Loyalty

Since people value the protecting members of one's family, friends, neighbors, and fellow citizens, loyalty is to be rewarded and betrayal is to be punished.

Respect Of Authority

Since social order is necessary for the survival of humankind, people ought to behave within agreed upon behavioral guidelines and respect authority.

Purity And Sanctity

Certain aspects of life are sacred and things that defile that sanctity are bad. Purity in thought and action is good, so one ought to strive to avoid contaminating one's thoughts and body, as well as avoiding behaviors that are degrading.

So how is it that two people can value the same underlying principles, read precisely the same Bible verses in an identical version of the Bible, and yet come away with completely different interpretations of what they just read? It is the differences in priorities that make the difference in the way the two groups think and act even though they both have the same principles at their core. Conservatives tend to have loyalty, authority, and purity as their highest priorities. Liberals are more inclined to have as their highest priorities preventing harm and ensuring fairness. This is not to say that conservatives reject the importance of harm prevention or don't care about fairness; merely that conservatives see them as usually less of a priority than the other three principles. [113] Both groups value all the principles, but where they differ is in the order of priority.

My Interpretation Isn't Biased; You're The One Who Is Biased!

"in·ter·pret v
1. to establish or explain the meaning
or significance of something
2. to ascribe a particular meaning or
significance to something."[114]

When anyone interprets something he or she is putting his or her own meaning on it. Therefore, interpretation is a subjective, not an objective, process.[12] "This is a rock," is

12 "sub·jec·tive adj. 1. based on somebody's opinions or feelings rather than on facts or evidence 2. existing only in the mind and not independently of it."
"ob·jec·tive adj. 1. free of any bias or prejudice caused by personal feelings 2. based on facts rather than thoughts or opinions." *Encarta World English Dictionary*

an objective statement, whereas, "This is a pretty rock," is a subjective claim. When reading the Bible most people don't realize they are interpreting the words according to their own biased world-view. The concept of bias only comes to mind when their interpretation conflicts with someone else's interpretation, at which point most people accuse the other person of being biased: "It's right there in black and white! The meaning couldn't be more clear! Only a biased mind like yours could come away from reading that verse with such twisted understanding of it."

In 2009 some people were so convinced that a biased view of the Bible was being put forth that they wanted to have their own translation that better fit their world-view. They warned: "The committee in charge of updating the bestselling version, the [New International Version], is dominated by professors and higher-educated participants who can be expected to be liberal and feminist in outlook. As a result, the revision and replacement of the NIV will be influenced more by political correctness and other liberal distortions than by genuine examination of the oldest manuscripts. As a result of these political influences, it becomes desirable to develop a conservative translation that can serve, at a minimum, as a bulwark against the liberal manipulation of meaning in future versions." They were concerned that, "Liberal bias has become the single biggest distortion in modern Bible translations." Therefore they proposed a "fully conservative" translation of the Bible with some underlying principles including:

Providing a, "strong framework that enables a thought-for-thought translation without corruption by liberal bias,"

Avoiding, "unisex, 'gender inclusive' language, and other modern emasculation of Christianity,"

Avoiding, "dumbing down the reading level, or diluting the intellectual force and logic of Christianity,"

Using, "powerful new conservative terms as they develop,"

"Explaining the numerous economic parables with their full free-market meaning," and,

Identifying, "pro-liberal terms used in existing Bible translations, such as 'government,' and suggest more accurate substitutes"

Was I Made In God's Image Or The Other Way Around?

In his dictionary of psychological terms, Dr. Arthur Reber defined projection as, "The process by which one's traits, emotions, disposition, etc. are ascribed to another."[115] People project these characteristics on those around them-spouses, other family members, co-workers, Jesus and God. This tendency to project characteristics onto others is nothing new. Eight hundred years before Jesus, the Greek poet Hesiod observed the same thing: "We men have made our gods in our own image. I think that horses, lions, oxen too, had they but hands, would make their gods like them. Horse-gods for horses, oxen-gods for oxen." Although projection is normal we still ought to be aware that it can cause problems as Michael Gerson warned: "For millennia, artist, thinkers and politicians have shaped their image of Jesus, often into a mirror of themselves. But the goal of Christianity is to allow him to shape us, not the other way around."[116]

> "God made man in his own image
> And man returned the compliment."
>
> Blaise Pascal[117]

Our Father Who Art In Heaven

"God, at least in the half-assed way we conceive of him,
is a being, who made us in his own image,
and he is male, even he-man."

Brian Bouldrey
Monster: Adventures In American Machismo[118]

When asked, eighty percent of Americans reported they think of God as a male, so when they pray to, "our father who art in heaven," they automatically ascribe the attributes, both positive and negative, of their earthly fathers onto their heavenly father. This is so common that when I am working with a patient on spiritual issues I will ask her to write words or phrases that describe her father. Then in the next session I ask for a description of her concept of God. Usually the two descriptions are almost identical. Of course this overlap is wonderful if she had a father who was kind, loving, gentle, compassionate, fair, and attentive. But what if she had a father who was distant, violent, shaming, judgmental, blaming, and full of rage? Then she is likely to expect God to behave in the same way. Since Jesus was a male, she is equally likely to project on to him the characteristics of her father and other male authority figures.

"But who do you say that I am?"

Jesus (*Matthew* 16:15)

People, who have had an abusive father figure and project that image on to God or Jesus, sometimes turn to Mary (the mother of Jesus) in order to have a kind and gentle spiritual image in their lives. Others attribute motherly characteristics to God as did Pope John Paul I when he stated, "He is Father. Even more, God is Mother, who does not want to harm us." Of course, the usefulness of thinking of God as a mother figure is helpful only to the extent that one had an accepting, loving, kind mother in one's life. Unfortunately, in some people's experience, a mother is someone neglectful, who stood by and did nothing to stop abuse that was taking place, or was the perpetrator of abuse.

In the many decades that Father John Clay was a parish priest, he heard countless stories of people who were harmed by their family members, clergy, or other authority figures; he saw how these experiences negatively affected their ability to form or maintain a comforting relationship with God. During services he acknowledged the presence of these wounded people in his congregation:

> Are you feeling angry at the church? There are many ways that we are wounded by abuse we receive as children or later in life. Though some abuses cause deeper wounds than others, they are all damaging. There is physical abuse and sexual abuse. There is emotional abuse where nothing is done physically, but the words and actions make a person feel unworthy, ashamed, worthless, no good, stupid, and undeserving of good treatment. There is also abandonment and rejection. There is the crazy-making behavior where the words are loving and the actions hurtful. This isn't everything, but it gives us a good idea about what abuse is like. Religious or spiritual abuse can involve any of these with the added hurt of this being done by someone who is seen as representing the church or religion. This can alienate a person from church or religion and deprive them

of the value that church and religion had been or could be for them. This leaves a great emptiness that holds anger, confusion, cynicism, and despair. Something that goes still deeper sometimes occurs. Since church and religion are associated with God, a person can feel alienated from and abandoned by God. Sometimes it will feel like God is hating them or punishing them. Such an image of God is worse than no God at all. For a person's faith and trust in God to be destroyed is the ultimate wound. The ultimate Love is seen as the Ultimate Hate.

Questions To Help In Personal Reflection Or Group Discussion

What was your reaction to Whose Side Is God On In This Game?

Rate the following values in order of importance for you from most important to least important.

Harm and care
Fairness and reciprocity
Group loyalty
Respect of authority
Purity and sanctity

How does your priority list affect the way you see the world?

How does your priority list affect your understanding of these topics?

The treatment of homosexuals
Legalized abortion
Sex education in public schools
The teaching of evolution in public schools
The use of the military
The role of government
The role of women in society
The cause or purpose of AIDS
Events such as earthquakes and hurricanes

What did you think of Father Clay's words?

How is your view of God and Jesus similar to your view of your father?

How is your view of God and Jesus dissimilar from your view of your father?

How is your view of God and Jesus similar to your view of your mother?

How is your view of God and Jesus dissimilar from your view of your mother?

An Angry God

Leo (July 23-August 22)
"God will appear to you in a dream and tell you that loving you is the part of His job He hates the most."
Horoscope from *The Onion*, 2009

One of the most important principles taught by Jesus was his view of God as being more like a devoted father to be respected and loved than a lord to be feared. Despite this, there is a long history of people looking for evidence of an angry God in the Bible. They view personal and world events as the result of the actions of a jealous, short-tempered God who judges harshly and is quick to punish. Sixteenth century minister John Calvin was such a man. He was sure God was angry, and worked long and hard to convince others of the extent of God's anger. Calvinism held that all humans, except for a select few, deserved damnation and would spend eternity suffering in Hell. He was even sure that babies who died in the womb, at birth or shortly thereafter, would immediately go to Hell to be with the rest of the damned in order to, "glorify [God's] name by their own destruction."[119] From the 1720s through the 1740s, America, especially New England, experienced a revival of Puritan style religion that became known as "The Great Awakening." It began as the result of theological disputes, including the belief that the religion being taught at Harvard was too liberal, which lead to the founding of Yale as a place where a more conservative version of Christianity could be taught. One of the graduates of this new school was Jonathan Edwards who became famous and popular for his fire-and-brimstone sermons that left listeners in tears, whether from religious joy or fear is difficult to determine. His most famous sermon was titled, "Sinners in the Hands of an Angry God:"

> The God that holds you over the pit of hell, much as one holds a spider, or some loathsome insect, over the fire, abhors you, and is dreadfully provoked; his wrath towards you burns like fire; he looks upon you as worthy of nothing else, but to be cast into the fire; he is of purer eyes than can bear to have you in his sight; you are ten thousand times so abominable in his eyes as the most hateful venomous serpent is in ours. You have offended him infinitely more than ever a stubborn rebel did his prince.[120]

"Belief in a cruel god creates a cruel man."

Thomas Paine

The Angry God Of The Old Testament

Adam & Eve

In the first book of the Bible, *Genesis,* God was portrayed as a generous creator of a wonderful garden filled with plants, animals, and two people; all of which God declared was, "very good" (1:31). God informed the newly created people that they could eat freely of every tree of the garden except the tree of knowledge. Apparently God thought warning the humans would be enough to prevent them from eating of the tree of knowledge and therefore provided no safeguards. But then a snake convinced Eve to eat the forbidden fruit; she in turn convinced Adam to do so, whereas they both gained awareness of good and evil thereby becoming more God-like. God was so angry about what the humans had done, that they were banished from the garden. To ensure that they didn't eat from the tree of life-thereby gaining eternal life-God placed a cherub[13] with a flaming sword to guard the tree (3:22-24). Although God started out as kind and generous in only three chapters he had already neglected to have the forbidden fruit guarded, banished humans from the garden, and provided them with no apparent method for reconciliation or forgiveness.

The Great Flood

By chapter six of *Genesis* God had decided it was a mistake to make humans as well as the other animals and was making plans to destroy all of them except a small group that would be allowed to escape (6:7 & 13). By the end of chapter seven God had, "blotted out every living

13 Although the *Encarta World English Dictionary* and greeting card companies think of a cherub as, "a chubby-faced child with wings," they weren't so mild mannered in Biblical times.

thing" that wasn't on the ark that Noah and his family had built (7:23).

Lot's Wife

After the floodwaters receded, God reassured Noah that never again would a flood destroy humans and the other life forms; but that didn't mean that God stopped killing people (9:8-17). By chapter eighteen God was again fed up with human behavior and decided to destroy the cities of Sodom and Gomorrah. Had not Abraham negotiated with God, everyone would have perished. Abraham convinced God to spare the lives of one family. Lot and his family were allowed to flee Sodom, but were warned not to look back. But like Eve, Lot's wife gave into to temptation, looked back, and for her disobedience, God killed her by being turning her into a pillar of salt.

The Pharaoh Of Egypt

In the second book of the Bible, *Exodus,* God continues to be angry, punitive, and very active. God caused seven years of famine; turned all the water into blood,; covered the land with frogs; brought forth swarms of gnats, flies, and locusts, caused boils to form on both humans and animals; brought down hail and fire from the sky killing the livestock and crops; and murdered the first born child of every Egyptian family. At first it appeared that the pharaoh was not very bright, a slow learner, or incredibly stubborn because he didn't let Moses take his people out of Egypt, despite all of God's efforts. But the pharaoh wasn't acting of his own free will, because God had "hardened" the pharaoh's heart on more than one occasion (*Exodus* 5: 21; 10:1; 10:20). This is an interesting bit of information; one would think if God could harden the leader's heart it would be within God's power to cause the pharaoh's heart to soften. If God had the power to get the Jews out of bondage by affecting the heart of Egypt's supreme leader, what reason would God have to engage in all the destructive acts described in *Exodus*? There were two reasons: to prove to the Jews that God was the LORD, and for "sport" (10: 1-2). God repeatedly sent Jewish leaders to tell the pharaoh to free their people in God's name while at the same time God saw to it that the pharaoh wouldn't cooperate. This kind of behavior reminds me of some of the fathers I have worked with in psychotherapy who manipulate and punish their children in order to demonstrate to other family members that the he has the most power in the family, and for his own sadistic pleasure. This is exactly how God was portrayed in *Exodus*. God was made out to be a force to be obeyed out of fear, rather than out of respect, gratitude, and affection.

The Suffering Of Job

The story of Job was considered so significant that an entire book was dedicated to it. In the very first verse Job was described as a man who was "blameless and upright, one who feared God, and turned away from evil" (*Job* 1:1). He rose early each morning to make offering to God. In fact Job was such a good man that God actually bragged to Satan about him. But Satan wasn't impressed; he claimed the only reason Job appeared to be upright and proper was because God had blessed him, and were God to make Job's life miserable Job would stop behaving according to God's laws and would curse God. In an effort to call Satan's bluff God misused his power by torturing Job, not to mention killing many animals and people in the process. First God had thieves steal Job's livestock, and murder his servants. Then God caused a powerful wind to knock down Job's brother's house, killing all those inside. Despite all these losses, Job continued to praise and worship God. God boasted to Satan that Job had maintained his integrity despite God's willingness to "destroy him without cause" (2:3). Satan claimed that

God hadn't properly tortured Job, so God invited Satan to torment Job in any way he could think of as long as he didn't kill him. Satan wasted no time and covered Job's entire body with, "loathsome sores," that were so disfiguring that his friends didn't recognize him when they saw him (2:7 & 12). Despite his suffering, Job refused to curse God. Job believed God wasn't responsible for his suffering; he thought God would, "not reject a blameless man, nor take the hand of evildoers" (8:20; 9:2). Rather than comfort Job or even ask his forgiveness God taunted him, "Where were you when I laid the foundation of the earth?" and continued to mock Job for another 121 verses (38:4-41:34). After that, God decided to forgive Job and, "gave him twice as much as he had before" (42:10). After, "all the evil that the LORD had brought upon him," Job was expected to let by-gones be by-gones because God had given him some gifts. In the book of *Job* God was depicted as an arrogant father abusing his child while demanding respect and assuming that the child wouldn't protest the mistreatment. This is a common pattern in family in which there is physical and/or sexual abuse. After perpetrating against the child, the parent attempts to alleviate his or her guilt by giving gifts to the child and expecting everything to go back to how it was prior to the abuse.

Satan does his worst (Photo by Mic Hunter).

What Is The Appeal Of These Stories?

It is understandable to me that some people who were raised in abusive families would gravitate to these sections of the Bible when formulating their view of God. Here they find Biblical validation of the correctness of their childhood experiences; a father figure who is quick to use violence and humiliation towards his children, and supposedly behaves this way because he loves them and is doing so for their own good.

The Wrath Of God In Modern Times

Once people have developed the attitude that God is angry and punitive it affects not only their interpretation of Bible stories but also their understanding of current events.

They're Just Getting What They Have Coming

In January of 2010 an earthquake devastated the impoverished nation of Haiti. It killed 220,000 people, injured 300,00 and left 1,000,000 homeless.[121] Even before the quake Haiti was considered to be the poorest country in the Western Hemisphere, with 80% of the population living under the poverty line and 54% in abject poverty. At that time half of the population was under the age of eighteen. In the years preceding that catastrophe the country has been battered by one hurricane after another. Even with all their problems Haitians have a reputation for being intensely religious, with 96% of the population being Christian.[122] Televangelist Pat Roberson on his program "The 700 Club" informed viewers that the earthquake, as well as the condition of the country prior to the disaster, was the result of the pact with the devil that the enslaved Haitians had made in the 19th Century in order to be freed from French domination:

> Something happened a long time ago in Haiti, and people might not want to talk about it. They were under the heel of the French. You know, Napoleon III and whatever. And they got together and swore a pact to the devil. They said, "We will serve you if you will get us free from the French." True story. And so, the devil said, "OK, it's a deal." And they kicked the French out. You know, the Haitians revolted and got themselves free. But ever since, they have been cursed by one thing after the other. Desperately poor. That island of Hispaniola is one island. It's cut down the middle. On the one side is Haiti; on the other side is the Dominican Republic. Dominican Republic is prosperous, healthy, full of resorts, et cetera. Haiti is in desperate poverty. Same

> island. They need to have -- and we need to pray for them -- a great turning to God.[123]

Later a spokesperson for the program insisted that Mr. Robertson had not explicitly stated that the earthquake was the result of the wrath of God.[124] Regardless, that is the logical conclusion as traditionally those who make a pact with the devil are rewarded in this life, not trapped under fallen buildings without food, water, or medical attention. It would seem if anyone made a pact with the devil it would be the people of the Dominican Republic who seem to have all the goodies. Mr. John George of Northfield Minnesota went even farther in assigning blame for the earthquake and its effects. In a letter to the editor he wrote; "The thing we Americans refuse to recognize is that *our* sin contributed to this disaster." And asked; "How about it Americans? When are we going to repent?"[125] Both of these men could have compared the plight of the long-suffering Haitians to the Old Testament story of Moses and the Jews-another people who suffered under a cruel regime, had to endure great hardship, but because they were faithful to God, were led to freedom. I doubt that Mr. Robertson would claim that the Israelites made a deal with the devil and that is how they escaped Pharaoh and his troops at the Red Sea. Similarly, the plight of the Haitians could have been compared to the story of Job who endured one ordeal after another despite being an innocent faithful person. But Mr. Robertson and Mr. George, like their counterparts in the Bible, assumed that the people of Haiti were just getting what they had coming to them. This philosophy has two self-centered advantages; first if bad things only happen to bad people, then all one has to do to be spared is to be good. Second, since when bad things occur, those who are injured, hungry, grief stricken, and homeless are to blame for their condition, they aren't worthy of compassion; therefore the rest of us can claim to be freed of any obligation to care for them. In other words, it is God's will that these sinners suffer, rather than it is God's will that we care for our fellow human being regardless of what brought about their suffering.

God Sent A.I.D.S To Punish Homosexuals And…

In the 1980's Acquired Immune Deficiency Syndrome (A.I.D.S.) was first identified in homosexual and bi-sexual men and became known as "the gay disease." Some Christians quickly announced that God had sent this disease specifically to punish homosexuals for their sinfulness. When it became known that A.I.D.S. was also being spread between I.V. drug users when they shared needles, some people claimed that God sent A.I.D.S. to punish drug users for their sinfulness. When the Joint United Nations Program on HIV/AIDS reported that sex between men and women was the "driving force" of the epidemic, some people explained this fact by claiming it was merely God's desire to punish those who engaged in sex with prostitutes or outside of marriage.[126] Maybe God was angry at heterosexual African-Americans; in 2009 one study found seventy-five percent of their patients with A.I.D.S. were black and sixty percent of them were women who had become infected when they had sex with men.[127]

If the virus that causes A.I.D.S. was sent to punish these three groups of people God certainly utilized a long complex method. I say that because recently it was determined that the H.I.V. virus that causes A.I.D.S. has existed in humans for about one hundred years before it was identified.[128] It is a mutation of a virus that has existed in chimpanzees in Africa for even longer. No human had to have sex with a chimp to acquire the virus, all that was necessary was to be exposed to chimps' blood when chimps were butchered and eaten. Despite this discovery, some people continue to insist that God specifically sent the H.I.V. virus to punish homosexuals, drug addicts, and sex addicts. But what of those people who became infected with H.I.V. as a result of receiving contaminated blood during a medical procedure, or when they had sex with their spouse not knowing he had engaged in sex with another man, a female prostitute, or an I.V. drug user? Wasn't God also punishing innocent people? In some people's minds, God wasn't wrongly punishing them because they had been tolerant of sex outside of marriage, I.V. drug use, or homosexuality so they deserved to become ill.

God Sent Terrorists To Punish Us All

Fred Phelps, a pastor at a church in Topeka, Kansas, and his followers were passionate about the issue of homosexuality. So much so that they showed up at the funeral of Matthew Shepard, a gay college student who was beaten and left to die on a prairie fence in Wyoming. Phelps and his flock made the trip so they could inform the friends and family members of the murdered young man that; "God hates fags," "Gays are vomit-eating dogs," and "Gays are worthy of death." Eight years later they were still attending funerals to make their hatred of homosexuals known. However, they were no longer only attending the funerals of known homosexuals; now they were appearing at the fresh grave sites of military personnel killed in the Middle East. They had determined that these deaths were the divine retribution for America's tolerance of homosexuality. Phelps actually thanked God for the existence of I.E.D.s (Improvised Explosive Devices) and their deadly effect on American citizens. [129]

God Sent Staphylococcus To Punish Us For…?

Staphylococcus, better know simply as staph, is a bacteria that is pretty much everywhere. It is present on your skin even as you read these words. In most cases it doesn't do any mischief, in fact, when things are in balance it is actually helpful in the body fight against other forms of bacteria. By 2005 it was killing more people in America than was A.I.D.S. When the first drug-resistant strain was found in the 1960's, it was only dangerous to elderly patients in hospital settings who already had weakened immune systems from other illnesses. Did God send drug-resistant staph to punish those people for being weak, for being old, or for unknown sins they had committed? By 2006 there was a much more dangerous form of staph created called community-acquired M.R.S.A. (Methicillin Resistant Staphylococcus Aureus). This version of staph was infecting 100,000 people a year and killing 19,000 of them. It was affecting both heterosexuals and homosexuals, old and young, Christians and non-Christians. People became infected even though they weren't sexually active, didn't use I.V. drugs, and hadn't even stepped foot in a hospital. Just going to public places such as schools and gyms put people at peril. Merely being a human being on planet Earth in the beginning of the 21st Century was enough to put one at risk of getting infected.[130] What act, if any, was God punishing by sending drug-resistant staph? Perhaps God didn't send drug-resistant staph to punish us, but instead it was created by humans through our use of anti-bacterial soaps and the excessive feeding of antibiotics to farm animals.

What Did Jesus Have To Say About The Wrath Of God?

Many people are familiar with the story of Jesus bringing eyesight to a man blind from birth. Most people focus on the miraculous aspect of the story while overlooking an important aspect also included in the account. In the time of Jesus, it was widely believed that if someone had a physical deformity or handicap that it was a punishment from God for sins committed by either the affected person or that person's parents. But apparently Jesus didn't hold this view (*John* 9:1-1). When his disciples asked Jesus who had sinned the man who was born blind or his parents,

Jesus rejected that explanation, insisting that neither the man nor his parents had caused the blindness.

No, I Insist. I Am Unworthy.

"There's a war inside me…
Do I push it down or let it run me right into the ground?
I feel like I wouldn't like me if I met me…
I feel like you wouldn't like me if you met me…"
Song lyrics from "You Wouldn't Like Me" by Tegan and Sara

There are two common responses shown by people who believe in an angry God. The first is to be angry right back at God by rejecting religion and the concept of God. The second type of response is to fear God and go to extraordinary lengths in a never-ending attempt to appease God. These perfectionists struggle in world that consists of extremes, an all or nothing existence of good or evil, saint or sinner. They recoil at the idea that all people have a mixture of both positive and negative characteristics. I have worked with numerous people who have no difficulty believing Jesus walked on water, cured illness, rose from the dead, and performed other miracles, but when it comes to believing that Jesus or God accepts and loves them right now, without any changes being necessary, they balk. They deny the power of God to love them with a thousand "yes, buts." They see being accepted by God as something that must be earned and if it occurs, will only happen after they have made major changes. They are convinced that God sees them in exactly the same way they see themselves-flawed, unworthy, and unlovable. Bernard Bush counseled, "We cannot assume that [God] feels about us the way we feel about ourselves, unless we love ourselves intensely and freely."[131]

A Loving God

While it is true that there are numerous references to God as wrathful and dangerous there are also plenty of descriptions of God as loving and safe. Paul described God as, "the God of love and peace" (2nd *Corinthians* 13:11). In *Timothy* he wrote, "For God has not given us a spirit of fear, but of power and love and of a sound mind" (1:7). In my opinion the most important information in the entire book of *John* are the three words, "God is love" (*1st John* 4:8). Since there are verses that depict God as wrathful and dangerous, as well as verses that portray God as generous and loving, it comes down to a very important decision; which view of God will be the one by which you live your life? Will you live in fear of a wrathful God, quick to take offense and ever vigilant for any indication of sin so that divine punishment can be dispensed. Or live a life based on the belief that God loves you and therefore is compassionate, kind, generous, and quick to forgive? How could Jesus tell his followers that we are to forgive, "unto seventy times seven," and to love our enemies, if God is unwilling or incapable of doing so? I find it impossible to believe the God of which Jesus spoke would impose eternal punishment on those who committed finite offenses, particularly if these actions were the result of ignorance, mistakes, or acts of desperation. It is written that God said, "Thou shalt not steal," but would God eternally punish someone who stole medication to save the life of a loved one? I think not. The God of my understanding is one who can forgive those I couldn't forgive, and love those who I could only hate. The God of my understanding offers acceptance unconditionally. Anthony de Mello believed the awakening of the Spirit occurred when people make a fundamental shift in their view of their relationship with God; "The great turning point in your life comes not when you realize that you love God but when you realize and fully accept the fact that God loves you unconditionally."[132]

In the book of *Mark* it is reported that God said to Jesus, "You are My beloved son, and with you I am well pleased (1:11). How would it affect your life if you believed God saw you this very same way; "You are my beloved child, and with you I am well pleased"?

Questions To Help In Personal Reflection Or Group Discussion

How does your life reflect the lessons in the story of the Garden of Eden?

How does your life reflect the lessons in the story of the Great Flood?

How does your life reflect the lessons in the story of the destruction of Sodom and Gomorrah?

How does your life reflect the lessons in the story of the Jews in Egypt?

What reason do you think God had for hardening the heart of the pharaoh?

Which groups of people do you believe God sent A.I.D.S. to punish?

Men who have sex with men

Men who have sex with male prostitutes

Men who have sex with female prostitutes

Men who are I.V. drug users

Women who are I.V. drug users

Women who are prostitutes

Women who have sex with I.V. drug users

Women who have sex with men to whom they aren't married who have had sex with prostitutes and/or I.V. drug users

Women who have sex with their husbands who have had sex with prostitutes and/or I.V. drug users

Men and women who have been infected due to tainted blood they received during a medical procedure

Medical personnel who become infected because of exposure to tainted blood during the course of their work, such as in the case of accidentally being stuck with a needle.

If you believe God is punishing one or more of these groups of people, but not the others, explain that belief.

Thinking back to the earlier story in Section I of Brryant the eleven month-old baby who was infected when his father injected him with HIV tainted blood in an attempt to kill him, what sins do you think Brryant might have committed that brought on God's wrath?

People used to debate questions such as, "Could God create a rock so heavy even He couldn't lift it?" I have a similar question for you; could God create a person so sinful He couldn't love and forgive that person?

Suffering

Nobody Knows The Trouble I've Seen

Dr. M. Scott Peck began his book, *The Road Less Traveled,* with the claim-"Life is difficult."[133] This simple sentence would be an appropriate opening line for the Bible because both the suffering of individuals and entire ethnic groups is a major theme in the Bible. The second oldest known joke book, *Liber Facetiarum (Book of Humor)* was published in 1484 A.D. It contained 273 jokes collected by Gian Francesco Poggio Bracciolini, who was at that time secretary to the Pope.[134] One of these jokes addressed the issue of God and suffering: A monk attempts to comfort a seriously ill man saying, "God inflicts misfortune on those he loves." The suffering man responds, "I am not surprised if God has few friends; if He treats them in the manner he treats me, He will have even less"[14] Suffering is so much a part of the Bible there is an entire book titled *Lamentations.* The word lamentation means, "an expression of grief or sorrow."[135] Chapter three, verse sixteen certainly fits that definition: "He has made my teeth grind on gravel, and made me cower in ashes; my soul is bereft of peace, I have forgotten what happiness is."

The Suffering Of Jesus

Based on the number of words in the gospels used to describe the death of Jesus the authors of the gospels didn't think the gory details were of much importance. The torture of Jesus was so immaterial to the authors of the books of *Luke* and *John;* they didn't even mention it. The books of *Matthew* and *Mark* both described the torture

14 Hey, I never claimed it was a funny joke.

in only a few words, "having scourged Jesus, delivered him to be crucified" (27:26 & 15:15). Then Roman soldiers put a crown of thorns on his Jesus' head, spat upon him, and taunted and ridiculed him (27: 29 –30 & 15:17-19). In the time of Jesus, it was common practice for those condemned to crucifixion to be whipped prior to being nailed to a cross. He was not getting any worse treatment than thousands of others before him. The process of being nailed to the cross and the slow painful death were not even mentioned; the entire death scene was a mere fifteen words; "And when they had crucified him, they divided his garments among them by casting lots" (27:35 & 15:24).

Despite the lack of interest in the details of the torture and killing of Jesus shown by his early followers some of those who came later seemed preoccupied with it. Their focus remained on how he suffered and died rather than on how he loved and lived. A recent example of this was the movie *The Passion Of Christ* that focused on the end of Jesus' life with an emphasis on his suffering. The director Mel Gibson insisted it was a historically accurate depiction of the last hours of Jesus, but as we have already seen the writers of the gospels gave almost no details of those events, so in effect the creators of the film had to make up what happened because one can't make a full length feature film based only on the few words provided in the Bible. The film portrayal of violence was so unrelenting and graphic that in order to get an R rating instead of an X rating a full five minutes of it had to be cut. One reviewer described it as long minutes, "of exaggerated blood-soaked violence as Jesus is tied to a post, whipped with a stick, then sadistically flayed again with a whip that has metal barbs at each end, his flesh torn out by the hooks. When he is finally nailed to the cross in slow motion hammer strokes, we breathe a sigh of relief because emotional numbness has taken over and we know the end is close."[136] One reviewer timed the movie at two hours and six minutes, during which time Jesus was beaten for forty-five minutes and whipped 115 times before being nailed to a cross with four spikes.[137] Whereas some people were horrified that children watching the Super Bowl football game caught a glimpse of singer Janet Jackson's nipple when she had a "costume malfunction" they saw no problem with bringing children to see a movie in which Jesus was graphically tortured.

A German portrayal of Jesus being beaten (Photo by Mic Hunter).

Whose Butt Would Jesus Whup?

What motivates people to focus more of their attention on the passion of Jesus instead of his compassion? There are two main reasons for focusing on the suffering of Jesus; every minute spent thinking about his suffering and dying is a minute we don't have to spend living up to his example. It is much easier to focus on the suffering of Jesus two thousand years ago than to pay attention to the suffering that is going on all around us from poverty, ignorance, homelessness, war, violence, and illnesses of the body and of the mind. Another reason to focus on the suffering of Jesus is to assure us that Jesus was a "real" man. In the book of *Matthew* Jesus said, "Learn from me, for I am gentle and humble in heart" (11:29). All this talk about non-violence, and loving doesn't exactly give Jesus the reputation for being macho, and that makes some men nervous; they don't know if they want to identify with a man like that. It is this anxiety that led to an article titled, "Jesus Christ: Milquetoast, Mealy mouth, Namby-pamby, Molly coddler, Hippie-wimp Or Bold & Brave Preacher, King, Captain And Judge" in which the author warned:

> The false prophets of this sinful and adulterous generation would have you believe that Jesus Christ the Lord was a simpleton, soft-on-sin wimp, who never said anything bad about anybody; who guaranteed love, forgiveness and heaven to everyone; and who only came to provide peace on earth. This is a satanic lie.[138]

Militaristic Language

Many modern day Christians continue to use militaristic language when talking about Jesus; Reverend Jeff McCoy of the New Hope Church in Minnesota noted that the theme for his 2010 Easter service was, "the war of the lamb."[139] I know of a group of men who refer to themselves as, "prayer warriors for Jesus." How can a person claim to be a warrior in the name of the Prince of Peace, the man who preached non-violence and died rather than use violence in order to save himself? That is like claiming to be dictators for democracy. Jesus even forbade others from using violence in order to save him. When the soldiers came to take Jesus into custody one of his disciples not only pulled his sword, but also cut off the ear of one the intruders. Jesus told him to put away his sword and offer no resistance (*Matthew* 26: 51-52).

Some Christians don't have to face this contradiction of using the language of warfare in the same sentence with Jesus' name because instead of a pacifist Jesus they have a tough kick-butt-and-take-names type of Jesus. In an article about the town where Matthew Shepard was beaten to death for being gay the author described a church service he attended:

> At the Harvest Foursquare full-gospel church that Sunday, people wore nametags and expressed a serene camaraderie. Then they sent the children downstairs to play while the "illustrated sermon"- a dramatization of Christ's Passion and death-took place. It was a stunning performance, beginning with the Jesus character racked with sorrow in the Garden. The narrator said Jesus suffered like any man. Then he said, departing from the script, "Every time I see an image of a feminine Jesus, it makes my blood boil. Jesus wasn't a weakling. Jesus was a man. If Jesus was here today, he could take on any man in this room." Later, when the Jesus character was tied to a post, flogged by two men-soldiers who took "sensual pleasure" in every fall of

> the whip, the narrator said-"Jesus didn't cry out for mercy...Jesus was a man. Jesus was a man's man.[140]

Worship Or Warship?

> "At the smack down on the Mount,
> The lion shall lie down with the lamb,
> But only one of them will leave!
> You can turn your other cheek,
> And then come back with a powerful roundhouse to his face!"
>
> "*Wait, Wait, Don't Tell Me*" on N.P.R.[141]

Tom Skiles was a man who, "loved every minute of kicking ass for the Lord." In 2009 Pastor Skiles presided over, "Easter In the Octagon: The Ultimate Fighter," at the Spirit of St. Louis Church. The church's web site proclaimed: "For years the church has taught us to be 'the nice guy' when we have really been called to be Ultimate Fighters. But what do we fight for? Join us on Easter and throughout April, as we 'jump into the Octagon of Life' and learn how to be the 'The Ultimate Fighter!'" Pastor Skiles believed his message of becoming a fighter for Jesus would appeal to both men and boys:

> The Ultimate Fighting is something we're doing to promote to the guys. We want to make Easter relevant again. We don't want to make it about lilies and nice dresses. When they walk in we'll have a chain link fence set up, it'll be set up like an octagon. We'll talk about fact that Jesus didn't tap out-he was an ultimate fighter.[15] We're doing Easter

15 "Tap" means to give up and end the bout.

> Smack Down for our kids. It's not going to be an egg hunt. It'll be a Smack Down. It'll be a cool event. Kids love wrestling. We got inflatable boxing ring and all that stuff.

When asked to describe the type of fighter Jesus was Pastor Skiles responded: "Vicious but yet forgiving. I always make fun of people's images of Christ. The hippie Christ. The Christ with the long flowing air, like he came straight from the salon. I make fun of that. I don't think he was that kind of man. I think Jesus was a man's man. Him and his disciples. I tell people they probably had teeth missing."[142] If Jesus and his followers were involved in ultimate fighting it is likely they had plenty of injuries; ultimate fighting involves throws, chokeholds, punches, and kicking that nearly always leads to the spilling of blood, and sometimes to broken bones and unconsciousness.

Pastor Skiles was not alone in his belief that violence and Jesus go together like bread and wine. Brandon Beals, the lead pastor at Canyon Creek Church outside of Seattle, put it this way; "Compassion and love — we agree with all that stuff, too, but what led me to find Christ was that Jesus was a fighter." The web site to Martial Arts Ministries had a section for, "Wee Warriors," to promote fighting to very young boys. In Memphis Pastor John Renken lead Xtreme Ministries, a church that doubled as a martial arts academy. The school's motto was, "Where Feet, Fist and Faith Collide." Prior to each cage match Pastor Renken prays over each of fighters; "Father, we thank you for tonight. We pray that we will be a representation of you." Not only does he provide spiritual guidance, but also martial arts encouragement: "Hard punches! Finish the fight! To the head! To the head!" Proponents of using ultimate fighting as method of following Jesus found support for their position in the Bible, citing, "fight the good fight of faith" (*Timothy* 6:12).

One might think that these ministers were members of some radical fringe group, but in fact of the 115,000 white evangelical churches in America 700 provided full contact fighting for their members, and the youth ministry of the National Association of Evangelicals, which represented more than 45,000 churches, endorsed it.[143] As violence became ever more accepted in some churches Pastor Ken Pagano of the New Bethel Church in Louisville, Kentucky took the next logical step and wore a pistol on his hip when he spoke from the altar. He encouraged his parishioners to bring their firearms to services in order to celebrate the role weapons played in the history of America.[144] Apparently one of the roles guns play in America is enforcing church attendance; Michael Colquitt, age 32, got a judge to issue an order of protection against his father. According to Michael his father, Reverend Joe Colquitt, a Baptist minister in Alcoa, Tennessee, was in the habit of threatening him a gun because of his poor church-attendance.[145]

A Focus On The Suffering Of Jesus + Belief In An Angry God=?

Throughout history many Christians focused more on the suffering and death of Jesus than on the messages he taught when he was alive. Eventually, some people began to associate the experience of suffering with holiness, and this view was reinforced because of the stories of saints included self-imposed suffering. Adrian, the patron saint of prison guards, was a Roman officer who was so impressed with the bravery of his Christian captives that he decided to become imprisoned with them. This so impressed his wife, Natalia, that she shaved her head, disguised herself as a man, went to visit him where she kissed the chains that bound him to the wall, and encouraged him to endure his suffering (Apparently, she didn't value suffering enough to be imprisoned herself, but she was happy to support her husband's efforts at martyrdom.)

When her husband's legs were cut off, she prayed that his hands also be amputated as would befit a true saint. Her prayers for her husband's further mutilation went unanswered, but when he died she was able to make off with one of his hands as a relic. For her efforts she too was made a saint.[146] In Paul's *Letter To The Romans* (5:3-4) he proclaimed, "...We rejoice in our suffering, knowing that suffering produces endurance, and endurance produces character, and character produces hope..." Saint Dominic was known for his daily practice of whipping himself bloody with three iron chains. Saint Teresa was famous for beating herself, rubbing stinging nettles on her skin, and rolling naked in thorns. Before long Christian hermits began to follow the example of the sainted and began whipping themselves as they contemplated the suffering of Jesus and the wickedness of humankind. The practice then spread to monks, priests, and nuns. By the eleventh century Italian Benedictine Peter Damian had officially established that voluntary self-flagellation was an acceptable practice for those in the religious life. When asked where in the teaching of Jesus believers were directed to undergo whipping as a means for obtaining the grace of God he responded, "Did our Redeemer not endure scourging. Weren't the apostles and many of the sainted and martyrs flogged?" He could think of no better way to follow in the footsteps of Jesus than to suffer as he suffered.[16] According to historian Niklaus Largier, "Flagellation came to be practiced in almost every order and every monastery in Europe." Dominican nun, Catherine von Gebersweiler, wrote in the fourteenth century about the self-flagellation she and her fellow sister performed; "Others tortured their flesh by maltreating it daily in the most violent fashion, some with blows from rods, others with whips equipped with three or four knotted straps,

16 Another way would be feeding the hungry, clothing the naked, comforting the sick, etc.

others with iron chains, and still others by means of scourges arrayed with thorns." Eventually not only clergy but also lay Christians began to see physical suffering as a path to God; Henry Suso carved "Jesus" in his chest and pressed a cross with nails sticking out of it into his back.

At first acts of self-injury were committed in private, but as the practice became more acceptable it began to take place in public. Elizabeth von Oye, a Swiss nun, was well known for whipping herself that bystanders in the chapel would be splattered with her blood. In the year 1260 a throng of citizens with the approval of the city authorities marched through the streets of Perugia, Italy whipping themselves in an attempt to save the town from the wrath of God because one of the town's citizens, Raniero Fasani, claimed he was told by an angel that the town would be destroyed unless the inhabitants repented for their sins.

Eventually self-injury served as a multipurpose act; punishment for personal sin, atonement for the wickedness of humankind in general, a method for experiencing what Jesus had endured and thereby becoming closer to him, and, when committed in front of others, a statement of one's commitment to spiritual purity no matter what the cost. What did God think about all this? According to Dominican nun Catherine von Gebersweiler "torturing" oneself brought joy to God: "For God takes pleasure in these exercises of humility and worship and does not fail to hear the groaning of those who are filled with penance." Self-injury became so prevalent as a method of repenting that it threatened to surpass in popularity non-violent methods such as confession. During the fourteenth and fifteenth centuries a sect of Christianity known as the Cryptoflagellants preached that anything the church offered was useless because the one and only way to salvation was through self-flagellation. [17] The Pope didn't take too

17 I know, the name sounds like a race of robots from space, but "crypto" merely means "secret."

kindly to this claim so he labeled them heretics and had them burned at the stake. [147]

Modern Day Self-injury

Pope John Paul II was probably the most popular Roman Catholic leader of the 20th Century. Although it was not public knowledge when he was alive, after his death in 2005 as a result of being considered for sainthood, those intimately associated with him began disclosing that he engaged in self-flagellation. Sister Tobiana Sobodka reported on several occasions she over heard the Holy Father as he whipped himself. This was confirmed by Bishop Emery Kabongo, who served as the pope's secretary; who stated the pope beat himself as a sign of his "remorse for his sins," and to prepare himself prior to ordaining priests.[148]

Even If You're Not Going To Whip Your Back, You Can Still Whip Your Mind

In her memoir, Darcey Steinke, the daughter of a Lutheran minister, wrote of herself; "I love my neighbor as I love myself-which is to say, minimally, if at all, and in between fits of out-and-out loathing."[149] Nowhere in the Bible is there any reference to Jesus teaching that torturing oneself brought joy to God; quite the opposite-the God of Jesus was a loving force. Unfortunately despite this New Testament portrayal of God some people continue to torture themselves, not with whips but with their thoughts. In their heads is an never ending thought loop that tells them they were born from sin, are unworthy of God's love, their desires-particularly sexual ones-are evil, and are doomed to a horrible afterlife. Many of them strive to be perfect. I don't mean perfectly human, but perfect period. But there are those of us who not only don't think we need to be perfect to be good followers of Jesus, we don't need Jesus to be perfect either. In 2007 twenty-six percent of born again Christians, and forty-one percent of others Christians polled agreed with the statement, "While he lived on earth, Jesus committed sins, like other people." [150] But it wasn't it written in *Matthew* that Jesus said, "be you perfect' (5:48)? Well, yes and no. In most of the versions of the Bible that were based on translations from Greek or Latin into English "perfect" was the word used, but according to speakers of Aramaic-the language Jesus spoke when addressing his students-the phrase is better translated as, "be you all-embracing."[151] Although becoming all embracing is not exactly easy it is certainly a more realistic goal than perfection.

Questions To Help In Personal Reflection Or Group Discussion

How does engaging in fist fighting in church fit with your understanding of the teachings of Jesus?

Do you think the passion of Jesus (his death) or the compassion of his life is more important?

How did you react to reading about people torturing themselves in the name of Jesus?

Which do you think is more disturbing for a child to see, a woman's bare nipple or someone being tortured?

Do you think Jesus committed any sins? If so, which sins might he have committed?

How would God love you more if you were perfect?

Do you spend your day acting and thinking as if God expects you to be perfect or accepting that you can be only perfectly human and that is enough?

Do you think God wants you to suffer? If so, how does suffering help you to better practice the teachings of Jesus?

Do you agree with Paul's claim, "...we rejoice in our suffering, knowing that suffering produces endurance, and endurance produces character, and character produces hope..."

If you think God wants you to suffer, does life already provide enough suffering or is it desirable to inflect suffering on oneself?

Do you think Jesus would rather you try to be "perfect" or "all-embracing?"

Stages Of Faith

In addition to one's attitudes, another major influence on how a person views God, Jesus, and the Bible is what stage of faith one has achieved. Knowing about the stages of faith makes it easier to have empathy and compassion when interacting with those whose beliefs differ from one's own, as well as better understanding one's own spiritual growth. In his classic book, *Stages Of Faith: The Psychology of Human Development and the Quest for Meaning,* James Fowler proposed that, just as there are developmental stages that children go through as they learn, there are stages of faith. These stages of faith aren't about the content of one's faith-what one believes-but rather how and why one believes. He understood these stages to be hierarchical-meaning the second stage builds on the first one, the third on the second, and so on. He proposed they are in a sequence that can't be changed; meaning a person doesn't skip over a stage, but must move through each one in order. Learning math follows a similar pattern; a person can't learn addition without understanding the concept of numbers, and one can't grasp multiplication without first comprehending addition. Merely aging isn't enough to cause a person to move from one stage into the next. Therefore not everyone moves through all the stages; some people reach a stage and never experience any reason to examine their understanding of God, spirituality, or religion. People move from one stage into the next when the current stage no longer works for them. When things no longer make sense using the old way of believing then they face a crisis of faith during which they are forced to re-examine their understanding of the way the universe is ordered. A person in one stage of faith development will understand the teaching of Jesus much differently than a person in another stage of development.

Long before Dr. Fowler lived, Jesus declared, "Blessed are the pure in heart: for they shall see God," indicating that he understood some people would not pay any attention to him and even those who did listen would hear his message differently depending on what stage of faith development they had obtained. The more his students grew spiritually, the easier it became to recognize God in the people and things around them. When people have a very specific, but narrow, concept of God it is more difficult for them to find God in all things as God Will Save Me illustrates.

God Will Save Me

Thomas was sitting on the front porch of his house that was located close to a river. Due to heavier than normal rain the river was rising out of its banks threatening to flood the area. As Thomas sat watching the river creep ever closer to his porch a man in a four-wheel drive truck pulled up. The driver called out, "Hop in and I'll get you out of here before you get caught in the flood." "Naw, you go on. I have faith God will save me," responded Thomas dismissing the driver with a wave of his hand. It didn't take long till the water had risen so high that Thomas was sitting on the roof of his house in order to keep dry. As he was sitting there a boat pulled along side the roof. A woman in the boat yelled to Thomas over the roar of the flood, "Get in and I'll take you to safety." But once again Thomas waved his hand dismissively telling the woman in the boat, "Thanks for the offer, but God won't let me die. I have faith God will save me." Shaking her head in disbelief the woman guided the boat away. Still the water kept rising. At last Thomas was calmly standing on the brick chimney of his house totally surrounded by swiftly moving water. Then he heard the unmistakable sound of a helicopter and looked up to see a Coast Guard rescue crew lowering a cable with a harness attached. Unable to shout loud enough to be heard over the racket from the helicopter's spinning blades one of the crew signaled to Thomas to put the harness on so he could be lifted to safety. Still looking up Thomas hollered at the top of his lungs exaggerating the movements of his mouth so he would be understood, "I DON'T NEED YOUR HELP. I HAVE COMPLETE FAITH GOD IS GOING TO SAVE ME. GO HELP SOMEONE WHO ACTUALLY NEEDS HELP," The helicopter flew away leaving Thomas all alone with nobody in sight. "They just don't understand. My faith in God is going to save me. I just know it," he thought with complete serenity. But mere moments later he died a painful death from being swept by the surging floodwaters through a forest of submerged trees.

Some time later Thomas was standing dripping wet before Saint Peter at the gates of Heaven. "What happened? I'm not supposed to be here. I shouldn't have died; I had complete faith in God, but God let me down," alleged Thomas as he stomped his foot and shook his fist in anger. When Thomas finally stopped complaining Saint Peter sighed and with the look of someone who had heard this exact objection more times than he wanted to remember said, "What? God sent a truck. Not good enough for you. Then a boat came. Again not what you had in mind. Finally a helicopter appears, but do you accept God's help? No. You were too busy declaring how faithful you were to actually grasp the fact that God was trying to save you. But you didn't accept the help you were offered because it didn't come in the form you had imagined. Now get in here; you're making a mess dripping water everywhere."

Roger Williams' Spiritual Crisis

Most people don't answer Jesus' question, "But who do you say that I am?" (Matthew, 16:15), only once in their life; the struggle to repeatedly answer that question is what causes a person to move from one stage to another, and how one answers the question will be a reflection of which stage of faith has been reached. This is exactly what occurred in the life of Roger Williams, one of the Puritans in the Colonial days of America, who had a well deserved reputation for having been intense about their religious beliefs. Mr. Williams was a man who more than fit this stereotype when he arrived in the Massachusetts Bay Colony in 1631. He came to the New World because he couldn't find a congregation anywhere in Europe that was up to his standards. When he arrived in Massachusetts the Puritan congregation offered him the position of minister that he promptly refused after deciding the members weren't puritanical enough for him. "In a community of religious fanatics, the outspoken Williams became the guy who all the other Puritans wished would lighten up about religion," was the way Sarah Vowell described him.[152] In only four years he made himself such a pest with his religious superiority that the General Court of Massachusetts Bay banished him from the colony. He fled to the south through the winter snows and would have died had not members of the Narragansett tribe taken him in. As you might imagine being banished by Christians to certain death only to be saved by heathens gave Mr. Williams something on which to meditate during the long New England winter. Eventually he and others obtained a charter from the King of England to form a new colony named the Rhode Island and Providence Plantations, later shortened to Rhode Island. One might expect that Mr. Williams and his fellows would create a society that demanded absolute adherence to rigid narrow Puritanical beliefs and practices. But banishment had lead Mr. Williams to experience a spiritual crisis and undergo a spiritual wakening. Ms Vowell summarized the effect of his transformation:

> Williams's settlement offered what he called, "soul-liberty." A man with the narrowest of minds presided over the most open-minded haven in New England. His own unwavering zealotry made him recognize the convictions of others, however wrong-headed. Others not sharing his beliefs would be tortured eternally, "over the everlasting burnings of Hell," and this he figures, was punishment enough." Soon Rhode Island became a refuge for all manner of religious outcasts including Quakers, Baptists, and Jews. Unlike any of the previous English colonies Rhode Island's charter from King Charles II included a guarantee that all of its residents would not be, "molested, punished, disquieted or called in question for any differences of opinion in matters of religion."

Stage One-God Exists & Is Magical

Professor Fowler's research found that these stages exist regardless of the culture or religion(s) to which the person is exposed. Therefore even children from families that are non-religious or even anti-religious still develop Stage One characteristics such as the idea that a god of some type exists. Stage One beliefs tend to develop between the ages of three to seven. During this time children are learning that adults view god, as well as other topics such as death and sex, as important. Children of this age have vivid imaginations so they can easily imagine a god that is unrestrained by the laws of nature, basically a super-hero capable of grand acts, someone to be viewed with respect, and who may bestow wonderful favors. But because of their ability to imagine things so vividly they can also create terrifying images of a god that is dangerous because he capable of great acts of violence and killing, and so must be feared and appeased.

In America most Christian children are exposed to the story of Santa Claus at the same age they are being taught about the life of Jesus. A person's first spiritual crisis may occur, when upon learning that Santa Claus is a fictional character and therefore concludes that Jesus must also be imaginary. It is easy for children to confuse these two figures because they are taught they both have a lot in common:

Both are kind and generous;
Both know if children have been naughty or nice;
Both see to it that children get what they deserve-Santa leaves gifts or a lump of coal, while Jesus gives eternal life or ever lasting punishment;
Both live in far off places-the North Pole and Heaven;
Both can be contacted-children write letters to Santa and pray to Jesus to express their desires;
Both can do amazing things-in only one night Santa can travel the world over leaving presents for every good

boy and girl, while Jesus can walk on water, turn water into wine, and bring the dead back to life, and:

In paintings and other art forms both are shown with beards.

Regardless of whether a child has a spiritual crisis or not it is normal to move into the second stage of faith merely as a result of the development of more sophisticated thinking that naturally occurs in the aging process.

Stage Two-God Knows Whose Is Naughty & Nice

By age ten most children's minds have developed to the point where they understand that there are rules by which the universe works. Peek-a-boo is not longer any fun because a child of this age understands that even though a person's face is hidden from view the person still exists and therefore the child is not surprised when the person's face comes back into view. At this age children are very interested in sorting out what is real and what is merely make believe. Therefore they are constantly demanding to know "why" and want proof of claims made by others. They approach the topic of God in the same way; they want to know why God does or doesn't do certain things.

People in Stage Two, regardless of their age, are able to tell stories about God, but these are not much more than retellings of stories that they have heard from others. Basically God is the way God is because that is what someone told them. God is viewed in literal human terms; God is the father, not like a father. The rules by which one ought to live one's life are seen as inflexible, not subject to questioning, nor dependent on situations; in other words it is never acceptable to break a rule no matter the circumstances. For people in Stage Two, there are two kinds of people, the good people who follow the rules, and the bad people who don't. Usually, the relationship between God and humans is seen in simple terms; people get what they deserve-God rewards good people and punishes bad people. The concepts of Heaven and Hell fit well into Stage Two thinking. For those in Stage Two prayer is viewed primarily as a way to gain God's favor and earn credit that may be cashed in when one needs special assistance or forgiveness from God.

One of the limitations of Stage Two is the tendency to try to be perfect in order to gain God's approval. Rather than believing it is acceptable in God's eyes to be perfectly human, and therefore a being that will make mistakes, there is the belief that one must be perfect and never commit an error. When a person with this belief inevitably falls short of perfection he or she usually sinks into relentless self-incrimination and shame, followed by promises to "never do that again or even think about it." This pattern can lead to an overwhelming sense that one will never be good enough to gain God's acceptance.

Stage Three-My God Can Beat Your God

"When I was a child,
I spoke as a child,
I understood as a child,
I thought as a child:
But when I became a man,
I put away childish things."

1st Corinthians 13:11

Research has found that although most people have moved into Stage Three by the time they enter their teen years, there are adults whose view of God remains in Stage Two for their entire lives. Stages One and Two are characterized primarily by child-like thinking whereas Stage Three is the adolescence of faith. As anyone who has been around teenagers knows they are very focused on the behavior and opinions of their peer group. Furthermore, despite having relatively little experience with the world, adolescents believe they understand reality better than adults. They are convinced when they become adults and in charge of things they will run the world properly and eliminate all the problems caused by their foolish parents. People, regardless of their age, who have developed Stage Three faith may exhibit a similar pattern of thinking and behaving about their religion; they are sure they have it right and anyone who disagrees with them is wrong, if not down right evil. Take for example the governor of Iowa, William Harding, who issued a decree in 1916 that made it illegal to speak any language other than English in schools, in places of worship, or even over the telephone. He explained, "There is no use in anyone wasting his time praying in other languages than English; God is listening only to the English language."[153] Governor Harding didn't disclose exactly when God stopped listening to languages other than English, but hopefully it wasn't during the time of Jesus. For a more recent example, we need look no further than Rochester, Minnesota. In 2003 a small group of Buddhist monks, some of whom had survived the attempted genocide perpetrated by the Khmer Rouge in Cambodia, legally immigrated to America. Once here they built a temple where they engaged in prayer and meditation with the goal of offering loving kindness to all living things. Although most of town's people welcomed their new neighbors, a small group of citizens didn't approve of non-Christians living among them. They expressed their disapproval by regularly smashing the monks' mailbox, breaking the lights on the outside of the temple, pulling up the flowers and trees the monks had planted, and spray-painting a cross and "Jesus saves" on the drive way leading to the temple. When the head monk was asked how they dealt with the seven years of on-going vandalism he responded, "The vandals know what they are doing is not right. We will pray for them to do good things instead of bad."[154]

Since people in Stage Three place so much importance on what others think those in this stage are vulnerable to what Sharon Parks called "the tyranny of the they."[155] These people are tempted to go along with whatever those around them are doing whether they truly believe in it or not.

Those in Stage Three haven't really examined their beliefs. They believe what they believe and will defend it, but they aren't able to explain how they know these things to be true other than pointing to an external authority. "Jesus loves me, this I know, for the Bible tells me so," is an example of Stage Three faith. This statement relies on the authority of the Bible alone rather than having a foundation in the Bible combined with personal experience that confirms what is contained in the Bible. Interviews conducted in churches and synagogues in America indicate that most members of these institutions are in Stage Three. This makes sense since these religious organizations function best when their members want to fit in with others and don't question the teaching of the religion because there is an assumption that everyone believes, or should believe, the same thing about God and Jesus.

There are three common reasons people question their Stage Three beliefs. The first is when one has a personal experience that doesn't fit with a Stage Three view of the world. An example would be the person who has been taught by her religious leaders that people get what they deserve; the good are rewarded and the bad are punished. But then something bad happens to her or a loved one and she can't see any reason God would want to punish someone who for all intents and purposes appears good, particularly when many people who appear to be bad, or at least are clearly doing bad things, seem to have an easy life. A second common motivation for questioning one's faith is when one is exposed to people who have a different understanding of God. This can occur when one travels, enlists in the military, enrolls in college, or anything else that leads to interacting with those who have beliefs that are different from one's own. I knew of a man who had been raised in a Protestant church who began dating a woman who was Roman Catholic and started attending mass with her. Not having been raised Catholic he was unfamiliar with all the rituals associated with this religion. When the congregation would engage in a particular ritual he would inquire, "Why are we doing this?" Inevitability she would respond, "Because that what the priest wants us to do." Not satisfied he would press the point, "But what is the meaning of the act? What does it symbolize?" She couldn't tell him; she engaged in the actions because she had been told to without any understanding of their significance and she wasn't motivated to find out what the rituals were supposed to symbolize. This woman was being exposed to someone who had different religious beliefs, but it never caused her to examine what she had been taught; therefore she remained in Stage Three. If she had been curious she could have examined her beliefs and one of two things would have occurred. She would find that some or all of the tenets of Catholicism made no sense to her and she would seek a new system of faith. On the other hand after examining her beliefs she could have gained a deeper and more personal understanding of all that Catholicism has to offer and grown spiritually while remaining a Catholic.

For some people marriage leads to religious conflict. Once I received a telephone call asking if as a therapist I had any experience working with, what the caller described as "mixed couples." I thought he meant couples of different races, but what he actually meant was a couple consisting of someone raised in the Methodist

Church and the other brought up in the Baptist Church. They had assumed that since they were both Christians their belief systems were identical. After marrying they began to find out there were differences and conflict ensued with each convinced of the correctness of their own beliefs. Each was determined to convert the other to the true faith and thereby save their spouse's soul. The therapy sessions consisted of both of them examining their faith systems, determining which aspects of them were was relevant and which weren't. Fortunately, once they were able to stop insisting that the other one was wrong and examined their own beliefs they were able to find enough in common that not only did the conflict that had threatened to destroy their marriage end, but they both grew in their understanding of their individual spirituality.

One of the most common events that cause people to question their Stage Three beliefs is when they are faced with seemingly contradictory explanations for the nature of the world. For example, what does one do when a well-respected schoolteacher explains the variety of life on Earth by invoking evolution and an equally admired religious leader insists that all life was created in one twenty-four hour day? Wrestling with an apparent dilemma can lead to Stage Four where the person develops a more complex understanding of God and creation. In Stage Three the two stories of creation need not be contradictory because each provides useful, although different, information about how to understand life.

When church officials make changes in the dogma that had long been held sacred it can throw a person in Stage Three into a crisis. For example, when the Episcopal Church leaders adopted a *Book Of Common Prayer* or when the Vatican II counsel made significant changes to what was expected of Roman Catholics. What is a person to do who has staunchly followed the teachings of a religion when church leaders decide that some aspect of the teachings no longer applies? How could it be that what was once a sin now is no longer a sin? If that part of the dogma can change what else might change? When faced with a crisis of faith some people in Stage Three cope by increasing their reliance on external authorities. For others, their crisis of faith leads them to reduce their dependence on authority figures for answers and increase their personal reflection. Such examination can lead a person into Stage Four.

Stage Four-My Experience Lead Me To Know This

Stage Four faith development is so advanced few people are able to obtain it before age thirty, if at all. As with the earlier stages this one is triggered by some event that causes upheaval in one's life, such as a divorce, or the death of a parent or spouse. Even with a major event causing a crisis of faith, establishing Stage Four usually takes five years or more. It is a process, not an event.

People in Stage Four take complete responsibility for their beliefs; "I believe this because I have examined it, questioned it, and determined that it makes sense." If they are members of a spiritual community it is because they actually share similar beliefs with the other members rather than they profess to believe something merely in order to be accepted into the group.

Persons in Stage Four of faith are willing to acknowledge that they don't have all the answers. Take for example the following portion of a speech Senator Ted Kennedy gave when he was invited by Dr. Jerry Falwell to speak at the Liberty Baptist College in 1983: "I am an American and a Catholic; I love my country and treasure my faith. But I do not assume that my conception of patriotism or policy is invariably correct, or that my convictions about religion should command any greater respect than any other faith in this pluralistic society. I believe there surely is such a thing as truth, but who among us can claim a monopoly on it?"

Fellow Minnesotan, Garrison Keillor, contrasted Stage Three and Stage Four when he wrote:

> The fundamental religion of most of mankind is the faith that God has revealed Himself to us and not to the barbarians. Our tribe is the one God chose and so if we vanquish the other tribes and rain fire and destruction on them, we're only carrying out God's will. There is a countervailing faith that says that God is in and of the world and has bestowed vast gifts to be shared with others, and that our understanding of God is faint and incomplete and so we should walk softly and not assume too much.[156]

Whereas a person in Stage Three is likely to insist, "My way is <u>the</u> truth," a person in Stage Four would only claim, "My way is true for me." Therefore, those in Stage Four are open to learning from the theology of others, even when it appears to contradict their own beliefs. This openness can lead to accusations of backsliding from people in Stage Three.[157] However, those in Stage Four don't have a need to defend the faith since in their eyes the faith doesn't need defending. They know the strength of one's faith isn't measured by how strenuously one rejects or denigrates the faith of others.

I know of a congregation that believed it was useful for the spiritual development of children for them to have an understanding of all the major religions of the world. Therefore in Sunday school they studied a different religion for an entire year. Rather than merely reading about it they engaged in some of the rituals associated with that religion. After having learned about these various religions the children, who by now were young adolescents, choose a member of the church with whom to meet each Sunday in order to discuss what they had learned and how it had affected their relationship with God and religion. The role of the adult wasn't to tell the adolescent what to believe, but rather to assist in the examination of these complex concepts and their practical application to everyday life. After the adolescents had learned about the various religious options and fully examined their personal beliefs they were invited to join the church as full members if they found its teachings acceptable. The members of this congregation were preparing their children with an education that would make it easier for them to eventually develop into Stage Four believers. Similar to the children of this congregation, members of Twelve Step-based programs are exposed to Stage Four concepts. Take for example this passage that is used in some Sex Addicts Anonymous meetings:

> "Over time, we establish a relationship with a Power greater than ourselves, each of us coming to an understanding of a Higher Power that is personal for us. Although the steps use the word 'God' to indicate this Power, SAA is not affiliated with any religion, creed, or dogma. The program offers a spiritual solution to our addiction, without requiring adherence to any specific set of beliefs or practices. The path is wide enough for everyone who wishes to walk it."

Although individual members may be at earlier Stages of faith, this statement is indicative of Stage Four thinking, in that members are encouraged to find their own understanding of God rather being told what they must believe. The wording ("over time" and "coming to") indicates that this understanding will involve a process rather than being a one-time event.

Stage Five-If I Think I Understand God, Then My God Is Too Small

Development of Stage Five is so complex Professor Fowler took fourteen pages to describe it. Perhaps the easiest way to grasp the characteristics of Stage Five is to use an analogy. For years scientists argued over whether light is a particle or a wave. Those who believed light is a particle conducted experiments that showed that light is indeed a particle. Meanwhile those who believed light is actually a wave asked questions from that standpoint, created experiments that not surprisingly got results that confirmed their beliefs. Faced with these seemingly contradictory results these two groups continued to run experiments that re-confirmed their beliefs rather than challenge their understanding of light. However, when all of the data from both sides of the debate were examined with an open mind it became clear that both sides were correct. It wasn't a matter of *or*, it was a matter of *and*. Light functions sometimes as a wave and sometimes as a particle. So whether light is a particle or a wave depends which method of examination is being used as well as on which moment in time it is being examined. Like a scientist who can grasp that light is both a wave and a particle a person in Stage Five of faith development is able to simultaneously and comfortably embrace two or more spiritual beliefs that at first appear to be contradictory. Whereas those in the earlier Stages of Faith see only contradiction (two things that can't possibly both be true) people in Stage Five see paradox (two things that on the surface appear to contradict one another but in fact are both true). In their search for truth people in Stage Five are willing to examine how well their beliefs hold up in the real world, and when appropriate change their beliefs, regardless of how long they have held them, in order to adopt something better. Such people are open to learning faith traditions other than the one they learned as children. While not seeing any need to convert to another religion they are able utilize aspects of other religions in order to makes theirs more comprehensive. In other words they are humble enough to know their religion isn't the only way to understand God. However, people in the earlier stages of faith tend to think along the lines of, "I know this to be true, there is only one God. Therefore, since you pray differently than do I, you are praying to a false god." People in Stage Five comfortably declare that we all worship the same God regardless of what name we use when praying, that all religions contain some aspects of the truth and therefore are legitimate paths to God. Their thinking concerning there being only one god has changed so that they think along the lines of, "I know this to be true, there is but one god, therefore, regardless of by what name you address god, or by what rituals you perform we are all addressing the same god. My god is your god and your god is my god." Such people come to know that God is too complex to completely understand, but are able to accept this great mystery and acknowledge not having all the answers. Those in this Stage are able to declare, "Any god that I could fully comprehend wouldn't be much of a god." Although they utilize symbols, rites, and rituals they are more interested in direct contact with God. They do this by acting on the teachings of their religion instead of merely discussing the meaning of the sacred texts. Their spirituality is completely integrated into how they live their lives; it has become who they are, rather than something they do. Bill W. saw a similar process occurring in Alcoholics Anonymous noting, "You don't join A.A., you become A.A."

Examples Of Stage Five Thinking

More than two hundred years before the birth of Jesus, Emperor Asoka of India, a Buddhist, put forth a royal decree, "It is forbidden to decry other sects; the true believer gives honor to whatever in them is worthy of honor." More recently when Rev. Billy Graham was asked if he believed people of other religions, such as Jews, Muslims, Buddhists, Hindus, or atheists would be admitted into heaven he responded: "those are decisions only the Lord will make. It would be foolish for me to speculate on who will be there and who won't...I don't want to speculate about all that. I believe the love of God is absolute. He said He gave His son for the whole world, and I think He loves everyone regardless of what label they have... As time went on, I began to realize the love of God for everyone, all over the world."[158]

Born of an Indian Hindu father and Spanish Catholic mother, Raimon Panikkar was educated in Spain by Jesuit monks. They inspired a love of learning in the young boy, who went on to earn three doctoral degrees. After being ordained as a Catholic priest he traveled to India. There he experienced a spiritual awakening; "I left Europe [for India] as a Christian. I discovered I was a Hindu and returned a Buddhist without ever having ceased being a Christian." He spent the remaining years of his life teaching at Harvard and The University Of California, where, despite being accused of being a radical, he highlighted the similarities between all religions and downplaying the differences.[159]

Just as individuals go through stages of faith development, so too do organizations-even entire religions. In 2006 Rev. Jerry Campbell was granted the dubious honor of becoming the president of the Claremont School of Theology. Since the school already had a 125-year history it was an honor to follow in the footsteps of the Methodists who came before him. The dubious nature of the situation was the fact that the school had low enrollment, was deep in debt, and therefore closing it was being seriously discussed. Having obtained at least a Stage four level of faith, Rev. Campbell proposed that not only could the school be saved, it could do so by becoming the first of a new type of school of theology-one that offered training in more than one religion. He proposed that the school train future Christian pastors, Jewish rabbis, and Muslim imams side-by-side. At first the board members of the United Methodist Church wanted nothing to do with such a radical idea, but complied after being promised that the funds they provided would only be used to educate Christians. When prospective students learned that the Claremont School of Theology was joining together with the Claremont Academy for Jewish Religion, and the Islamic Center of Southern California enrollment increased ten percent. This collaboration not only created the first multi-faith theology school, but also created the first accredited imam-training school in America. Not satisfied with only bring together the clergy of three major religions, the professors at Claremont began searching for Buddhist and Hindu faculty to be even more inclusive.[160]

Stage Six-God Is Universal

Professor Fowler named Stage Six "universalized faith" because to those people who have obtained it the barriers and categories that normally divide one group of people from another are viewed as meaningless. Humankind is viewed as one family, with no group or individual seen as unworthy of compassion and even love. People in Stage Six have a passionate, even radical, commitment to justice and making the world a better place, so much so that they are assassinated for their beliefs. Those few people who obtain Stage Six are focused, not on the afterlife, but rather on life in all its forms in the here and now. They are not waiting for someone supernatural to take action;

they themselves take meaningful action because they believe God's will can be done on Earth as in Heaven in the present.

It is rare to find a person in Stage Six. Jesus, the Buddha, and Mohammad no doubt achieved this level of faith.[18] Anyone who has been in the presence of someone in Stage Six instantly knew there was something very special about that person. As you can imagine people go away from these meetings inspired, saying, "It seemed like he was speaking directly to me. He treated me like I was the most important person in the world. I felt at peace and close to God."

"Beliefs separate.
Loving thoughts unite."

Paul Ferrine, 1994 A.C.E.[161]

A Summary Of The Stages Of Faith

Dr. Scott Peck in *The Different Drum: Community Making And Peace* noted how psychological growth and spiritual development are similar, and this is true of all cultures and all religions. If a girl is fortunate enough to be born into a family that is relatively stable and secure, by mid-childhood she has become a law-abiding, rule-following person. If her family supports and encourages her uniqueness and independence by adolescence she has become an up-and-coming skeptic who openly questions the laws, rules, and the myths she had been taught. If her church or parents do not excessively resist her skepticism she will become an adult who begins to understand

18 Because I believe Jesus had reached Stage Six development I don't believe he said, "I am the way, the truth, and the life. No one comes to the Father but by me" (*John* 14:6). I can't imagine from the things he taught that he would make such a claim that is so exclusive and would exclude so many people.

the meaning and spirit of what underlies all that she has been told, read, and observed. If she was not fortunate enough to be raised in such a family and spiritual community she likely will become stagnated at a low level of spiritual development.[162]

Clash Of Faiths Or Differences In Stages Of Faith?

Chief Red Jacket

In 1805 the leaders of the Seneca tribe met with a missionary who was insisting that they convert to Christianity. Chief Red Jacket reportedly responded:

> Brother, you say there is but one way to worship and serve the Great Spirit; if there is but one religion, why do you not agree, as you can all read the book [Bible]? ...We also have a religion which was given to our forefathers, and has been handed down to us their children. We worship that way. It teaches us to be thankful for all the favors we receive; to love each other, and to be united.

Since the Seneca's religion included being grateful, loving others, and treating others as family, it seems to me that Jesus would have approved of it regardless of what name it went by. Although Red Jacket found the religion he was already practicing was more than adequate, he was a spiritually advanced person, so he was open to the possibility that Christianity might have something valuable to offer:

> Brother, we are told that you have been preaching to white people in this place; these people are our neighbors, we are acquainted with them; we will wait a little while and see

> what effect your preaching has upon them. If we find it does them good, makes them honest, and less disposed to cheat Indians, we will then consider again what you have said.
>
> He then parted with these words:
>
> Brother, you have now heard the answer to your talk, and this is all we have to say at present. As we are going apart, we will come and take you by the hand, and hope the Great Spirit will protect you on your journey, and return you safe to your friends.

Unfortunately, the missionary refused to shake the Chief's hand because, "there is no fellowship between the religion of God and the works of the devil."[163]

Help Wanted: Atheists Need Not Apply

Mr. H.K. Edgerton desperately wanted to file suit against Cecil Bothwell a member of the city council of Ashville, North Carolina. Mr. Edgerton wasn't concerned about any of the councilman's stand on city issues, but he was disturbed by the fact that Mr. Bothwell was an atheist. "I'm a Christian man. I have problems with people who don't believe in God," explained Mr. Edgerton. In order to rid the city government of anyone not of his faith, Mr. Edgerton cited the portion of North Carolina's 1868 Constitution that disqualified anyone from holding State office, "who shall deny the being of Almighty God." His planned lawsuit relied on this obscure phrase even though it was no longer included in the State Constitution when it was revised in 1971, and despite the fact that the U.S. Constitution, which supercedes State Constitutions, forbids States from requiring any kind of religious test for holding office.[164]

This story is an example of Stage Three thinking; Mr. Edgerton's only objection to the councilman was that he didn't worship the God Mr. Edgerton was convinced he should worship. It was a case of-You aren't exactly like me, therefore you are bad, and should be punished for it.

Thank You For Four Decades Of Work, But You're Still Going To Hell

In medieval times when the great cathedrals were being built it was common practice for the stonemasons to carve the likenesses of their loved ones or co-workers on gargoyles and other architectural accents. In 2010, stonemason, Emmanuel Fourchet who was a restoring Saint Jean's Roman Catholic cathedral in France followed this tradition by carving a gargoyle in the likeness of one of his fellow stonemasons. He did this as a way to, "pay tribute to his decades of work on the cathedral." The man being so honored, Ahmed Benizizine, had already spent forty years restoring the church. Underneath the sculpture was the inscription; "God is great," written in French and in Arabic. The reason the phrase was written in Arabic was because Mr. Benizizine was a Muslim. This kind gesture may have passed unnoticed into history if it weren't for the extreme-right wing group Identity Youth of Lyon who were outraged that the likeness of a Muslim would be permitted on a Catholic Church. But what did the rector of the cathedral think of the gargoyle when he learned of it? The Rev. Michel [sic] Cacaud merely shrugged his shoulders and noted, "There is no religion that doesn't say 'God is great'" [165]

In this story the people that objected to the inscription believed, because of Stage Three thinking that there is only one true religion, and to acknowledge a different religion is to lessen the validity of one's own religion. They couldn't grasp what Rev. Cacaud understood-all religions believe God is great because we are all worshiping the same God.

Do You Smell Something Burning?

In 2010 Pastor Terry Jones, of the ironically named Dove World Outreach Center, announced plans for International Burn A Qur'an Day on the ninth anniversary of the 911 attacks. He claimed: "We have nothing against Muslims. They are welcome in our country. They are welcome to worship." However, he still encouraged people throughout the world to burn Islam's holy book because, "Islam is of the devil. It is causing billions of people to go to hell." Mr. Jones was so confident that he was correct, he wrote a book titled, *Islam Is Of The Devil,* and at his church in Gainesville, Florida he sold coffee mugs and tee shirts with that statement printed on them.

Although the members of his congregation were supportive of his plan, not everyone in America thought it was such a great idea. In the secular world General David Petraeus, the U.S. and N.A.T.O. Commander in Afghanistan, Secretary of State Hillary Rodham Clinton, and U.S. President Obama all warned that such a provocative act would be a recruiting bonanza for anti-American terrorist groups and would undoubtedly put American service members at greater risk. Political conservatives Glenn Beck and Sarah Palin were against it as well. The Associated Press announced it would not publish any photos of the event. Fox News reported it wouldn't cover the event at all.

Responding to news of the plan to burn the Qur'an demonstrations erupted in Afghanistan as outraged Muslims burned effigies as they chanted "Death to America." Muslim leaders warned of serious repercussions if the event took place. Pakistan's President Asif Ali Zardari warned the event was sure to, "inflame sentiments among Muslims throughout the world and cause irreparable damage to interfaith harmony and also world peace."

Nor were most Christians thrilled about the idea of burning another religion's holy book. The Rev. Richard Land, head of public policy for the Southern Baptist Convention, America's largest Protestant group, described the event as abhorrent. George Wood, general superintendent of the Assemblies of God, one of the largest Pentecostal denominations warned that the holy book burning would damage Christian-Muslim relations. The Vatican took a public stand against it. The National Association of Evangelicals issued a statement urging the book burning be canceled, "in the name and love of Jesus Christ," and called for its members, "to cultivate relationships of trust and respect with our neighbors of other faiths. God created human beings in His image and therefore all should be treated with dignity and respect." The Gainesville Interfaith Forum, a group of Christians, Muslims, Jews, and Hindus announced they planned to hold a rally, "for peace, understanding, and hope," the night before the scheduled Qur'an burning.

How did Mr. Jones respond to this out pouring? He claimed that all these Christians were merely failed religious warriors that had given up the fight against forces bent on silencing Christians. His response demonstrated the arrogance common of people in Stages Two and Three. He was the pastor of a church of meager fifty people. He called himself "doctor" even though he had only an honorary degree, meaning he didn't attend any schooling to obtain it. Furthermore, the organization that granted him the honorary degree, the California Graduate School of Theology, that had, according to its website, had never applied to be federally accredited. Despite his lack of credentials or even training Mr. Jones was convinced that he knew more than all the combined individuals and organizations that begged him to re-think his actions. He was sure he was totally in the right and all of them were completely wrong. But then, who among us has never been determined to take some action even though all those around us warned that it was ill advised?

Mr. Jones behavior showed indications of both Stages Two and Three. He said he would only change his plans if he received, "a sign from God." Rather than be open to what that sign might be, he decided it would be the halting of the construction of an Islamic center that Mr. Jones considered to be too close to the site of the former World Trade Center. Mr. Jones didn't seem to consider worldwide commendation of his plans to be a sign from God. One day before the scheduled event Mr. Jones called it off, at least temporarily, with the vague explanation; "It's not the time to do it." But only hours later he was reconsidering his decision. Still later he insisted; "We are, of course, now against any other group burning Qur'an. We are absolutely strong on that."[166] This behavior was another indication of someone with stage three faith. When faced with overwhelming pressure he changed his mind about following through on the action, but really didn't have an understanding of the reasons his behavior was inappropriate. All he knew was that people were telling him he was up to no good and that he was getting in trouble. So he changed his position, but not because he had gained any insight." He then became adamant about his new position; even though he would unable to express the reason he held this new position that only days before had been contrary to everything he believed. It is situations like this that can lead a person into a crisis of faith, and that facilitate spiritual growth and movement to a higher level of faith. Hopefully, that was the outcome for Mr. Jones.

A Process Rather Than An Event

Spiritual development tends to be gradual; people have one foot in the earlier stage and one foot in the next. In other words spiritual growth is a process rather than an event. One exception is when a person suddenly moves from Stage Three to Stage Four in a dramatic shift in perception and behavior called a conversion. The twelfth Step in Twelve Step mentions having a "spiritual awakening."[19] Some members jokingly describe this awakening as, "a blinding flash of the obvious," when they move into a new stage of faith. One of the co-founders of Alcoholics Anonymous, Bill W., credited his own spiritual awakening with restoring his mental health and preventing him from drinking himself to an early grave. But that is not to say that Bill prior to his awakening was actively searching for spiritual growth:

> I had always believed in a Power greater than myself. I had often pondered these things. I was not an atheist. With ministers, and the world's religions, I parted right there...To Christ I conceded the certainty of a great man...His teaching-most excellent. For myself, I had adopted those parts, which seemed convenient and not too difficult; the rest I disregarded.[167]

But then, as they say, the plot thickened; Ebby, an old drinking buddy arrived at Bill's door. Bill was surprised to see his old chum since he had heard he had been locked up for "alcoholic insanity." Then came an even bigger surprise, Ebby hadn't had any alcohol for two months and was happy about it! He calmly declined a glass of gin when Bill offered it to him. Bill could see that besides the fact that Ebby had just refused a free glass of gin there was something else different about him; he was, "inexplicably different." When Bill inquired what had happened to cause such as a drastic change he was "aghast" at

19 "Having had a spiritual awakening as the result of these steps, we tried to carry this message to alcoholics, and to practice these principles in all our affairs" (A.A., 1976, p. 60). Of course in other fellowships the word *alcoholic* is replaced with a term relevant to the affliction that fellowship addresses.

Ebby's answer- "I've got religion."[168] Only because Ebby didn't insist that Bill believe exactly what he believed was Bill willing to continue listening. What made all the difference to Bill was Ebby's unwillingness to argue over what was the one true notion of God and his, "novel idea," that Bill was free to choose his own conception of God.[169] Bill was so impressed with Ebby's dramatic change that he entered a hospital in order to be medically monitored while he went through the process of detoxification after his decades of heavy drinking. At the hospital Bill turned his will and his life over to the care of the God of his understanding which he referred to as the Father of Light."[170] Once he did so, "the effect was electric. There was a sense of victory, followed by such a peace and serenity, as I had never known. There was utter confidence."[171] Although Bill's spiritual awakening was, "sudden and profound," he always acknowledged that in most cases, "God comes to most [people] gradually."[172] The philosopher William James termed this type of spiritual awakenings as, "the educational variety."

An example of someone being at the crossroads of stages of faith is when C.S. Lewis was asked by the B.B.C. to explain Christianity to listeners. On one evening he began his description by indicating what Christians don't need to believe:

> If you are a Christian you do not have to believe that all the other religions are simply wrong all through. If you are an atheist you do have to believe that the main point in all the religions of the whole world is simply one huge mistake. If you are a Christian, you are free to think that all those religions, even the queerest ones, contain at least some hint of the truth...But, of course, being a Christian does mean thinking that where Christianity

> differs from other religions, Christianity is right and they are wrong. As in arithmetic-there is only one right answer to a sum, and all other answers are wrong; but some of the wrong answers are much nearer being right than others.[173]

Although previous to this talk Mr. Lewis was an atheist he made the effort to examine that belief system and, after determining it was inadequate to explain things, he became a Christian. In this talk Mr. Lewis shows signs of being in more than one stage of faith simultaneously. After becoming a Christian he continued to examine his beliefs that allowed him to move through the first three stages of faith. He was open to the idea that all religions, "even the queerest ones, contain at least some hint of the truth," which is an indication of Stage Four. However, he still insisted there was only one truly right answer to spiritual questions, and further that all Christians share this belief, which is an indication of Stage Three faith development.

Questions To Help In Personal Reflection Or Group Discussion

What do you think about the idea of stages of faith? How useful a concept is it?

In which stage do you believe you are currently?

Think of a person you know who has obtained a high stage of faith, what is it about the way this person behaves that indicates to you that he/she is spiritually advanced?

Would you be willing to speak with this person and inquire what actions he/she took that lead to this spiritual growth you admire?

Can you give an example of some spiritual concept of which over time you changed your understanding?

Does this represent a change in stages of faith?

Have you ever experienced a crisis of faith? If so, how did you cope with it?

Did it lead to you moving from one stage to another?

What do think of those whose spiritual beliefs differ from yours?

Is there someone in your life with whom you have conflict over spiritual matters? If so, how might this conflict be better understood as a matter of being in different stages of faith rather than who is right and who is wrong?

Has reading this book lead you to question any of your spiritual beliefs? Is so, has it been helpful?

Have you had a spiritual awakening? If so, was it sudden or the educational variety?

How do you think Jesus would behave in the situation where the Buddhist monks were being harassed by those who sprayed-painted "Jesus saves" on the drive way of the their temple?

Section III

Living Life According To The Principles Taught By Jesus

(Warning-Not An Easy Task)

Applying The Principles Jesus Taught

"I doubt if there is in the world a single problem, whether social, political, or economic, which would not find ready solution if men and nations would rule their lives according to the plain teaching of the Sermon on the Mount."

U.S. President Franklin D. Roosevelt

The principles taught long ago in the past by Jesus are only relevant to the degree that they can be applied to our lives in the present. If they aren't applicable and practical in our daily lives then they are nothing more than quaint stories of the past. Dr. Scott Peck insisted that all genuine spirituality is radical; "If a so-called religious belief is not radical, we must suspect that it mere superstition, no deeper than the belief that a black cat means bad luck...the profession of a religious belief is a lie if it does not significantly determine one's economic, political, and social behavior."[174] I believe the principles that Jesus taught have passed the test of time and are as relevant to our lives today as they were to the people who actually heard him speak. Since then the principles have remained constant, but over time how they have been interpreted, understood, and applied has changed. For example, Martin Luther, the man for whom the Lutheran Church was named, wrote: "Idiots, the lame, the blind, the dumb, are men in whom devils have established themselves-and all the physicians who heal those infirmities, as though they proceeded from natural causes, are ignorant blockheads, who know nothing about the power of the demon."[175] Although in his day many people would have agreed with him in the 21st century it is widely accepted that physical deformities and handicaps are caused by birth defects or illness rather than demon possession.

What If Jesus Came Back?

Ever since Jesus left people have been anticipating and predicting his return. Some imagine a grand dramatic return; something like what Michelangelo would paint on the ceiling of the Sistine Chapel. Others fear he wouldn't be treated any better than he was the first time.

> If Jesus Christ were to come today, people would not even crucify him. They would ask him to dinner, and hear what he had to say, and make fun of it.
>
> Thomas Carlyle (1795-1881)

> If Christ should appear on earth he would on all hands be denounced as a mistaken, misguided man, insane and crazed.
>
> Henry David Thoreau (1817-1862)

> If Christ came back today and started teaching, we would put him on the cross quicker than we did 2,000 years ago
>
> The Reverend Billy Graham [176]

> If Jesus were alive today, we would kill him with lethal injection...We would have to kill him for the same reason he was killed the first time. His ideas are just too liberal.
>
> Kurt Vonnegut, Jr. [177]

Whether these are accurate predictions of what Jesus would face were he to reappear today is debatable, but in any case, as of today it is up to us to live our lives in a manner as to honor his teachings and thereby keep his message vibrant and relevant.

I find it puzzling that people keep finding signs of Jesus in strange places: in Salford, England a person reported an image of Jesus appeared when a pancake was burned in a pan; also in England, in the town of Old Hatfield, a partially burned fireplace log was supposed to resemble Jesus; an image of Jesus was reported to have been sighted in a bucket of sauce at Brownie's Famous Pizzeria in Old Forge, Pennsylvania; a person in Lockport New York claimed an image of Jesus and his mother Mary was visible in a piece of fruit that was sliced open on a Christmas morning, and; in Rockford, Illinois, an image proposed to resemble Jesus was identified in a MRI that was made as part of an examination of a patient's spine.[178] This interest in finding images of Jesus is puzzling because it seems to me if Jesus, or anyone else for that matter, was going to send a supernatural message to us he wouldn't use pizza sauce as the medium. Furthermore, nobody actually knows anything about Jesus' physical appearance-every image is nothing more than a guess. For years artists were certain he was clean-shaven, and then it became fashionable to portray him with a beard. Finally, I don't think we need to look for images of Jesus in burned pancakes when, if we open our eyes, there are reminders all around us of the many opportunities to practice his teachings by assisting those who are lonely, poor, hated, imprisoned, and sick.

Where Did You Learn *That*?

Children have a tendency to learn more by watching the way someone behaves than from listening to what they are told. When I was sixteen and had just obtained my driver's license I was driving with my dad as a passenger. "How fast are you going?" he inquired leaning over to check the speedometer. "Just 70," I casually replied. "Is that what they are teaching in drivers' education classes now? Driving 70 in a 55 mile per hour zone?" he asked. "No," I admitted. "Well, then," he demanded, "Where did you learn to drive like that?" "Well...from you, I guess. I've never seen you drive the speed limit unless there was a cop car in sight," I answered, knowing although it was a true statement it probably wasn't in my best interest to be speaking the truth right then.

> "Example, the surest method of instruction."
>
> Pliny The Younger (62-113 A.C.E.)

Jesus Was A Good Role Model, But Who Is Modeling Being A Follower Of Jesus?

One might logically assume children who are attending Sunday school, church services, or other religious events are not only hearing about the principles taught by Jesus, but also embracing them as guides to living. However, according to a Junior Achievement/Deloitte poll from 2009 that assumption is wrong. One in every ten of the teenagers polled reported they have no role model whatsoever. Same-age peers were seen by thirteen percent of the teens as their primary source for determining appropriate values and behavior. Only three percent indicated they looked to the leaders in their place of worship for guidance on how to live. In terms of what teenagers constituted acceptable behavior the researchers found:

> Thirty-eight percent said breaking rules at school was permissible in order to succeed;
> Nearly half stated lying to parents was appropriate behavior;

Approximately eighty-six percent stated they were more accountable to themselves than to parents, friends, or society as a whole;

About twenty-seven percent of these adolescents believed physical violence was an appropriate method for solving problems or obtaining one's way, and;

Twenty percent indicated they had committed acts of violence towards at least one other person in the previous year.

One very important finding from the survey was that fifty-four percent of these adolescents reported they viewed their parents as role models.[179] Of course this begs the question, "How well are their parents doing at living a life based on the principles taught by Jesus?"

People might take comfort in the idea that behaviors such as ignoring rules cheating, and using violence is something that adolescents will stop as they mature, but unfortunately they don't. According to The Josephson Institute that studies the ethical beliefs and behaviors of high school students, those people who cheated as high school students grow into adults who lie to their customers and spouses, and cheat on their taxes, insurance claims, and expense accounts.[180]

"[A majority of people] are not theoretical atheists;
they are practical atheists.
They do not deny the existence of God with their lips,
but they are continually denying his existence
with their lives."

Dr. Martin Luther King, Jr.[181]

Questions To Help In Personal Reflection Or Group Discussion

What do you think of the quotes on the return of Jesus?

What do you think would happen if Jesus would return to earth today?

How do you think Jesus would react to the way his teachings have been interpreted and practiced?

What would be the first statement you would make to Jesus?

What would be the first question you would ask Jesus?

What is the first statement you would expect Jesus to say to you?

What is the first question you would expect Jesus to ask you?

How would you answer that question?

What was your reaction to the results of the survey on adolescents and their role models?

If you have children, whom do you think they look to as an example of how to live?

In thinking about your own behavior over the previous year, which behaviors would you want children to follow and which of your behaviors wouldn't you want them to imitate (dishonesty, cheating, breaking rules/laws, smoking, etc)?

How do you justify continuing the behaviors in which you wouldn't want your children to engage?

~

Can We Wage War In The Name Of The Prince Of Peace?

"Much less evil would be done on earth
if evil could not be done in the name of good."

Marie von Ebner-Eschenbach

Doesn't The Bible Indicate That God Takes Part In War?

The Bible, at least the Old Testament, described a God that played favorites in times of war, not merely lending moral support, but actually taking part in battles and directly killing. In the book of *Joshua* God was reported to have, "cast down large hailstones from heaven on [the enemy of the Israelites] and they died...There were more who died from the hailstones than the children of Israel killed with the sword" (10:11). God even caused the sun to stand, "still in the midst of heaven," so Israelites had plenty of light in order to have, "revenge upon their enemies." If there remained any doubt as to whose side was in the right verse 14 made it clear, "...the LORD fought for Israel." In *Psalms* the writer clearly believed God would favor one side over the other:

> Your hand will find out all your enemies; your right hand will find out those who hate you, you will make them as a blazing oven when you appear. The LORD will swallow them up in his wrath; and fire will consume them. You will destroy their offspring from the earth, and their children from among the sons of men (21:8-10).

The Old Testament made it abundantly clear that the Jews of that time were convinced that God took their side during wars. However in the New Testament Jesus not only said nothing about God taking part in war, he went so far as to encourage the loving of one's enemies. Repeatedly Jesus gave his disciples the radical directive to pray for those who hated them and persecuted them, and to love their enemies, (*Matthew* 5:44 & *Luke* 6:27 & 35).

Them Versus Us Or What Part Of "Love Thy Enemy" Don't You Understand?

"in·fi·del n (disapproving)
1. Somebody who has no belief in the religion of the speaker or writer, Especially Christianity or Islam
2. Somebody who has no religious beliefs."[182]

"Infidel, *n*. In New York, one who does not believe in the Christian religion; in Constantinople, one who does."
Ambrose Bierce, *The Devil's Dictionary,* 1881

Given Jesus' directive to love your enemy one might think "holy war" would an oxymoron, but the concept of holy war has long been popular with Christians.[20] The First Crusade was launched in 1095 A.C.E. with the words, "God wills it," spoken by Pope Urban II. [183] He assured those who were willing to be martyrs in the struggle against unbelievers who illegitimately occupied the holy land that they would receive great rewards in Heaven.[21] The Crusades

20 Of course, holy war is not limited to Christians; both ancient, and some contemporary; Muslims endorse the concept of holy war.
21 If that bargain sounds familiar it might be because nearly a millennium later Osama bin Laden and other Islamic extremists made the same guarantee to Muslims.

were brutal. In 1099 A.C.A. Raymond d'Aguilers, a French cleric described how the Christian troops dealt with the Muslims and Jews they encountered:

> Piles of heads, hands, and feet were to be seen in the streets...Men rode in blood up to their knees and bridle reins. Indeed, it was a just and splendid judgment of God that this place should be filled with the blood of unbelievers, since it had suffered so long from their blasphemies.[184]

Throughout history people who consider themselves followers of Jesus have insisted that God was supportive of their various missions. Kaiser Wilhelm II of Germany was one of the major instigators of World War I, which was one of the most deadly conflicts in human history, and helped set the stage for the slaughter of millions more during World War II. He justified his actions by explaining he received his power from God. "[The emperor's crown] is granted by God's Grace alone and not by parliaments, popular assemblies, and popular decision... Considering myself an instrument of the Lord, I go my way." German soldiers carried on their belt buckles a constant reminder of Wilhelm's view of Christianity; "God is with us." [185]

Know Your Saints

Saint Barbara

Patron Saint of

ammunition manufactures,

artillery, and detonations[186]

Them Versus Us, Or "Jesus Loves Us Better Than He Loves You"

" her·e·tic n
Somebody who holds or adheres to an opinion or belief
That contradicts established religious teaching,
Especially one that is officially condemned by
religious authorities.[187]

Throughout history Christian leaders have not only encouraged violence against those who were not Christians (infidels), but also against Christians who didn't follow the teachings of the form of Christianity dominant at the time (heretics). Pope Gregory IX, the pontiff from 1227-1241 A.C.E. and best known as the instigator of the infamous Inquisition stated, "It is the duty of every Catholic to persecute heretics." By heretics he meant Catholics who strayed from the strictest most conservative Church teachings. If he were Pope today, he undoubtedly would pronounce as heretics most American Catholics and all Protestants.

How Could *They* Believe God Is On Their Side?

"God has sent one of the attacks by God
And has attacked one of its best buildings.
And this is America filled with fear
From the north, south, east, and west,
Thank God."

Osama bin Laden,
On the 9/11 attacks[188]

"God is on our side,
And Satan is on the side of the United States."
Saddam Hussein, President of Iraq, in 2003 [189]

The belief that God supports a war makes it easier to start one and to keep fighting once it gets started. Those who believe they are carrying out God's will are likely to draw strength and determination from this belief and continue to fight even against seemingly hopeless odds. They believe that since God is on their side they cannot possibly lose and hold out for a miracle from God, thereby needlessly prolonging the war.

Since the founding of America our presidents have had to balance their Christian beliefs with pressure to go to war. Some of these men were humble enough to not assume that God automatically supported America's war efforts. Former president John Adams in a letter to former president Thomas Jefferson wrote, "Power always thinks it has great soul and vast views beyond the comprehension of the weak; and that it is doing God's service, when it is violating all His laws." During the American Civil War a man asked president Abraham Lincoln if he thought God was on the side of the North and the president responded, "Sir, my concern is not whether God is on our side; my greatest concern is to be on God's side, for God is always right."

"Onward Christian soldiers,
Marching as to war,
With the Cross of Jesus going on before."

Onward Christian Soldiers
Words by Sabine Baring-Gould (1865)
Music by Arthur Sullivan (1871)

"Seize your armor, gird it on.
Now the battle will be won.
Soon, your enemies all slain.
Crowns of glory you shall gain."

Soldiers of the Cross, Arise
Words by William How (1863)
Music by William Gilchrist (1895)

Czech soldiers march to "holy" war
(Photo by Mic Hunter).

War And Prayer

In 1904 satirist Mark Twain wrote a short story titled *The War Prayer*. However at his direction it wasn't published until after his death in 1910 because even he, someone who had spoken out against racism, religious hypocrisy, and many other controversial topics, thought being critical of Christians who supported war would get him in too much trouble if he were still alive. Prior to his death his family members begged him never to publish it fearing it would destroy his reputation for all time. I have no doubt if a contemporary author published a similar article it, too, would be met with outrage and he or she would be labeled a traitor and a heretic.

The War Prayer (Abridged)

> It was a time of great exulting and excitement. The country was up in arms, the war was on, in every breast burned the holy fire of patriotism...daily the young volunteers marched down the wide avenue gay and fine in their new uniforms, the proud fathers and mothers and sisters and sweethearts cheering them with voices choked with happy emotion as they swung by; nightly the packed mass meetings listened, panting, to patriot oratory which stirred the deepest depths of their hearts, and which they interrupted at briefest intervals with cyclones of applause, the tears running down their cheeks the while; in the churches the pastors preached devotion to flag and country, and invoked the God of Battles, beseeching His aid in our good cause in outpourings of fervid eloquence which moved every listener.
>
> It was indeed a glad and gracious time, and the half dozen rash spirits that ventured to disapprove of the war and cast doubt upon its righteousness straight way got such a stern and angry warning that for their personal safety's sake they quickly shrank out of sight and offended no more in that way.
>
> Sunday morning came... The service proceeded; a war chapter from the Old Testament was read; the first prayer was said...None could remember the like of it for passionate pleading and moving

and beautiful language. The burden of its supplication was, that an ever-merciful Father of us all would watch over our noble young soldiers, and aid, comfort, and encourage them in their patriotic work; bless them, shield them in the day of battle and the hour of peril, bear them in His mighty hand, make them strong and confident, invincible in the bloody onset; help them to crush the foe, grant to them and to their flag and country imperishable honor and glory…

"O Lord our Father, our young patriots, idols of our hearts, go forth to battle – be Thou near them! With them – in spirit – we also go forth from the sweet peace of our beloved firesides to smite the foe. O Lord our God, help us to tear their soldiers to bloody shreds with our shells; help us to cover their smiling fields with the pale forms of their patriot dead; help us to drown the thunder of the guns with shrieks of their wounded, writhing in pain; help us to lay waste their humble homes with hurricanes of fire; help us to wring the hearts of their unoffending widows with unavailing grief; help us to turn them out roofless with their little children to wander unfriended the wastes of their desolated land in rags and hunger and thirst, sports of the sun flames of summer and the icy winds of winter, broken in spirit, worn with travail, imploring Thee for the refuge of the grave and denied it – for our sakes who adore Thee, Lord, blast their hopes, blight their lives, protract their bitter pilgrimage, make heavy their steps, water their way with tears, stain the white snow with the blood of their wounded feet! We ask it, in

> the spirit of love, of Him Who is the Source of Love, and Who is the ever-faithful refuge and friend of all that are sore beset and seek His aid with humble and contrite hearts. Amen."

Modern Christians & War

Although Aldous Huxley wrote the following in 1937, it just as well might have been written today:

> The church allows people to believe that they can be good Christians and yet draw dividends from armament factories, can be good Christians and yet imperil the well-being of their fellows by speculating in stocks and shares, can be good Christians and yet be imperialists, yet participate in war. All that is required of the good Christian is chastity and a modicum of charity in immediate personal relations.[190]

Fifty years later Dr. Scott Peck wondered if America ought to change the motto on our money from "In God We Trust" to "In God We Partially Trust or "In Weapons We Trust."[191] American revolutionary patriot Thomas Paine, best known as the author of *Common Sense*, had the same view of Jesus' teaching on non-violence as many contemporary Christians-he would be delighted to practice non-violence if only everyone else would do so first:

> Could the peaceable principle of the Quakers be universally established, arms and the art of war would be wholly extirpated: But we live not in a world of angels...I am thus far a Quaker, that I would gladly agree with all the world to lay aside the use of arms, and settle matters by negotiation: but unless the

> whole will, the matter ends, and I take up my musket and thank Heaven He has put it in my power.

Jesus and his early followers lived under the occupation of another country's armed forces. If ever violence were to be justified it would be under these conditions, but I don't see anywhere in the Bible where Jesus said, "Love thy enemy, but only after your enemy loves you." Nor have I seen any evidence that Jesus expected his followers to begin being non-violent only after others had done so. His message was let peace begin with each of us today, not sometime in the future after others have taken the risk of being the first to laying down their weapons. Jesus didn't merely preach non-violence he practiced it-even when his life was in danger. When he was being taken into custody one of his followers drew a sword and Jesus said to him, "Put your sword back into its place; for all those who take up the sword shall perish by the sword (*Matthew* 26:52). Most of us today are don't have the courage and faith that Jesus had-we want a guarantee of complete safety before we are willing to risk being non-violent.

"The atomic bomb is a marvelous gift
that was given to us by a wise God."

Phyllis Schlafly

Even If Jesus Isn't Pro-War The Ministers Certainly Are

During the George W. Bush administration when it came to going to war, many Christian leaders were supportive, even enthusiastic. Charles Stanley, former president of the Southern Baptist Convention and pastor of the First Baptist Church of Atlanta, claimed in one of his weekly sermons before millions of television viewers, "We should offer to serve the war effort in any way possible," and, "God battles with people who oppose him, who fight against him and his followers."[192] Jerry Falwell wrote an essay entitled "God is pro-war." In October of 2002, five evangelical Christian leaders sent President George W. Bush a letter supporting a pre-emptive invasion of Iraq because it was, "a just war." It was written by Richard D. Land, president of the Ethics & Religious Liberty Commission of the Southern Baptist Convention, and co-signed by: Chuck Colson, founder of Prison Fellowship Ministries; Bill Bright, chairman of Campus Crusade for Christ; James Kennedy, president of Coral Ridge Ministries; and Carl D. Herbster, president of the American Association of Christian Schools. All over America sermons rallied evangelical congregations behind the invasion of Iraq. In 2003 an amazing eighty-seven percent of all white evangelical Christians in the United States supported the president's decision to go to war, three years later polls indicated that sixty-eight percent of white evangelicals continued to support the war.[193] Of course, not all Christian leaders were pro-war. Pope John Paul II said that invading Iraq violated Catholic moral teaching and threatened, "the fate of humanity." His successor Pope Benedict XVI was less resolute, but still said there were, "not sufficient reasons to unleash a war against Iraq,"[194]

> "[Terrorists] are evil people.
> And we're not going to win this fight
> by turning the other cheek."
>
> Vice-President Dick Cheney, 2009

Kill Them Or Convert Them?

A Christian missionary in an article carried by the Baptist Press News Service, wrote, "American foreign policy and military might have opened an opportunity for the Gospel in the land of Abraham, Isaac and Jacob."[195] Evangelist

Franklin Graham, the son of Billy Graham, and Marvin Olasky, a former advisor to President Bush on faith-based policy, and editor of the conservative *World* magazine, were excited that the American invasion of Iraq would create exciting new prospects for proselytizing Muslims.[196]

In January of 2010, ABC News reported that the sights on some firearms used by the US military in Iraq and Afghanistan had been inscribed by their manufacturer with Bible verses. Soldiers referred to these weapons as "Jesus rifles." The Pentagon quickly promised to stop using these weapons, but claimed it would take a year to remove the Bible verses from all its weapons.[197]

Bring On The End Times

Some people believe the only way that the Kingdom of Heaven can be established on Earth is for a horrible war between the forces of good and evil to take place, and this cosmic battle will take place in the Middle East. These people believe the first requirement for this to take place was fulfilled when the country of Israel was founded. This began a series of ongoing wars between them and other countries, as well as certain ethnic and religious groups. When America invaded Iraq Tim LaHaye, the co-author of the *Left Behind* series, saw it as, "a focal point of end-time events." He believed its special role in the earth's final days would become clear after invasion, conquest and reconstruction of the country.[198] Mr. LaHaye and a number of other Christians didn't consider all this enthusiasm for war as incongruous with the teachings of Jesus; in fact since they were convinced a massive war in the Middle East was necessary for Jesus to return, any attempt at peace was viewed as misguided or evil.

Some people aren't content to wait for Jesus to return in his own time; they want him back, and they want him back now. Therefore, they are willing to do whatever it takes to bring on the end-times. One such group was the self-proclaimed "Christian warriors," known as, "The Hutaree militia." They were convinced that politicians and members of law enforcement agencies were conspiring with Satan and the Anit-Christ, and that Jesus wanted them to be ready to "defend" themselves, "using the sword," and other "equipment." By other equipment they meant automatic weapons and homemade bombs. Their plans for self-defense included placing a phony 911 call and killing the police officer that responded. Phase two included planting bombs at the officer's funeral in order to kill as many other officers as possible, thereby setting off a general armed uprising against the government by other Christians.[199]

He Can Shoot Straight, But…

Although many Christians were supportive of the war effort some of them were less than supportive of all the troops. Navy veteran Cecil Howard Sinclair served in the first Gulf War and when he died, his family wanted to have a memorial service at the High Point Church in Arlington, Texas. The surviving brother, who worked at the church, and their sister had everything prepared and were shocked when they were informed twenty-four hours before the service that the event couldn't take place because pastor Gary Simons had learned that Mr. Sinclair was gay by reading his obituary that listed his "life partner" as a survivor. Pastor Simons explained the church believes homosexuality is a sin, and had the service been held there it would have appeared to be an endorsement of, "that lifestyle." He further explained, "We did decline to host the service - not based on hatred, not based on discrimination, but based on principle… It's not that we didn't love the family." At the time the church boasted 5,000-members, but not one of them protested the actions of the pastor.[200] I had to wonder if the church had previously allowed memorial services for someone who had committed sins such as murder or adultery, and if so, why homosexuality was determined to be so much worse than these acts?

Wage Peace

Statues of St. Francis of Assisi are sold in garden shops for people to put in their yards. He is usually shown surrounded by little woodland creatures gathered peacefully all around him. Most people know nothing about his stand on war; he didn't believe it was possible to wage a "holy" war. He was so against war that he made the refusal to bear arms a prerequisite for membership in his Order. Francis' kindness and gentleness did more to promote the teachings of Jesus than the actions of tens of thousands of knights and infantrymen that waged war in the name of Christianity:

> "... [Francis] renounced violence and war, and announced that he and his followers would be people of nonviolence and peace. In his most dramatic episode, he joined the crusades, not as a warrior but this time as a practitioner of Gospel nonviolence. In 1219 A.C.E. he began a yearlong, unarmed walk right through a war zone from Italy to northern Africa, where he managed to meet the Sultan, Melek-el-Kamel, and the leading Muslim of the time... The Sultan was so impressed by Francis' kindness and gentleness, that he announced, "If all Christians are like this, I would not hesitate to become one." [201]

If Francis were alive today he probably would be called many things, a coward, a traitor, and an unrealistic dreamer. The best he could hope for would to be thought of as a conscientious objector. Department of Defense statue 1300.6 defines a conscientious objector as a person who has, "a firm, fixed and sincere objection to participation in war in any form or the bearing of arms, by reason of religious training and belief." I once asked a man who had gone through the steps necessary to be officially recognized as a conscientious objector based on his belief in the non-violent teachings of Jesus if people ever ridiculed him? "All the time," was his response. Then I asked him what was the most common thing people said to him. "Usually they ask me in an angry tone, 'where would the world be if all the Americans had refused to fight in World War II?' And I respond, 'Where would the world be if all the German and Japanese citizens had refused to fight?' "

As noble as being against war may be-it is not enough. Jesus highlighted this fact when he said; "Blessed are the peacemakers, for they shall be called the children of God" (*Matthew* 5:9). Being non-violent is a start, but more is required, one must take action to stop and prevent war. The phrase, "Give peace a chance" makes for a great song lyric, but peace doesn't happen by chance. In order to obtain peace on Earth and good will towards all people we must wage peace with more effort than do those who wage war. This brings us back to Jesus' teaching that faith without works is dead. Believing in peace is pointless unless we are willing to take meaningful action. Throughout history people have noted the effect of inactivity on the condition of the world and stressed the importance of taking action.

Inaction In Action

"Depart from evil, and do good."
Psalms 34:14

"The only thing necessary for evil to triumph is
for good men to do nothing."
Edmund Burke, British statesman (1729-1797 C.E.)

"Plato for thought, Christ for action."
American religious reformer Bronson Alcott's
Journal entry for March 23, 1869 C.E.

"Bad men need nothing more to compass
their ends than that good men
should look on and do nothing."
John Stuart Mill, (1806-1873 C.E.)
Rector of the University of Saint Andrews, Scotland

"When 'Do no evil' has been understood, then
learn the harder, braver rule, 'Do good.'"
Arthur Guiterman, Irish poet (1871-1943 C.E.)

Questions To Help In Personal Reflection Or Group Discussion

Do you believe there is such a thing as a holy war? If so, how does one determine when a war is holy and when religion is merely being used as an excuse to go to war?

How did you respond to Mark Twain's *The War Prayer*?

What is your stand on war?

What have you done to promote war?

What have you done to promote peace?

How do the economics of your life contribute to war?

The Role Of Women

Who Was Made In The Image Of God, & Who Wasn't?

Anyone who has attended more than a couple of American weddings has probably heard Paul's verses from *1 Corinthians* (13:1-6):

> If I speak in the tongues of men and angels, but have not love,
>
> I have become sounding brass or a tinkling symbol.
>
> And if I have prophecy and know all mysteries and all knowledge, and if I have all faith so as to remove mountains, but have not love, I am nothing.
>
> And if I dole out all my goods, and if I deliver my body that I may boast but have not love, I gain nothing.
>
> Love is long suffering, love is kind, it is not jealous, love does not boast, it is not inflated.
>
> It is not discourteous, it is not selfish, it is not irritable, it does not enumerate the evil.
>
> It does not rejoice over the wrong, but rejoices in the truth.
>
> It covers all things, it has faith for all things, it hopes in all things, it endures in all things.

Despite these lovely words, elsewhere in the same book Paul made it clear that men and women were not equal in the eyes of God. He came to this conclusion because in the book of *Genesis* the first male was made in the image of God, but the first female was created from the man's body (the rib from Adam). Paul denied that woman was created in the image of and likeness of God, noting, "For a man indeed ought not to cover his head, forasmuch as he is the image and glory of God: but the woman is the glory of the man"(*1 Corinthians* 11:7). Two hundred years after Paul, Clement of Alexandria, a man often referred to as a Father of the Church, and sainted, vigorously insisted that every woman ought to be overcome with shame at the mere though that she was a woman. One thousand years after Paul, Saint Bernard was sure it was easier for a man to bring the dead back to life than to live with a woman without endangering his soul. At about that same time, Saint Thomas of Aquinas, who is still considered to be the model teacher those studying for the priesthood and is considered to be one of Christianity's greatest theologians, was preaching that women were inferior to men in body, mind, and morality. He complained, compared to men, women were, "less capable of restraint and self-control." Therefore it was clear to him that, "women are meant to be servile and under male domination."[202] He disagreed with the story of creation found in *Genesis* 2 that reported Eve was created to ease Adam's loneliness. Instead he insisted that the only reason woman had been created was to be impregnated and raise the resulting children. When it came to companionship, he insisted, "Man is best served by man."[203] By the twelfth century, Gratian, known as "The Father of Science of Canon law," was busy writing a book that quickly became the standard textbook for students of Christian law throughout Europe for the next nine hundred years. In it he wrote that mutuality between spouses was impossible because women were inferior to their husbands since, "woman was not made to God's image."[204]

Which Story Of Adam & Eve Do You Believe?

So, who was created in the image of God and who wasn't? To answer that question one has to turn to the book of *Genesis* where Adam and Eve make their first appearance. But wait, which story of Adam and Eve? There are two versions of the story of the creation of humankind in *Genesis*. In the first version God, "created man in his own image, in the image of God created he him; male and female he created them" (1:27). In this telling of the story, it appears that male and female are created of the same stuff at the same time. It would then follow that being made by the same God, of identical material, and at the same time, males and female would be equal beings. But that is not the account of the story typically quoted. Church officials, particularly those who are male, usually prefer the description of creation found later in *Genesis*. In chapter two, God created man, and unlike in the previous version, the material and method used was identified; "And the LORD God formed man of the dust of the ground, and breathed into his nostrils the breath of life; and man became a living soul (2:7). Then God created a garden, brought forth trees, and four rivers (2:8-17). But God realized, "It is not good that the man should be alone; I will make him a helper for him" (2:18). Now you might think that this is when Eve makes her entrance, but you'd be wrong; God didn't form woman, but instead created the animals. "And out of the ground the LORD God formed every beast of the field, and every fowl of the air (2:19). Next God had the man name all the animals, but not one of them seemed to be an appropriate helper, Finally after fourteen verses God decided to create woman. "And the LORD God caused a deep sleep to fall upon Adam, and he slept: and he took one of his ribs, and closed up the flesh instead thereof; And the rib, which the LORD God had taken from man, made he a woman, and brought her unto the man. And Adam said, 'This is now bone of my bones, and flesh of my flesh: she shall be called Woman, because she was taken out of Man'" (2:21-23). In this version of the story woman was formed with a different method and from material unlike that which was used to create man and the other animals. No explanation for these differences was provided in the text, so one is left to make one's own determination if these details are important and if so, what they mean. Historically, this story had been used to show that women weren't made in the image of God, and therefore are less worthy than men. Of course, that is merely one possible understanding of the story. Another interpretation is the first female was unique among all God's creatures because she was made of living material rather than dust, and she was God's final handiwork thereby completing creation.

Are Some Of Us Are Made More In The Image Of God Than Others?

When asked eighty percent of surveyed Americans, both males and females, reported that their image of God was masculine. The Bible is full of references to God in masculine form: "I, the Lord, the first, and with the last; I am He" (*Isaiah* 41:4). One usually overlooked reason for the use of masculine terms when discussing God is the fact the Hebrew language requires that all nouns and verbs be either masculine or feminine. In other words, there are no gender-neutral nouns or verbs in the language. Whereas English has masculine (he, him, his), feminine (she, her, hers), and sex-neutral (it) terms to choose from, those writing in Hebrew were forced to choose each time they wrote whether to categorize God as male or female, they had no other choice.[205] Despite this limitation in the structure of the Hebrew language to provide sex-neutral <u>words</u> the Canonized Bible still contains gender-neutral <u>images</u>. In the description of Moses' first personal contact with God, God chooses to appear in a form that is neither male nor female-a burning bush (*Exodus* 3:1-12). Most readers focus on the report that the bush is burning but is not consumed; as one would normally expect to happen, but few readers ever notice that a burning plant is a sex-neutral image. In addition when God spoke to Moses God's self-identification was neither male nor female-"I am Who I am."

Women As Clergy? God Forbid!

Approximately one thousand ninety four years after the birth of Jesus, four hundred and sixty-six years after King Henry VIII founded his church, twenty years after other Anglican Churches, and following seventeen years of intense debate, women in the Church of England were permitted to be ordained as priests. At that time England had already survived eleven years of Margaret "Iron Lady" Thatcher as Prime Minister. But having a woman in the country's highest office was one thing, after all, that was only politics, but when it came to religion there was much more at stake. Therefore, five hundred male priests upset over the idea of female priests left the Church of England in protest, two-thirds of them becoming Roman Catholics. Despite this mass exodus the members of the Church's governing body, made up of clergy and laypersons, voted in 2008 to remove any Church law that discriminated against women. That meant that a woman could hold any office in the Church-even becoming a bishop.[22] In the next sixteen years more than two thousand five hundred women became Anglican priests. This meant that nearly one third of the working priests in the Church of England were women. Despite their numbers these women were not accepted by thousands of Anglicans; some male priests and lay people of both sexes refused to

22 The Anglican Church hierarchy doesn't include the office of pope.

take Communion from the hand of a woman. That same year three hundred dissenting bishops from twenty-seven Church provinces met as the Global Anglican Future Conference in order issue a statement accusing the rest of the Anglican Church of "false gospel" because of their acceptance of women clergy. When the official Bishop Conference was held a month later, a fifth of the bishops stayed away to make clear their disapproval of women clergy.

It was not as if other churches didn't have conflict over the role of women. In America the Episcopalians, who had been permitting female bishops for some time, had four entire dioceses flee the Church when Katherine Jeffers Schori was elected presiding bishop. Some of the clergy and lay people who didn't leave the Church refused to accept the legitimacy of a female bishop, and since one of the roles of bishop was to ordain priests, anyone who she ordained they considered not to be a rightful clergy member. [206]

The head of the Roman Catholic Church, Pope Benedict XVI was aware of the conflict over women clergy in the Anglican Church, and offered to admit Anglican priests, if they were male, into the Catholic priesthood. Furthermore, they could remain married and wouldn't be required to be celibate. He was prepared to recruit married men from another religion before he was willing to permit nuns or other female members of his religion to be ordained as priests or serve Mass.

The usual justification for not ordaining female priests in some Episcopalian and Anglican dioceses, and the entire the Roman Catholic Church is the belief that Jesus had only male disciples and apostles; but what if this is a mistaken belief? In this section we will examine what the Bible can tell us about the historical role of women in what became known as Christianity. You might find yourself surprised, shocked, disturbed, or comforted.

What Was The Status Of Women In Biblical Times?

Most people believe that in first century Palestine all women were powerless and at the mercy of men. Reverend Henley described the place of women during Biblical times this way: "In that time and culture, women had no value as people. They were someone's daughter and then someone's wife. Generally, women were of no more value than the sheep and goats, a servant, or any other property. And, if they did not 'fit' into an 'acceptable' category, they were regarded with pity sometimes, but mostly were treated with disrespect or contempt, by their neighbors."[207] Although in those days there certainly was more oppression of women than there is today, things were not as clear-cut as most people believe. The role of women under Roman law was quite clear- they were the property of men and subservient, however in the conquered lands distant from Rome these laws weren't strictly enforced. Public documents from the first century after the birth of Jesus indicate women inherited property, entered into legal contracts, had wills, and even initiated divorce. By the second century after the birth of Jesus wealthy women were even able to obtain high levels of education.[208]

Those who wish to minimize the role of women in religion claim that women couldn't have been leaders in synagogues or the early Christian churches because females were segregated from males and regulated to passively sitting in balconies. However, over and over again when archeologists excavate first century synagogues in the Holy Land they find they were built <u>without</u> balconies.[209] Furthermore there is historical evidence that women were active religious leaders such as inscriptions in synagogues from <u>before</u> the time of Jesus showing women functioned as clergy. There were even two words for *priest,* one for males (*hiereia*) and one for females (*hieressa*). One clear example is the tombstone of a woman who died in the century before Jesus' birth, "O Marion, priest, good friend to all, causing pain to no one and friendly to your neighbors farewell!"[210] Another ancient tomb marker refers to "Sophia of Gortyn, elder and leader of the synagogue of Kissamos."[211] In the second century after the death of Jesus women were clearly still important religious leaders. A tomb inscription from that time tells how powerful a woman could be: "Rufina, a Jewess, head of the synagogue, built this tomb for her freed slaves and the slaves raised in her home. No one else has the right to bury anyone [here]. If someone should dare to do so, he or she will pay 1500 denars to the sacred treasury and 1000 denare to the Jewish people. A copy of this inscription has been placed in the [public] archives." Religious scholar Mary Thompson noted how these few words reveal so much information about the place of this woman in her community; she is the head of the synagogue, had the power to own and free slaves, the authority to impose a fine, and her actions were important enough to be a matter of public record.[212] Those who believe that women shouldn't hold high positions in religious settings have attempted to discount all this historical evidence. They claim when applied to women these titles were just honorary or merely inherited from their husbands who must have been the actual clergy. But there is no evidence to support these claims.

Was Jesus A Feminist?

> "What else is woman but a foe to friendship,
> an unescapable punishment, a necessary evil,
> a natural temptation, a desirable calamity,
> a domestic danger, a delectable detriment,
> and evil of nature, painted in fair colors!"
>
> Saint John Chrysostom
> (between 390 and 407 A.C.E.)[213]

According to the books of the Canonized Bible Jesus enjoyed the company of women. The longest personal exchange contained in the Gospels was his encounter with a woman at a well in Samaria. In those days it was scandalous for a Jewish man to speak in public with a woman who wasn't part of his family. The apostles weren't exactly pleased with Jesus for violating the social norms of the times; they "marveled" at him having a conversation with a woman in a public place. In the book of *Luke* when a female "sinner" washed Jesus' feet with her tears and dried them with her hair Simon insisted that Jesus couldn't be a prophet if he was willing to allow that from a woman. But Jesus responded that this woman had shown him more love than had Simon.

So we know that Jesus violated the social norms of the times by interacting with women who weren't his family members, but does that make him a feminist? Well, the answer to that question depends on one's understanding of *feminism*. Jesus wasn't a feminist if you agree with evangelist Pat Robertson who claimed, "Feminism encourages women to leave their husbands, kill their children, practice witchcraft, destroy capitalism and become lesbians."[214] But Jesus was a feminist if you agree with Cheris Kramerae's definition; "Feminism is the radical notion that women are human beings." According to *Galatians* (3:28) to the early followers of Jesus the usual categories used to divide people, religion, race, social status, or sex were no longer relevant. Regardless of the version of the Bible one consults the message is the same; we are all equals (*Galatians* 3:28).

Galatians (3:28)
"There is neither Jew nor Greek, there is neither bond nor free, there is **neither male nor female**: for you are all one in Christ Jesus"-*American King James Version*

"There can be neither Jew nor Greek, there can be neither bond nor free, there can be **no male and female**; for ye all are one man in Christ Jesus"-*American Standard Version*

"There is **no** Jew or Greek, servant or free, **male or female**: because you are all one in Jesus Christ"-*Bible in Basic English*

"There is no Jew nor Greek; there is no bondman nor freeman; there is **no male and female**; for ye are all one in Christ Jesus"-*Darby Bible Translation*

"There is neither Jew nor Greek: there is neither bond nor free: there is **neither male nor female**. For you are all one in Christ Jesus"- *Douay-Rheims Bible*

"There can be neither Jew nor Greek, there can be neither bond nor free, there can be **no male and female**: for ye all are one man in Christ Jesus"- *English Revised Version*

"There are neither Jews nor Greeks, slaves nor free people, **males nor females**. You are all the same in Christ Jesus"-*God's Word Translation*

"Because all of you are one in the Messiah Jesus, a person is no longer a Jew or a Greek, a slave or a free person, **a male or a female**."-*International Standard Version*

"There is neither Jew nor Greek, there is neither bond nor free, there is **neither male nor female**: for ye are all one in Christ Jesus"-*King James Bible*

"There is neither Jew nor Greek, there is neither slave nor free man, there is **neither male nor female**; for you are all one in Christ Jesus"- *New American Standard Bible*

"There is neither Jew nor Greek, there is neither bond nor free, there is **neither male nor female**: for ye are all one in Christ Jesus"- *Webster's Bible Translation*

"In Him the distinctions between Jew and Gentile, slave and free man, **male and female**, disappear; you are all one in Christ Jesus" -*Weymouth New Testament*

"There is neither Jew nor Greek, there is neither slave nor free man, there is **neither male nor female**; for you are all one in Christ Jesus" -*World English Bible*

"There is not here Jew or Greek, there is not here servant nor freeman, there is **not here male and female**, for all ye are one in Christ Jesus" -*Young's Literal Translation*

When Did *Galatians* 3:28 Become Obsolete?

When it comes to restricting the role of women in Christianity the two most often cited verses are from Paul; "the women should keep silent in the churches. For they are not permitted to speak, but should be subordinate, as even the law says... For it is shameful for a woman to speak in church" (*1st Corinthians* 14:34-35). Paul cites, "the law," in order to justify his claim. However, "the law" to which he is referring is Jewish law; whether one believes Jesus preached a new covenant between God and humans or started a new religion, his teachings rendered at least some of the aspects of the old law obsolete, and the unequal roles of men and women was one of them. A careful reading of the Bible, particularly the New Testament, shows that women played a significant role in the events portrayed. The actions of women were included in parables and other forms of teaching. In the gospels women who are identified by name are the main characters in nearly two-dozen events, and in another thirty-one incidents un-named women are the primary characters.

Female disciples were present at the crucifixion of Jesus while no male disciples witnessed the event.[215] In the first decades after Jesus' crucifixion it was considered proper for women to be religious leaders, not just of other women, but of men as well as this verse clearly indicates; "He began to speak boldly in the synagogue; but when Priscilla and Aquila heard him, they took him aside and explained to him the way more accurately" (*Acts* 18:26). Women held high rank, as Paul made clear; "I commend to you Phoebe our sister, who is also deacon of the church at Cenchreae..."(*Romans* 16).[23] Women even founded churches as Paul's Letter to Philemon was written to, "Apphia, our sister" and the church in her house.

Women witnessing the death of Jesus (Photo by Mic Hunter).

23 The word *diakonon* is sometime translated as deacon and other times as minister (Thompson, 1995).

Despite the claim in *Galatians* (3:28) that, "there is neither male nor female: for you are all one in Christ Jesus," many contemporary theologians continue to insist that God made men and women different not just physically, but spiritually. In 2004 the Vatican released a thirty-seven-page document titled, Letter to the Bishops of the Catholic Church on the Collaboration of Men and Women in the Church and in the World that asserted that the differences between men and women are so fundamental that they will endure even after death and in the afterlife. While asserting women could serve in positions of responsibility in politics, because women shouldn't be held to, "a passivity inspired by an outdated conception of femininity," and urged all governments to, "combat all unjust sexual discrimination," it still insisted that women could not serve as priests. It also suggested women cultivate "feminine values," including, "listening, welcoming, faithfulness, praise, and waiting."[216] While certainly excellent characteristics for which to strive, they need not have been labeled "feminine" since they would seem to be spiritual traits that all people, whether female or male, ought exhibit.

Are You A Follower Of Jesus Or Of Timothy?

Paul was certainly not the last Christian who sought to keep women from being powerful in the church. In our time those who seek to keep women out of leadership positions within religious settings cite *1st Timothy* 2:12; "I do not permit a woman to teach or to have authority over a man; she must be silent." Certainly the intent of this verse is clear and the justification for this exclusion of women was; "For Adam was formed first, then Eve." The author of *Timothy* claimed the order of creation was reason enough to keep women subservient. "I was here first," isn't a very sophisticated argument, and more importantly it ignores the teachings of Jesus. It is a hallmark of Jesus that he turned social convention upside down: "But many who are first will be last, and the last first" (*Matthew* 19:30); "So the last will be first, and the first last" (*Matthew* 20:16). The other justification from *1st Timothy* was the assertion; "And Adam was not the one deceived; it was the woman who was deceived and became a sinner." This statement completely ignored the wrongful actions of Adam in the story. Both he and Eve were told not to eat of the Tree of Knowledge, but both did:

> She took of the fruit thereof, and did eat, and gave also unto her husband with her; and he did eat…And the LORD God called unto Adam, and said unto him, Where art thou?…Hast thou eaten of the tree, whereof I commanded thee that thou shouldest not eat? And the man said, The woman whom thou gavest to be with me, she gave me of the tree, and I did eat. And the LORD God said unto the woman, What is this that thou hast done? And the woman said, The serpent beguiled me, and I did eat (*Genesis* 3: 6, 9, 11-13).

A French portrayal of God confronting Eve, while Adam tries to pretend the whole thing didn't happen (Photo by Mic Hunter).

Earlier in the story was a description of how the snake lied to Eve and convinced her to eat the fruit, but Adam was portrayed as not needing any convincing; "She gave me of the tree." In the Old Testament Adam was a co-conspirator, but by the time the books that became the New Testament were being written he had been transformed into a hapless victim of a sinful woman. Biblical scholars place the writing of *1Timothy* as sometime between 100 and 150 A.C.E. which means the earliest *1 Timothy* was written was decades after the death of Jesus. Notice the author cited an Old Testament story as his justification and doesn't even assert that Jesus held these positions on the role of women. The author made it clear it was his point of view; "**I** do not permit a woman to teach or to have authority over a man; she must be silent." Finally scholars can't even agree on who wrote *1 Timothy*; some insist that it was Paul, but others point to evidence that indicates he couldn't be the author. If it was Paul, remember he never met Jesus when Jesus was alive. Paul's understanding of the teachings of Jesus was based on visions of Jesus he claimed to have experienced. Regardless of whether it was Paul or not, the point is *1st Timothy* was not based on the words of Jesus. Ultimately the question is-are you a discipline of Jesus or of someone else?

Women As Disciples And Apostles

Most people think of the terms disciple and apostle as distinct terms and as applying only to men. However from careful reading it becomes clear that the term disciple was applied to more people than to the twelve best-known disciples; "And when it was day, he called his disciples and chose from them twelve, whom he named apostles" (*Luke* 6:13). At least some of the Biblical authors used the words disciple and apostle interchangeably. In the book of *Matthew* in one sentence the word disciple is used and soon thereafter in another sentence the same group is described as apostles (10:1-5). One Gnostic text, that was excluded when the Bible was canonized, was specific that Jesus had twelve male disciples and seven female disciples.[217] Regardless of the significance one gives a Gnostic text the books of the Canonized Bible also show women were considered apostles: "Now many signs and wonders were done among the people by the hands of the apostles... And more than ever believers were added to the Lord, multitudes <u>both men and women</u>, so that they carried out the sick into the streets, and laid them on beds and pallets, that as Peter came by at least his shadow might fall on some of them (*Acts* 5: 12 & 14-15). Paul referred to women as apostles. In his letter to the Romans he began by greeting Andronicus (a male's name) and Junia (a female's name), and went on to describe them as, "prominent among the apostles" (*Romans* 16:7). In his writings Paul repeatedly refers to women using the Greek word *synergos*, which means, *associate* or *co-worker*.[218] In the writing style of Biblical times the order of names was significant; the more important persons were always mentioned prior to the persons with less status. Therefore it was significant that in *Romans* (16:3) Paul addressed his letter to Prisca (female) and Aquila (male), "my co-workers in Christ." The woman's name preceding that of the man indicated she was of higher status than he. The order of their names was repeated in 18:18 and 18:26. Furthermore Paul referred to a woman Phoebe as a *diakonon* (deacon) (*Romans* 16:1). In *Timothy* there is a series of guidelines for the proper behavior of deacons and it is clear that women function in that role (1 *Timothy*. 3:11).

Women were even seen as being capable of prophecy; "He had four virgin daughters gifted with prophecy..." (*Acts* 21:9).

How Did It Come To This?

According to tradition the founders of the Chapel of St. Helena obtained some soil from the site where Jesus was crucified and had it spread out on the floor of the chapel. On the altar was placed a huge statue of St. Helena. Mediaeval pilgrim guidebooks that described the chapel warned that it was considered so holy that access to the chapel by women was forbidden. How did it come to this? Women were disciples of Jesus, witnessed his death when his closest male disciples had gone into hiding, were the first to visit his tomb, they set up churches in his name, were religious leaders, and were sainted, yet somehow it was decided that the presence of a female in a chapel named in honor of a sainted woman would make it less holy.

The Good Old Days Ain't What They Used To Be

When modern day people insist that women should get back to their, "traditional role," in the family and religion, to which tradition are they referring; the one during Jesus' time and right after his death when women were active leaders or to the later role in which they were thought to be second class in the eyes of God? Those who think feminism is a recent phenomenon have been selectively reading Biblical text and also not paying attention to changes in society over the previous one hundred years.

Results Of A 1903 Survey By *Ladies Home Journal* On The Most Desired Qualities In A Husband

Having strength of character-42%
Having good abilities in business-25%
Having respect for women-18%
Being loving-17%
Being honest-17%
Being broad-mindedness-16%
Having a sense of humor-15%
Having a love of home & children-14%
Being a Christian-14%
Being sympathetic-13%

"When religious institutions exclude women from their hierarchies and rituals, the inevitable implication is that females are inferior...Religious groups should stand up for a simple principle: any person's human rights should be sacred, and not depend on something as earthly as their genitals."

Nicholas D. Kristof[219]

Questions To Help In Personal Reflection Or Group Discussion

Do you think of God as male, female, or as not having a sex?

If God is a male does that mean that human males are more like God than are females?

If you think of God as a male how would it change your life if you began to think of God as female?

Were you surprised by the information that women played an active and significant leadership role among the early followers of Jesus? If you were surprised, how is it that those who provided your education on religion didn't include these facts?

What do you think is meant by *Galatians* 3:28? ("There are neither Jews nor Greeks, slaves nor free people, males nor females. You are all the same in Christ Jesus.")

What motivated past and current church leaders to minimize the role of women in religious matters?

Do you think it is appropriate for women to serve as disciples and apostles? If not, how do you justify excluding them?

What is your definition of a feminist?

Do you think Jesus was a feminist?

Would you rather have you daughter or sister marry a Christian who didn't respect women, or a man who was not a Christian, but respected women? Explain your answer.

Jesus' Other Mary

We have seen how the role of women as disciples of Jesus declined from the time when Jesus was alive when they were peers with men to the current situation where in some circles it is only appropriate for them to be submissive. To further examine this process we will now look at the role the infamous Mary of Magdala played in the life of Jesus. Her story contains the ingredients of power, status, gender role expectations, spirituality, and sexuality- all in all a recipe for controversy.

Detail from a German church (Photo by Mic Hunter).

They're Everywhere

Mary is a very common name in the Bible. The two most important women named Mary in the New Testament were Mary, the mother of Jesus, and Mary of Magdala, also known as Mary Magdalene.[24] Unlike the other women named Mary in the Bible (the wife of Clopas, the mother of Joses, and the mother of James) Mary of Magdala isn't identified in relationship to a man; this means there was something very special about her. Mary of Magdala was mentioned fourteen times in the books of the New Testament, and was involved in more of the significant events of Jesus' life than was even his mother. Mother Mary's presence at the crucifixion of her son was mentioned in only one of the gospels, while all four books reported Mary of Magdala was present.

The Sainted Whore

For hundreds of years Mary of Magdala wasn't thought of as a prostitute. Probably because she was born of a wealthy family so she had no financial need to sell her body and more importantly nowhere in the Bible was she described as a prostitute, an adulterer, or a harlot.[220] But when in a sermon Pope Gregory the Great (540-604 A.C.E.) proclaimed she had been a prostitute both Catholics and Protestants accepted it as fact for hundreds of years. In 1969 officials of the Catholic Church announced that Mary had never been a prostitute. But a reputation, particularly a bad one, is difficult to alter. Despite some people's attempts to rehabilitate her reputation in 2008 she was still described on www.Catholic.org as a "notorious sinner." What would lead anyone, Pope or not, to claim

---

24 I refer to her as Mary of Magdala because using Mary Magdalene makes it appear that she had a last name. At that time neither men nor women had last names; instead people would be described in relationship to another person (son of...) or by the places where they lived.

Mary of Magdala was a prostitute? One reason might be simple confusion. But since there were so many women in the Bible named Mary to avoid misunderstandings the writers often included descriptors, such as "Mary mother of James," in an attempt to be specific about which Mary was being discussed. A more insidious reason for labeling Mary of Magdala a harlot would be to lessen her status in the eyes of the reader, to make her a less appealing as a person, and a less significant character in the story of Jesus. To this end people point to the story of the woman washing the feet of Jesus and drying them with her hair. Certainly a very sensuous act, one might even say sexually provocative, but in any case it was not Mary of Magdala who did it. Neither the book of *Mark* (14:3-9) nor the book of *Matthew* (26:3-13) identified the woman. In the book of *Luke* Mary of Magdala was present and identified by name, but the woman who was washing his feet is un-named (7:36-50). In the book of *John* the name of the woman doing the washing is named Mary, but she is clearly identified as Mary of Bethany, which makes sense since the events described took place in her family's house. The other verses that are used to justify labeling Mary of Magdala a prostitute are found in the book of *Luke* where it was reported that "seven devils" had "gone out" of her (8:1-3). That her condition was described as seven devils was an indication that it was a serious problem, but exactly from what she was suffering was not detailed so every reader is free to impose his or her own meaning on the passage such as claiming it meant Mary was a sinful prostitute. However, most Biblical scholars understand the passage to mean that she was cured of a serious illness, rather than her condition had anything to do with sex or sin.

A More Accurate View Of Mary Of Magdala

Over and over in the Bible Mary of Magdala was portrayed not only as an important part of Jesus' inner circle, but also as a leader. One of the most interesting aspects of Mary of Magdala's life is what isn't written about her in the Bible-what is missing is any justification for her high status-it appears to be readily accepted by the authors of the gospels-if her prominent role hadn't been widely accepted at the time it seems they would have provided some form of explanation.

Mary Was A Disciple

The Greek word for disciple means, "one who is learning."[221] Within the gospels Mary of Magdala, as well as other women, were described as disciples; it wasn't until many years later that church officials began to use the word only in reference to men.

Mary Was A Minister

The definition of ministering is, "to administer something, for example, aid, medicine, or a sacrament."[222] In three of books in the Bible prior to the death of Jesus Mary of Magdala was reported to have ministered (*Luke* 8:1-3; *Matthew* 27:55; *Mark* 15:41).

Mary Was An Apostle

We often hear the phrase, the apostle Paul, but who has ever heard the expression, the apostle Mary? Paul considered himself to be an apostle; "For I am the least of the apostles" (*1 Corinthians* 15:9), and, "nor did I go up to Jerusalem to those who were apostles before me" (*Galatians* 1:17). If one defines an apostle as someone who actually interacted with Jesus, then Mary of Magdala had much more of a claim to the title than did Paul. Whereas Paul's only contact with Jesus was through apparition,

Mary actually spent time with Jesus when he was alive. Despite all this evidence Pope John Paul II wrote in 1988 that during early Christianity's, "most arduous test of faith and fidelity" [the Crucifixion], Mary, "proved stronger than the Apostles," thereby indicating he didn't consider Mary to be an apostle herself, otherwise he would have written she proved stronger than the other Apostles.[223]

Mary Was A Saint

For many years Mary of Magdala was very popular, second only to Mother Mary; barrel-makers, gardeners, glove makers, hairstylists, perfume manufactures, sailors, weavers, wine-growers, and, of course, prostitutes, all considered her their patron saint. On July 22nd, her saint's day, it was common practice to read the Biblical poem about sex-*The Song of Songs*. By the twelfth century there were one hundred and thirty churches dedicated to Mary of Magdala.[224] Since she was so admired it may come as no surprise that bones purported to be from her body were considered very valuable relics. Over the centuries so many churches claimed to possess at least some of her bones it is said that if they were all combined five entire skeletons could be assembled and there still would be additional bones left over.

Mary In The Gnostic Books

In the Gnostics Books that weren't included when the Bible was canonized, Mary played an even more central and important role in the story of Jesus as an active and well-respected member of Jesus' inner circle. In the *Gospel of Mary* Jesus rose from the dead and appeared before his disciples, including Mary. He reminded them that the Kingdom of heaven is within each person, and that the search for the divine is an internal search so they ought to avoid depending on authorities for the answers. He then departs. At this point Peter, noting Jesus loved Mary above all women, asked her if Jesus told her anything in private. Mary reported he had and began to describe the soul's ascent to truth. (Unfortunately, the next four pages are missing so we will probably never know what all she said.) Peter then turned to the other males and asked if they believed her. Another disciple, Levi, responded, "If the Savior made her worthy, who are you to reject her?" In another text, titled *Faith Wisdom*, Jesus responded to forty-six questions presented him by his disciples. Of those forty-six questions thirty-nine of them were asked by Mary, further indicating she was an active, curious, and enthusiastic disciple.

Mary Was Jesus'...?

Even before the Gnostic books were rediscovered people wondered if Mary was Jesus' lover or even his wife. In *The Gospel Of Philip* she was described as the "companion" of Jesus and that he often kissed Mary on her mouth. [225]

What Finally Happened To Her?

According to legend, (since after the resurrection nothing about Mary's life was described in the Bible) fourteen years after the death of Jesus, Mary, her maid, Saint Lazarus,[25] Saint Martha,[26] and the corpse of Saint Anne[27] were sent adrift without oars or sail until they eventually landed on the shores of Southern France. There Saint Mary spent the rest of her life in contemplation. She lived in a cave where daily angels brought her the Holy Eucharist that served as her only food. At age 72 she was miraculously transported to the chapel of Saint Maximin, where

25 The man Jesus is reported to have brought back from the dead.

26 The sister of Lazarus, frequent hostess of Jesus (*Luke* 10:38-42, *John* 11:1-53, 12:1-9).

27 Jesus' maternal grandmother.

she received the last sacraments just before she died. [226] Notice how the story has her living an isolated life where she is not involved in preaching, writing, or otherwise continuing to spread the teachings of Jesus.

Questions To Help In Personal Reflection Or Group Discussion

Do you believe Mary was a prostitute? If she was, does that mean she couldn't be a part of Jesus' inner circle? Explain your answer.

Do you think labeling Mary a prostitute was an attempt to make her less appealing as a role model or to reduce her significance in the life of Jesus? Explain your answer.

Do you believe Mary was a disciple of Jesus? Explain your answer.

Do you believe Mary was an apostle? Explain your answer.

Even if it wasn't included in the Canonized Bible do you believe Mary was in a position to write a gospel? Explain your answer.

If Mary was Jesus' lover or wife how would that affect your view of her?

How would it affect your view of Jesus?

How would it affect your view of sex?

Jesus And Sex

For many people, the three words, "Jesus and sex," have no business being in the same sentence, let alone being an entire section of a book. Despite sex being something created by God there is a long history of Christian leaders bad mouthing it. Saint Gregory the Great, who became pope in 590 believed all sex, even for the purpose of conceiving a child, was evil. He liked to tell the story of a woman who had sex with her husband and shortly thereafter went to church, and because of that went insane. He believed all children were damned because they were the result of their parents' lust.[227] Although it was never mentioned in the Bible, tradition has it that Saint Mark was so sexually aroused when a beautiful woman kissed his hand that he cut it off. (Luckily for him Saint Mary restored his hand to its proper place.)[228]

Not all religions view sexuality so negatively, nor do they regard virginity and celibacy as more holy than sexuality. Take for example this Hindu text written sometime between 1192 and 1333 :

> The union of male and female, of man and woman, symbolizes the union of the gods themselves at the moment when the world was created. The gods smile upon your lovemaking, enjoying your pleasure! For this reason both husband and wife must strive to please each other and themselves when they embrace. If you are both satisfied, the gods will be satisfied.

What is the basis of the negative attitude towards sexuality exhibited by some Christians, and what are the consequences of such a viewpoint?[28]

The Old Testament

The first book of the Canonized Bible is *Genesis* and contains the story of Adam and Eve. After they eat of the tree of knowledge they know good and evil, realize they are naked and cover their bodies (3:5 & 7). Many people interpret their shame at being naked as an indication that the human body and sex are inherently shameful. However, prior to eating from the tree they were both naked and not ashamed (2:25). Furthermore they weren't banished from the Garden of Eden for being naked or having sex, but for disobeying God's directive not to eat of the tree of knowledge and to prevent them from eating from the tree of life and becoming immortal (3:23). Further evidence that God wasn't against sex can be found in verses in which God created male and female and said to them to "be fruitful and multiple" clearly indicating they were encouraged to have sex (1:27-29). Then there is *The Song Of Solomon* that described the delights of sexual activity. There was quite a bit of debate when church leaders were deciding which books to include in the Bible. Since *The Song Of Solomon* made no reference to God, many leaders thought it had no religious value and ought to be left out of the approved Bible. After it was accepted as part of the Bible, some clergy were uncomfortable with its obvious erotic focus. So they began insisting that it was actually written to symbolize of Jesus' love for the church,

28 Of course Christian clergy aren't the only ones who have a less than positive view of sexuality. Take as an example Iranian Muslim cleric Hojatoleslam Kaze Sedighi who warned, "Many women who do not dress modestly lead young men astray, corrupt their chastity and spread adultery in society, which increases earthquakes" (*Time* May 3, 2010).

even thought it contained such graphic sexual imagery, and it was written long before Jesus was born.

Verses From The Song of Solomon

How beautiful are thy feet with shoes, O prince's daughter! The joints of thy thighs are like jewels, the work of the hands of a cunning workman. Thy navel is like a round goblet, which wanteth not liquor: thy belly is like a heap of wheat set about with lilies. Thy two breasts are like two young roes that are twins. How fair and how pleasant art thou, O love, for delights! This thy stature is like to a palm tree, and thy breasts to clusters of grapes. I said, I will go up to the palm tree, I will take hold of the boughs thereof: now also thy breasts shall be as clusters of the vine, and the smell of thy nose like apples; And the roof of thy mouth like the best wine for my beloved, that goeth down sweetly, causing the lips of those that are asleep to speak. Behold, thou art fair, my love; behold, thou art fair; thou hast doves' eyes within thy locks. Thy lips are like a thread of scarlet, and thy speech is comely: thy temples are like a piece of a pomegranate within thy locks. Thy two breasts are like two young roes that are twins, which feed among the lilies. Until the daybreak, and the shadows flee away, I will get me to the mountain of myrrh, and to the hill of frankincense. Thy lips, O my spouse, drop as the honeycomb: honey and milk are under thy tongue; and the smell of thy garments is like the smell of Lebanon.

Let him kiss me with the kisses of his mouth: for thy love is better than wine. Because of the savior of thy good ointments thy name is as ointment poured forth, therefore do the virgins love thee. Draw me, we will run after thee: the king hath brought me into his chambers: we will be glad and rejoice in thee, we will remember thy love more than wine: the upright love thee. Thy cheeks are comely with rows of jewels, thy neck with chains of gold. He shall lie all night betwixt my breasts. Behold, thou art fair, my love; behold, thou art fair; thou hast doves' eyes. Behold, thou art fair, my beloved, yea, pleasant: also our bed is green. I sat down under his shadow with great delight, and his fruit was sweet to my taste. His left hand is under my head, and his right hand doth embrace me. O my dove, that art in the clefts of the rock, in the secret places of the stairs, let me see thy countenance, let me hear thy voice; for sweet is thy voice, and thy countenance is comely. My beloved is mine, and I am his: he feedeth among the lilies. Until the daybreak, and the shadows flee away, turn, my beloved, and be thou like a roe or a young hart upon the mountains of Bether. By night on my bed I sought him whom my soul loveth: I sought him, but found him not. It was but a little that I passed from them, but I found him whom my soul loveth: I held him, and would not let him go, until I had brought him into my mother's house, and into the chamber of her that conceived me. Let my beloved come into his garden, and eat his pleasant fruits. My beloved put in his hand by the hole of the door, and my bowels were moved for him. I rose up to open to my beloved; and my hands dropped with myrrh, and my fingers with sweet smelling myrrh, upon the handles of the lock. What is thy beloved more than another beloved, O thou fairest among women? My beloved is white and ruddy, the chiefest among ten thousand. His head is as the most fine gold, his locks are bushy, and black as a raven. His eyes are as the eyes of doves by the rivers of waters, washed with milk, and fitly set. His cheeks are as a bed of spices, as sweet flowers: his lips like lilies, dropping sweet smelling myrrh. His legs are as pillars of marble, set upon sockets of fine gold: his countenance is as Lebanon, excellent as the cedars. His mouth is most sweet: yea, he is altogether lovely. This is my beloved, and this is my friend, O daughters of Jerusalem.

The Virgin Mother

In two of the four gospels, *Matthew* and *Luke*, Jesus was born of a virgin mother (1:18-25 & 1: 26-35). Many Christians believe that Jesus had to be <u>born</u> of a virgin in order for him to be holy. Strictly speaking for Jesus to be conceived by the union of the Holy Spirit and an earthly mother all that would be required was a virgin conception. In other words it wasn't necessary for Mary to have been a virgin when she gave birth to Jesus for him to be extraordinary. Although none of the known early Christian creeds mention Mary the mother of Jesus remaining a virgin after the birth of Jesus by the 2nd century A.C.E. some Christians were claiming that she remained a virgin for her entire life. The first known written claim that Mary was a perpetual virgin was made by Christian theologian Epiphanius in 374 A.C.E.[229] This claim was puzzling since in the earliest gospel written Jesus was reported to have several brothers, James, Joses, Judas, and Simon, as well as some sisters (*Mark* 6:3)[29]. Unless they too were the result of virgin conception and birth in which case Jesus was not unique and Joseph was a very understanding man (*Mark* 6:3). The second written gospel also mentioned the siblings of Jesus, although Joses was listed as Joseph the more formal version of the name, much like referring to someone as "Bob" instead of "Robert."[230] These siblings were mentioned in a very matter of fact manner in the first two produced gospels, but within only a few years when the book of *Luke* was written they are no longer mentioned. Although early Greek speaking Christians acknowledged that Jesus did indeed have brothers and sisters they claimed they didn't have the same mother as Jesus. Church officials declared Jesus' earthly father Joseph fathered them during a pervious marriage.[231] Thereby insuring that no humans ever existed that had any DNA in common with Jesus. By the fourth century A.C.E. the Roman Catholic Church began to claim that when the Biblical text used the words "brother" and "sister" they were not to be taken literally, but were meant to be taken metaphorically; these people were the brothers and sisters of Jesus in the way all people are part of the Christian

29 Tradition holds their names were Mary and Salome (Tabor, 2006).

family.[232] By the twentieth century A.C.E. most people thought Jesus had been an only child; which lead Dory Previn to write the song *Did Jesus Have A Baby Sister?*

Did Jesus Have A Baby Sister?

By Dory Previn
(Abridged)

Did Jesus have a baby sister?
Was she bitter?
Was she sweet?
Did she wind up in a convent?
Did she end up on the street?
On the run?
On the stage?
Did she dance?

Did he have a sister?
A little baby sister?
Did they give her a chance?

Her brother's birth announcement was pretty big, I guess;
While she got precious little notice in the local press.
Her mother was the virgin when she carried him;
If the little girl came later then was she conceived in sin?
And in sorrow?
And in suffering?
And in shame?

What was her name?
Did she long to be the savior?
Doesn't anyone know?

Often when people speak or write about Mary they describe her as "without sin." By this do they mean she never dishonored her father and mother, didn't take the Lord's name in vain, avoided eating shellfish, shunned work on the Sabbath, or any of the other commandments found in the Hebrew Bible? No, what they usually mean is she never had sex.[30] In effect they are claiming that in the eyes of God sex between a woman and a man, even when married, is sinful. What is the impact of such a belief? I see it all the time; people come to my office because they feel shameful for being sexual, even with their spouse, and merely for having sexual thoughts. They don't think of their sexual union as making love, but only as committing a sin. I knew this sex negativity had really gone to ridiculous extreme when I saw a catalog for greeting cards for veterinarians who wanted to advertise their pet boarding services. One of the cards had a drawing depicting a snuggling cat and dog sleeping together in a bed. But for those customers who found that image too sexually provocative, the publisher was kind enough to have another version of the card where the animals were in separate beds.[233]

Know Your Audience

So the story goes that Jesus was walking through the streets of his hometown when he noticed a crowd of people yelling and threatening to stone an adulteress to death. He instantly put himself between the terrified woman and the mob and declared, "Let the one who is without sin cast the

30 Some people believe the phrase means she was not tainted by original sin, but then that means her mother would have had to been a virgin when she was carrying Mary.

first stone!" After a moment of silence a large stone came flying out of the crowd and hit the adulteress right on the head. Shocked Jesus scanned the crowd for the culprit who dared heave the rock, only to exclaim, "Mom! Cut it out, you're cramping my style."

Saint Augustine (354-430 A.C.E.), considered one of the most important figures in the development of Christianity, taught that sexuality was nothing more than an animal desire, not properly human in any way. He even insisted that merely to embrace of one's wife was a sin.[234] With the things church leaders throughout history have said and written, it is no wonder many people believe sex isn't a gift from God, but something sinful (Thoughts On Sex By Church Leaders). In the 1950's the Roman Catholic Archdiocese of Indiana declared sex outside of marriage was not only a sin, but promoted Communism! Indiana even had a law that called for fourteen years of prison time for anyone found guilty of encouraging masturbation for someone under the age of twenty-one.[235] In 2009 the Vatican invited those male Episcopal priests who were disgruntled over the Anglican Churches increasing acceptance of gay and lesbian church members to serve as Catholic priests. The Catholic leaders were willing to allow the Anglican priests to remain married even though Catholic priests are forbidden to be marry and are expected to be celibate. Lest one think that the Vatican was starting to view sex in a better light, it was made clear that these married men could serve as priests, but would be barred from becoming Catholic bishops.[236]

Thoughts On Sex By Church Leaders

"Holy virginity is a better thing than conjugal chastity...
A mother will hold a less place in the kingdom of heaven, because she has been married, than the daughter, seeing that she is a virgin."

Saint Jerome (340-40 C.E.)

"Virginity is natural and marriage came after the Fall."

Saint Jerome

"I am aware of some that murmur: if all men should abstain from intercourse, how will the human race exist? Would that all would abstain; much more speedily would the City of God be filled, and the end of the world hastened."

Saint Augustine in his book *On The Good Marriage*

"Virginity stands as far above marriage as the heavens stand above the earth."

Saint Joannes Chrysostomus in 390 A.C.E.

"Adultery in the heart is committed not only because a man looks in a certain way at a woman who is not his wife, but precisely because he is looking at a woman that way. Even if he were to look that way at the woman who is his wife, he would be committing the same adultery in the heart."

Pope John Paul II during his weekly audience in Rome in 1980 A.C.E.

Virgin *Father*?

Although Mary's sexuality, or lack thereof, gets a lot of attention, very few people bother to think about the sexuality of Mary's husband, Joseph. According to Saint Epiphanius (315-403 A.C.E.) Joseph was eighty-nine-years-old when he married Mary and was celibate all his life. It then follows that unless Mary committed adultery, she remained a virgin all her life.[31]

Sex: Obscene Or Just Indecent?

By federal law over-the-air television channels cannot air "obscene" material at any time and cannot air "indecent" material between 6 a.m. and 10 p.m. The Federal Communications Commission defined obscene material as portraying sexual conduct, "in a patently offensive way," and lacking, "serious literary, artistic, political or scientific value." Content deemed indecent is not as offensive, but still contains references to sex or excretions. (Notice that violence wasn't mentioned in either definition.) In 2009 The U.S. Supreme Court heard a case to determine if the

31 But then how does one explain her four other sons (*Mark* 6:3) and daughters (*Matthew* 13:56)?

First Amendment of our Constitution protected films that showed animal cruelty as free speech. The films involved actual dogfights, animals being tortured and killed, and small animals begin crushed by women in high-heeled shoes. Justice Antonin Scalia insisted, "It's not up to the government to tell us what are our worst instincts." Justice Scalia thought images of violence and death ought not be censored because the government isn't allowed to limit speech and expression, unless it involved sex or obscenity.[237] Actor Jack Nicholson summarized America's view of sex and violence; "Kiss a woman's [breast], they'll slap you with an X [rating]; cut it off you only get an R [rating]." In America as a society we have come to believe that sex is more disturbing than violence. This attitude that some people have, that in the eyes of God having sex with someone is worse than being violent towards someone, has serious consequences for individuals and our society as a whole.

Sex Education

Research from the University of Texas at Austin found that a majority of Americans who marry aren't virgins on the day of their wedding; including those who describe themselves as, "religious," and even those who had taken abstinence pledges.[238] Since a majority of those who marry aren't virgins at the time of their wedding it would seem that it would be a good idea to provide people with accurate and useful information about sexual matters not only before they are married, but before they have sex so they can make informed choices. But many people fear that providing accurate information about sexuality only encourages people to have sex.

Don't Make Sex Safer

In 2007 an FDA-approved vaccine was made available which protected again the two strains of a virus that were responsible for seventy percent of cases of cervical-cancer as well as two other strains. Nearly half of sexually active adults sometime during their life are infected with these viruses. Although in most cases the virus is harmless, it can lead to abnormal cells in the cervix lining that can turn cancerous, and can also cause cancer of the penis. Since males can pass the virus on to females Dr. Bradley Monk, associate professor in gynecologic oncology at the University of California at Irvine, strongly recommended that all everyone, females and males, obtain it.[239] Immediately five States allotted funds to provide no cost vaccinations for girls. However, many conservative Christians feared that vaccination would be made mandatory and would encourage premarital sex.[240] Dr. Monk was not convinced the risk of engaging in premarital sex outweighed the dangers of not protecting people from a wide spread sexually transmitted disease. He noted that inoculation does not necessarily lead to foolhardy behavior observing, "Just because you wear a seat belt, does that mean you drive recklessly? Or just because you give your son a tetanus shot, does that mean he is going to go out and step on a rusty nail? Of course not."

Condom Use

"When as an adolescent I had prayed a
pitiful prayer for a clean life, saying,
'Give me chastity and give me control over myself,
but not yet."

Saint Augustine, *Confessions*

Although not one hundred percent effective, condoms are useful if one wants to reduce sexually transmitted diseases and unwanted pregnancies. Dr. Taraneh Shafii assistant professor of pediatrics at the University of Washington interviewed more than 4000 teenagers concerning their sexual behavior over an eight-year period.

All of the teenagers had sex by the second year of the study, and sixty-two percent used a condom the first time they had sex. By the end of the study those who used a condom the first time they had sex and those that didn't use a condom had the same average number of sexual partners (5), but those who didn't use a condom starting with their original sexual experience were twice as likely to have contracted a sexually transmitted disease. [241]

Pope Paul VI predicted grave consequences would arise from the widespread and unrestrained use of contraception.

> Upright men can even better convince themselves of the solid grounds on which the teaching of the Church in this field is based if they care to reflect upon the consequences of methods of artificially limiting the increase of children. Let them consider, first of all, how wide and easy a road would thus be opened up towards conjugal infidelity and the general lowering of morality. Not much experience is needed in order to know human weakness, and to understand that men—especially the young, who are so vulnerable on this point—have need of encouragement to be faithful to the moral law, so that they must not be offered some easy means of eluding its observance. It is also to be feared that the man, growing used to the employment of anti-conceptive practices, may finally lose respect for the woman and, no longer caring for her physical and psychological equilibrium, may come to the point of considering her as a mere instrument of selfish enjoyment, and no longer as his respected and beloved companion.[242]

Did you notice that women were not mentioned, other than as the objects of sexual desire by men? There was no warning to women that without the fear of pregnancy they perhaps would be more interested in having sex and might become less respectful of men. It is as if women don't have an interest in sex.

When virginity and celibacy are held up as virtues, an indication of purity and spirituality and being sexual is viewed as a sign of the opposite, being immoral, impure, and anti-spiritual, we end up with a dichotomous Madonna/whore view of women. Either a woman isn't interested in sex and is a "good girl" or if she had any interest in sex then she is a "bad girl." In this view of sexuality there isn't a category for a good woman who is both spiritual and sexual.

The Consequences Of Ignorance

What happens when people don't have access to accurate education about sex and condoms or other forms of birth control? They don't have sex unless they want babies, right? I suppose that works well in theory, but in the real world people, married and unmarried, have sex and some women get pregnant even when they don't want babies. So these women give up their unwanted babies to couples who adopt them, right? Again, that is a great idea, but in many cases that isn't what happens; instead they have abortions whether it is legal or illegal. When some women don't have easy access to birth control such as condoms abortion becomes their form of birth control. In just one month in 2007 at one clinic in China sixty-five abortions were performed, and of these forty-two women had already terminated one or more pregnancies. One woman was having her sixth abortion. Another woman, who was a nurse so she knew how babies are made, was having her second abortion in eighteen months. Studies have found that between twenty and fifty-five percent of unmarried Chinese women have had at least one abortion. A study of 8,846 women in ten Beijing hospitals found that thirty-six percent had undergone more than one abortion within the previous six months. The Chinese Ministry of Health recorded 7.1 million abortions in 2005, but other research places the number of abortions closer to 13 million per year. Compare this rate in America where information on sex and birth control are more easily available. In 2002, there were 1.29 million abortions in America. Of course these are only the officially recorded abortions. In both countries there are unofficial ways of obtaining an abortion if one has enough money and the proper connections. [243]

Fully Human, Fully Sexual?

There used to be a form of Christianity called Docetism, that was declared to be heretical and has since all but died out. The members of this sect believed that Jesus' body was not real, because he was a phantom.[244] Of course not actually having a body would mean that Jesus couldn't eat, sleep, drink, or be sexual. But most people believe that Jesus had an actual body, therefore he ate, drank, became tired, slept, experienced pain, and had emotions. But many of these people believe for some reason Jesus never engaged in any sexual behavior. Tom F. Driver, an associate professor at Manhattan's Union Theological Seminary, objected to this common belief, "To put it bluntly a sexless Jesus can hardly be conceived as fully human."[245] What would be so disturbing about Jesus being fully human? Some people believe accepting Jesus as a sexual being is dragging him down to the level of mere mortals. Mr. Driver claimed these people miss the very meaning of the Incarnation: that God in Jesus did come down to man's level in everything except sin. The Gospels make it clear that Jesus was subject to all sorts of earthly temptations, "he was tempted in everyway we are" (*Hebrews* 4:15). Unless all sex is interpreted as sinful, a view rejected by most modern theologians, there is no Biblically supported reason to insist that Jesus didn't have sexual urges or even that he acted on them. Jesus began his ministry about age thirty. Most observant Jewish men would have been married by this time. None of the gospels mention anything to do with Jesus being sexual or married. How is one to interpret this? Does it mean Jesus had no sexuality, that the authors didn't think the topic of sex was relevant to his ministry, or that Jesus' message on sex was exactly the same as the message on other activities? In other words, anything can be overdone and become sinful; eat too much become a glutton, drink too much wine and become a drunkard. As a practicing Jew it seems Jesus would be familiar with, and influenced by, the guidelines in the Hebrew Bible. At the same time Jesus frequently violated The Law when he saw it as too repressive. The best example of this when it comes to sex is the woman who committed adultery and he refused to condemn her even though Jewish law called for her to be stoned to death. Jesus apparently saw sex itself neither as a barrier in the way of salvation nor as a condition of spiritual blessedness. He seems to have accepted it as a fact of life—not as divine or demonic.

> "If anyone thinks that Christians regard unchastity
> as the supreme vice, he is quite wrong. The sins of the
> flesh are but they are the least bad of all sins.
> All the worst pleasures are purely spiritual:
> the pleasure of putting other people in the wrong,
> of bossing and patronizing and spoiling sport,
> and back-biting, the pleasure of power, of hatred."[246]
>
> C.S. Lewis

Questions To Help In Personal Reflection Or Group Discussion

Do you think Adam and Eve were banished from the Garden because they were sexual?

How did you react to reading the Song of Solomon?

When the Bible was canonized what motivated church leaders to include these verses?

What do these verses tell us about God?

What do you think God's stance is on sex?

Do you think Mary was a virgin when Jesus was born? If so, how is that important to your understanding of Jesus?

Do you think Mary remained a virgin her entire life? If so, how does that impact your view of sex?

If she did have sex at some point in her life, does that make her less pure or holy in your opinion?

Do you think Jesus had siblings? If he did does that change your view of Jesus in anyway?

If Jesus had siblings were they born of Mary and Joseph?

Which do you find more disturbing media images of sex or violence?

Humans engage in all types of sinful behavior, over eating, being greedy, being cruel, etc. What is it about sex that so many people seem convinced it is a greater sin than lust for money, power, status, material goods, or anything else that distracts us from God?

Do you think Jesus had sexual thoughts and/or acted on them? If not, how would it affect your view of him if you learned he was a sexually active being?

~

If I Were A Rich Man

"The good Lord gave me my money."

John D. Rockefeller

Whose fortune in 1912 was $900,000,000[247]

Of Course If It Were Mine I'd Give It To You, But It's God's So Back Off

Reverend Kenneth Copeland preached the "prosperity Gospel" which proposed that following God's will would not only lead to spiritual rewards but earthly wealth as well. He insisted due to his role as the head of a mega-church in Texas he needed a private jet. So his church provided him a plane to allow him to speak at other churches without having to take commercial flights, but he also used it to fly from Texas to his house in Minnesota and his two houses in Florida that were worth more than $3 million. He also owned a stunt plane, as well as numerous luxury vehicles and boats. When the Internal Revenue Service and the Senate Finance Committee requested the church's financial records because they suspected that Reverend Copeland was abusing the church's tax exempt status he was outraged; "[The money] is not yours, it's God's and you're not going to get it." He was unapologetic for his extravagant lifestyle, "I think it's important that I not be embarrassed about the increase the Lord does bring me."[248] Of course Reverend Copeland wasn't the first member of the clergy who viewed God as his financial planner. In 1836 clergyman Thomas P. Hunter published *The Book of Wealth: In Which It Is Proved from the Bible That It Is the Duty Of Every Man to Become Rich.* No doubt

David Cerullo would agree with the message of *The Book Of Wealth*. He and his father, Morris Cerullo, a Pentecostal preacher, purchased the television studio of Jim and Tammy Bakker and founded their own prosperity gospel program. During one program after speaking in tongues he declared, if viewers donated money to him the "windows of heaven" would open up to them "one-hundred fold." All the while the screen displayed the message, "Call now with your $900 offering and receive God's debt cancellation!"[249]

A pot of money from the Czech Republic.
(Photo by Mic Hunter)

Hey, What Is That Camel Trying To Do?

I'm always puzzled by those people who consider themselves to be followers of Jesus, agree that none of the accounts of his life indicated he was a wealthy man, admit he repeatedly spoke of the importance of giving to the poor, can quote the verse about it being harder for a rich man to get into heaven than for a camel to pass through the eye of a needle, and claim that what they value above all else is their spirituality, but still insist that God wants them to be materially rich. When I point out this apparent contradiction I have been informed by more than one person, "Jesus wasn't against someone being rich, he just didn't want to anyone to be poor. He never said it was wrong to be rich." Given Jesus' numerous statements on helping the poor it seems to me that as long as poverty existed he would in fact be against anyone being rich. The Jesus portrayed in *Luke* (3:10-11) spoke about, what in our time would be called, wealth redistribution; when his followers asked, "What shall we do?" he answered; "He who has two coats, let him share with him who has none; and he who has food, let him do likewise." Even more radical is the story found in both *Mark* and *Luke* where Jesus tells a rich man who wants to become a follower to, "sell everything you have and give to the poor" (10:20-22 & 18:21-23). What did Jesus predict would happen if the wealthy man did as suggested? Did Jesus promise his riches would be returned to him a hundred fold; that God would reward him with a grand house, a large tract of land, and many precious items? No, Jesus said only that the man would have, "treasure in Heaven." He said nothing about being rewarded with material gain on Earth. But seriously, what kind of person would actually do as Jesus suggested? He'd have to be crazy.

"That's Crazy!"

After serving in the military during World War II Mr. Fran Heitzman returned to his hometown of Bloomington, Minnesota and started Oxboro Dry Cleaners. One of his first employees was Edwin Carr, who was qualified to do dry cleaning, was a hard worker, had a wonderful laugh, and a heart of gold. But there was one thing terribly wrong with Mr. Carr-he had black skin. The residents of the all-white neighborhood in which the shop was located didn't want their dirty clothes coming in contact with the hands of a black man. They presented Mr. Heitzman with a petition demanding that he get rid of Mr. Carr. Mr. Heitzman politely informed his customers if they didn't approve of his employees they could take their business elsewhere. Not only did Mr. Heitzman continue to employ Mr. Carr, but also the two became good friends over the many years they worked together.

After many years Mr. Heitzman retired from his business. He was restless so he founded Bridging Inc. a charity that took in a million dollars of donated furniture each year and turned it around and gave it to those who needed it. People who are poor or have lost everything in an apartment fire came in and got to choose what they wanted. Mr. Heitzman explained this policy; "When people come here, they go through our warehouse and pick out what they need. It's just like shopping. We don't give them a sofa and say, 'Here, you have to take this sofa.' One day, as she was leaving, a woman came up to me and said, 'Thank you. You have given me back my dignity.'" Once when Mr. Heitzman was assisting a single mother and her young daughter stock their kitchen he handed the girl some silverware, and she exclaimed, "Just think, Mom, now we won't have to share spoons when we eat." That night Mr. Heitzman went home and, "stole five sets of silverware from our kitchen drawer. It took my wife a year and a half to even realize that they were missing." Mr. Heitzman would tell anyone who would listen to him; "Everybody has too much stuff! Give it away! Help someone! Five thousand kids slept on the floor last night! In our country, that should never, ever happen! That's crazy!"[250]

Wealth & Self-centeredness

"God knows where the money is,
and he knows how to get the money to you."
Gloria Copeland, prosperity gospel preacher[251]

In the 1990's a new form of religious thought known as prosperity gospel began to be preached. By 2009 fifty of the two hundred sixty largest churches in America were preaching prosperity gospel. One study found that sixty-six percent of Pentecostal and forty-three percent of "other Christians" claimed that material wealth would be granted to those with enough faith. The same study found that seventy-three percent of Latinos agreed with the statement; "God will grant financial success to all believers who have enough faith." Prior to prosperity gospel nearly all religious leaders taught not only wasn't material wealth the goal of religious practice, but went as far as to claim that focusing on material gain interfered with spiritual development. But pastor Fernando Garay of Charlottesville, Virginia preached the exact opposite; "We love the money in Jesus Christ's name! Although he didn't cite any Biblical verses as evidence, he declared, "Jesus loved money too!" Pastor Garay assured his followers: "It doesn't matter what country you're from, what degree you have, or what money you have in the bank. You don't have to say, 'God, bless my business. Bless my bank account.' The blessings will come! The blessings are looking for you! God will take care of you. God will not let you be without a house!" He went so far as to claim if someone were to donated $100 to the church it would yield $10,000 in return: "This is not my promise. It is God's promise, and he will make it happen!" One member of the congregation announced that God had saved his life, but apparently didn't think that was blessing enough. In a manner that sounds more like a directive or a demand than a request he declared: "And now you [God] will give me a gift. I want to buy a house. Not a small one, but a really huge one."

Does the prosperity gospel harm anyone? Well, if it distracts people from developing spiritually then they are certainly harmed. And it should be noted that during the housing foreclosure crisis of 2009 , the pattern of foreclosures was highest in those areas where prosperity gospel was popular. Apparently Pastor Garay was mistaken when he claimed, "God will not let you be without a house."

When George Adams lost his job at an Ohio factory he moved with his wife and four preteen boys to Conroe, a suburb of Houston. They made this cross-country trip in order to join Lakewood Church the mega church run by televangelist and best selling author Joel Osteen, who was best known for preaching that one of God's top priorities was to shower material blessings on Christians. Mr. Adams happily agreed and proclaimed; "It's a new day God has given me! I'm on my way to a six-figure income!" Mr. Adams planned to use his forthcoming fortune to purchase his dream house- "Twenty-five acres, and three bedrooms. We're going to have a schoolhouse (in order to home school his children). We want horses and ponies for the boys, so a horse barn. And a pond. And maybe some cattle. I'm dreaming big--because all of heaven is dreaming big. Jesus died for our sins. That was the best gift God could give us. But we have something else. Because I want to follow Jesus and do what he ordained, God wants to support us. It's Joel Osteen's ministry that told me. Why would an awesome and mighty God want anything less for his children?"[252]

Did you notice that all of Mr. Adams' goals focused on himself and his family; he said nothing about using his promised wealth to assist the poor or sick. His plans were entirely about his pleasure and comfort. He insisted that God wanted to make him materially rich, but he didn't mention Jesus even though he considers himself to be a Christian. That lack of attention paid to Jesus is appropriate because Jesus didn't teach that God was a celestial sugar daddy. Jesus made clear his priority was spiritual wealth not material riches; "Do not store up for yourselves treasures on earth, where moth and rust destroy, and where thieves break in and steal. But store up for yourselves treasures in heaven, where moth and rust do not destroy, and where thieves do not break in and steal" (*Matthew* 6:19-20).

In his day Jesus saw how the quest for material wealth could make people self-centered. To illustrate this problem he told the story of the rich man and Lazarus (*Luke* 16:19-31). The rich man dressed in expensive clothes and ate elaborate meals every day while just outside his door was Lazarus, a homeless man who looked on longingly. Lazarus would have been satisfied with table scraps, but these were instead fed to the rich man's dogs. When the two men died, their circumstances were reversed: Lazarus was given consolation and the rich man was tormented. When Pope John Paul II was asked his interpretation of the parable he answered: "The rich man was condemned because he did not pay attention to the other man, because he failed to take notice of Lazarus, the person who sat at his door and who longed to eat the scraps from his table. Nowhere does Christ condemn the mere possession of earthly goods as such. Instead, He pronounces very harsh words against those who use their possessions in a selfish way, without paying attention to the needs of others."[253]

"Money is a good servant but a bad master."

French saying

Greed

Both *Matthew* and *Mark* contain nearly identical stories that illustrate Jesus' stand on material wealth. In both versions of the story Jesus first directed a rich man to give away his wealth if he wanted to become his disciple. When the man refused Jesus commented that it is difficult for the rich to enter the kingdom of heaven. The rich man wanted his possessions more than he wanted to be Jesus' disciple. Jesus knew that greed interferes with a person's ability to focus on spiritual matters. He warned that every minute spent focusing on material wealth was a minute not spent on spiritual matters; "Watch out! Be on your guard against all kinds of greed; a man's life does not consist in the abundance of his possessions" (*Luke* 12:15). Jesus knew whatever one puts at the center of one's life becomes one's god; "For where your treasure is, there your heart will be also"(*Matthew* 6:21). When a person moves from possessing material objects to being possessed by the desire for more material objects then that person has sinned by replacing the love of God with the love of material wealth. Jesus was quite clear about his stand on this matter: "No servant can serve two masters. Either he will hate the one and love the other, or he will be devoted to the one and despise the other. You cannot serve both God and money" (*Luke* 16:13). In the twenty-first century writer Bill Bryson described greed as when things are done for a better return on investment, rather than for making the world a better place.[254]

Then Come Follow Me

"Now a man came up to Jesus and asked, "Teacher, what good thing must I do to get eternal life?" "If you want to enter life, obey the commandments." "Which ones?" the man inquired. Jesus replied, "'Do not murder, do not commit adultery, do not steal, do not give false testimony, honor your father and mother, and love your neighbor as yourself." "All these I have kept," the young man said. "What do I still lack?" Jesus answered, "If you want to be perfect, go, sell your possessions and give to the poor, and you will have treasure in heaven. Then come, follow me" (*Matthew* 19:16-22).

"As Jesus started on his way, a man ran up to him and fell on his knees before him. "Good teacher," he asked, "what must I do to inherit eternal life?" "You know the commandments: Do not murder, do not commit adultery, do not steal, do not give false testimony, do not defraud, honor your father and mother." "Teacher," he declared, "all these I have kept since I was a boy." Jesus looked at him and loved him. "One thing you lack," he said. "Go, sell everything you have and give to the poor, and you will have treasure in heaven. Then come, follow me (*Mark* 10:17-21).

"No one is master of his wealth, but its servant; and no one can serve two masters."

Father Louis Evely[255]

How Much You Want Isn't The Same As How Much You Need

If money could buy happiness George and Marie Douglas-David with an estimated net worth of $329 million ought to have been blissful. But after only seven years they were in divorce court accusing one another of infidelity. George expected Marie to be happy with a mere $43 million, but she wanted $100 million. She pointed out if she had only $43 million she would be broke in sixteen years, what with the costs associated with her New York apartment, three homes overseas, and her weekly travel expenses. In court papers she listed her weekly expenses as $700 for limousine service, $1,000 for hair and skin treatments, $1,500 for meals and entertainment, $4,500 for clothes, and $8,000 for travel. At a time when over 47 million Americans lived in poverty, and the median household income for a family of four was $50,000 a year she told the court she required $53,800 a week for her individual "needs."[256] Ms Douglas-David certainly isn't the only person in America who vastly overestimates what it costs to satisfy her needs; over the past thirty years the income of the top 0.01% of the American population grew over 900%. Every year these 14, 588 mega-rich people received at least another $11.5 million, or to put it another way, 6% of all of the income of the country. In contrast the majority of citizens (90%) made an average of $32,421.[257]

More Money ≠ More Happiness

Does the amount of money one has correlate with the amount of happiness one experiences? Randy Newman addressed this question in his song *It's Money That I Love;* "They say that money can't buy love in this world, but it'll get you a half-pound of cocaine, and a sixteen-year old girl, and a great big long limousine." These things might be the ingredients for a pleasurable evening, but would they lead to long-term happiness? Most people don't understand that the relationship between financial wealth and happiness is nonlinear. As Daniel Gilbert, Harvard University psychologist and author of *Stumbling on Happiness,* explained; "Psychologists have spent decades studying the relation between wealth and happiness, and they have generally concluded that wealth increases human happiness when it lifts people out of abject poverty and into the middle class but that it does little to increase happiness thereafter."[258] In other words, doubling your income when you are poor does a lot to increase your happiness, but doubling your income when you are rich has very little effort on happiness. This is because satisfying needs is more meaningful than satisfying mere wants; getting enough food for one's hungry family members has more impact on happiness than purchasing them all a new gadget, especially if they already have many thingamabobs. Now you might be thinking, "Well, even if those rich people aren't happier the more money they have, I certainly would be!" Well, that's not what the research has found. When American multimillionaires were asked to rate their level of happiness on a scale of one (not at all satisfied) to seven (completely satisfied) the average score was 5.8. Comparing this number with the average score of homeless people in Calcutta, India (2.9) one might conclude that money does buy happiness, but that conclusion doesn't hold up when additional groups are asked about their happiness. Besides super rich Americans, other people who rated their happiness at around 5.8 were the Inuit of northern Greenland and the Masai of Kenya, cattle-herders who live without electricity or running water in huts made of dung. Only when people were in various levels of extreme poverty did money affect happiness; people who lived in the slums of Calcutta rated their happiness higher than those who were homeless (4.6 to 2.9).[259]

But what if we examine the happiness of regular people, not the mega-rich and the horribly poor? Social psychologist Ruut Veenhoven of Erasmus University in Rotterdam analyzed more than 150 studies on wealth and happiness before concluding economic indicators measure economies, but not the wellbeing of citizens. The gross domestic product (GDP) or gross domestic income (GDI) is a basic measurement of a country's overall economic performance using the market value of all goods and services within the borders of a country in a year. Sometimes it is also referred to as the standard of living. Regardless of what it is called, since World War II it tripled in America, despite this increase in overall material wealth during this same time period, surveys show the level of happiness, as a nation has remained pretty much the same. Ed Diener of the University of Illinois, and Martin Seligman of the University of Pennsylvania summarized the situation, "Although economic output has risen steeply over the past decades, there has been no rise in life satisfaction ... and there has been a substantial increase in depression and distrust."[260] Psychologist Kennon Sheldon's research consistently found that people who said money was the most important thing were also the people who scored lowest on happiness.[261] To put a number on all this, only about 1% of a person's happiness is the result of income.[262] This was illustrated by a study that examined lottery winners and people who had sustained serious physical injuries that found, as one might expect, that immediately after obtaining the prize the winners were happier than they had been before, and just as obviously, right after being injured those people were less happy than they had been. No surprises there. But between eight weeks and five years both groups had returned to the same level of happiness they had experienced prior to the positive or negative event.[263]

"We make a living by what we get,
but we make a life by what we give."
Sir Winston Churchill

When I'm Rich

Unless we have rich relatives, the only chance most of us have for becoming rich is winning a lottery, and the odds of that are pretty slim. Although as they say, "You can't win if you don't play," it is also true that your odds of winning are about the same whether you purchase a ticket or not. I have frequently heard people describe what they plan to do when they win the lottery even though the odds of picking the six numbers necessary to win the grand price in the Powerball™ lottery are 1 in 195,249,054.[264] I have never had anyone tell me their plans for when they are struck by lightening, even though the odds of that happening are much better than winning the lottery.[32] All these figures! Let's put a face on this issue (That's Not My Fantasy Of What Happens When I Win The Lottery). After looking at what happened to these big time winners it becomes apparent these people still had problems even after they became rich; they weren't necessarily happier than they had been. Amazingly for many winning doesn't even resolve their money problems; as evidenced by the fact that nearly one-third of lottery winners end up filing for bankruptcy.[265] In most people's fantasies about sudden wealth they never consider that the windfall could bring about unexpected problems that they wouldn't have had to face had they not obtained a vast sum of money. The operator of The United Kingdom National Lottery studied the winners of their prizes and found that two percent stated the change in their finances made them less happy.

---

32 Odds of being struck over an 80 year period are1 in 6250. National Weather Service, http://www.weather.gov/om/lightning.

That's Not MY Fantasy Of What Will Happen When I Win The Lottery[266]

In 2002 "Jack" Whitaker won a $314.9 million jackpot and walked away with $113.9 million, at which time he pledged a tenth of his lottery earnings to Christian charities. Shortly thereafter, his teenaged granddaughter died of a drug overdose, and he was arrested for drunk driving.

In 2004, Columbian immigrant Juan Rodriguez won $149 million in the New York Mega Millions lottery and took home $88.5 million. Soon thereafter, Iris, his wife of seventeen years, filed for divorce and demanded half of the winnings.

In 2005, Gerald Muswagon, won a $10 million lottery prize. He spent much of it on partying and giving it to friends. During that time he was arrested for dangerous driving and for fondling an under-age girl. Seven years after getting his riches he killed himself by hanging.

In 2006, Donald and Danette Sigmon won $800,000 in the Powerball Lottery. They attempted to tithe 10% of their lottery earnings to their church, but the pastor refused to accept it because it had been obtained through gambling. In addition to rejecting their donation, the members of the Baptist church they had long attended shunned them because they had sinned by playing the lottery.

There are a number of reasons that suddenly obtaining a large sum of money can negatively affect someone's happiness. First, it puts a strain on family relationships when suddenly requests, or even demands, for gifts and money come pouring in. Second, over half of winners quit their jobs, thereby eliminating the satisfaction of accomplishment that comes with being part of a team effort and completing a task. Furthermore by leaving their place of employment they cut themselves off from important social contact. They become further isolated when they begin to travel without their friends who can't afford lavish vacations. New social contacts prove difficult to develop because the newly rich wonder if these relationships are actually based on affection or on a desire to benefit from their wealth. Finally, any psychological problems that existed prior to winning may intensify afterwards.[267] Social scientists estimate that the quantity and quality of human relationship accounts for seventy-percent of an individual's level of happiness. But, as Eric Weiner noted, money tends to have a negative effect on relationships:

> So the greatest source of happiness is other people-and what does money do? It isolates us from other people. It enables us to build walls, literally and figurative, around ourselves. We move from a teeming college dorm to an apartment to a house, and, if we're really wealthy, to an estate. We think we're moving up, but really we're walling off ourselves.[268]

Material wealth permits people to work less, or in some cases, not at all. Most people predict that the more leisure time a person has the happier he or she will be. It is this belief that leads people to declare if they suddenly became wealthy they would immediately quit their jobs. Does the amount of one's leisure time correlate with one's level of happiness? Most people would predict that getting paid to do nothing would be the perfect arrangement and a guarantee of happiness. However, a number of studies of unemployed workers in Europe found that they were significantly less happy than people who were actively working. Due to unemployment benefits, these people were receiving approximately the same income as when they were working, but were less happy than when they were employed. [269]

No, YOU'D Be Different

"You wouldn't be one of those selfish lottery winners, though. Oh, no, you'd spread the wealth. Buy your mom that condo in Florida, your brother that sports car, and even throw a few thousand to some worthy cause. Darfur, maybe. You wouldn't be one of those squanderers, either. No, sir, you'd be responsible. You'd invest. Eventually, after a few years, you might even do some work again. On Tuesdays. In the afternoon. Maybe. Yes, if you won the lottery, you would be, in a word, happy."

Eric Wiener, in *The Geography Of Bliss*

All Right Already, What DOES Lead To Happiness?

Money can buy comfort, but it can't purchase contentment. In a study focusing on "positive feelings"-a measure of a society's happiness- found that America ranked twenty-sixth out of eighty-nine countries, even though we had the highest Gross Domestic Products per capita.[270] Nancy Gibbs insisted that, "happiness correlates much more closely with our causes and connections than with our net worth." To support her position she pointed out that according to surveys eight of the ten states that have the highest percent of happy Americans also rank in the top ten states for highest percentage of citizens who were actively involved in volunteer activities to help others.[271] In other words, what does bring about happiness is practicing the actions taught by Jesus.

The Expense Entailed In Obtaining Wealth

"My father told me that if you saw a man in a Rolls Royce you could be sure he was not a gentleman unless he was the chauffeur."

The Earl of Arran

Many people believe Jesus said, "Money is the root of all evil," but this phrase doesn't appear in any known version of the Bible. What does appear is the phrase, "for the love of money is a root of all kinds of evil." Early disciples of Jesus knew that there is frequently a spiritual expense paid in order to obtain and kept material wealth: "People who want to get rich fall into temptation and a trap and into many foolish and harmful desires that plunge men into ruin and destruction. For the love of money is a root of all kinds of evil. Some people, eager for money, have wandered from the faith and pierced themselves with many griefs" (*1st Timothy* 6: 9-10). Regardless of which version of the Bible one turns to, the message is the same; one who loves money will do whatever evil it takes to obtain it, will not focus on being Jesus' disciple, and will end up unhappy. Over 1800 years after Jesus, Ralph Waldo Emerson summarized *1st Timothy* 6: 9-10 in five words; "Money often costs too much."[272]

People who are striving to become materially wealthy and those who are making every effort to hold on to as much of their riches as possible are unlikely to put much energy into changing the system, even when it is an unjust system, because to make the system more just would mean they would have less. As the saying goes, "You can make money or you can make waves, but you can't make both." Too many people value their material wealth over fairness and the wellbeing of others. Contrast this with the early followers of Jesus who strived to live by the motto,

"If we have food and clothing, we shall be content with that" (*1st Timothy* 6: 8).

People pay for material success by accepting lengthy commutes, thereby sacrificing time that could be spent with family, friends, or on hobbies. According to the Bureau of Labor Statistics people with higher incomes devote relatively more of their time than those with lower incomes to activities associated with, "higher tension and stress," such as work, "obligatory" (not fun) shopping. Furthermore, people with higher incomes spend less time on enjoyable leisure activities such as socializing or watching television. In other words, they worked more, and played less. Men making more than $100,000 per year spent less than twenty percent of their time on leisure, compared to men making less than $20,000, who spent nearly thirty-five percent of their time in relaxation. Similarly, women making more than $100,000 spent only about twenty percent of their time being leisurely, compared to those making less than $20,000 who spent over thirty-three percent of their time kicking back.

But Greed Is Good

In the 1987 movie *Wall Street* actor Michael Douglass played Gordon Gekko who made the following claim when addressing a stockholders meeting:

> The point is, ladies and gentleman, that greed -for lack of a better word- is good. Greed is right. Greed works. Greed clarifies, cuts through, and captures the essence of the evolutionary spirit. Greed, in all of its forms -- greed for life, for money, for love, knowledge -- has marked the upward surge of mankind. And greed -- you mark my words -- will not only save Teldar Paper, but that other malfunctioning corporation called the USA.

There are certainly plenty of people who endorse greed, and even more who indulge in it even as they condemn it in others. But greed had no place in the teachings of Jesus. No where was it recorded that he said, "Make your fortune, and then help others." In the book of *Job* Eli'phaz gave a warning to the greedy: "You gave no water to the weary and you withheld food from the hungry, though you were a powerful man, owning land—an honored man, living on it. And you sent widows away empty-handed and broke the strength of the fatherless. That is why snares are all around you, why sudden peril terrifies you"(*Job* 22:7-10). Centuries later Jesus gave a similar warning: "Then he will say to those on his left, 'Depart from me, you who are cursed, into the eternal fire prepared for the devil and his angels. For I was hungry and you gave me nothing to eat, I was thirsty and you gave me nothing to drink, I was a stranger and you did not invite me in, I needed clothes and you did not clothe me, I was sick and in prison and you did not look after me' "(*Matthew* 25:41-43).

Those who lived after Jesus also taught of the spiritual importance of being generous with those less fortunate. In 1833 Chief Black Hawk of the Sauk tribe spoke of the differences between his religion and his understanding of white people's religion:

> We can only judge of what is proper and right by our standards of what is right and wrong, which differs widely from the whites', if I have been correctly informed. The whites may do wrong all their lives, and then if they are sorry for it when about to die, all is well, but with us it is different. We must continue to do good throughout our lives. If we have corn and meat, and know of a family that have none, we divide with them. If we have more

> blankets than we absolutely need, and others have not enough, we must give to those who are in want.[273]

Is American Style Capitalism Compatible With What Jesus Taught?

"When I gave food to the poor, they called me a saint.
When I asked why the poor were hungry,
they called me a communist."
Dom H. Camara, *Poverty and The Poor*

America is a capitalistic society, which is defined as "an economic system based on the private ownership of the means of production and distribution of goods, characterized by a free competitive market and motivation by profit." Lest you think this definition came from some communist philosopher it came from the *Encarta World English Dictionary* that was developed for the Microsoft Corporation. When he founded Microsoft Bill Gates' goal was, "to get a workstation running our software onto every desk and eventually in every home"[274] For the most part he has fulfilled his plan. When the company released an initial public offering (IPO) in the stock market it made four billionaires and an estimated 12,000 millionaires of Microsoft employees.[275]

As it turns out there are two styles of capitalistic societies, those that are cooperative, and those that are highly competitive. Countries such as Germany, Austria, Norway, and the Netherlands endorse the more cooperative form of capitalism. People in these countries remember that the root of the word *compete* is the Latin word *competure* which means, "to seek with," not to defeat. They believe that the various forces in the economy, business owners, stock holders, management, employees, consumers, and the government ought to work together to see that problems related to unemployment, the economy, and the environment are addressed in a way that every groups' needs are taken into account. German businesses focus on stakeholders rather than shareholders; therefore worker representatives sit on boards of directors, income is more equitably distributed among workers and management, and benefits are generous. You might think this style of doing business couldn't possibly succeed, but it does. Germany is, and has been for years, the world's leader in exports, and German companies are famous for producing high quality items (e.g. BMW, Braun, Mercedes Benz).

The more highly competitive form of capitalism that emphasizes the free market is found in America, Canada, England, and Australia. In these countries it is believed that supply and demand will solve society's economic and social problems and therefore most, if not all, involvement by the government is nothing more than interference. Research has found that people from the competitive form of capitalism tend to be more materialistic than those who live in the more cooperative type.

From 1947 until the 1980's The Union of Soviet Socialist Republics and the United States of America were engaged in what was called "The Cold War." It was primarily an economic contest between communism and capitalism. By the end of the 20th century the U.S.S.R. had all but broken up. By 1999 Russia and the U.S.A. were both competitive capitalistic style counties and were generating lots of wealth. Of all the countries on the planet that year the U.S.A. ranked <u>second</u> in the percentage of the country's population that was considered "well-to-do" (rich) and Russia ranked first. When it came to the percentage of the country's population considered poor, or near poor, America was number two and Russia was number one. These two countries had the highest percentage of wealthy people but also had the highest percentage of poor people.[276] How is that these two countries with all that wealth allowed so many of their own citizens to be poor? During the Cold War the citizens of the U.S.S.R. were sometimes referred to as Godless communists, but what was our excuse?

When asked about their values, citizens of competitive capitalistic counties report they appreciate money, power and achievement over personal relationships and community relationships to a higher degree than do those from cooperative capitalist cultures. According to the results of studies conducted by social psychologist Dr. Tim Kasser and his colleagues, "Our form of capitalism encourages materialistic values, and the research shows that people high on materialism...are more likely to engage in unethical business behaviors and manipulate people for their own purposes."[277] Striving for money, power and achievement instead of developing personal and community relationships goes against the principles that Jesus taught. Based on our behavior it seems clear that we endorse the tenets of John D. Rockefeller more than those of Jesus.

Wealth And The Old Testament

As a scholar of Jewish law Jesus was familiar with how material wealth was addressed in the Old Testament. Examination of a few of these verses makes it clear where Jesus developed his un-American views on poverty, material wealth, and the responsibilities of the those who are well off financially:

"Do not forget to do good and to share with others" (*Hebrews* 13:16);

"Keep your life free from the love of money, and be content with what you have" (*Hebrews* 13:5);

"Do not wear yourself out to get rich; have the wisdom to show restraint" (*Proverbs* 23:4-5).

Charging Interest

One of the commandments from God recorded in *Exodus* that almost never comes up in contemporary discussions on what is appropriate behavior for disciples of Jesus is, "Do not take advantage of a widow or an orphan. If you do and they cry out to me, I will certainly hear their cry... If you lend money to one of my people among you who is needy, do not be like a moneylender; charge him no interest" (22:22, 23, & 25). That last part about the <u>no</u> interest was so unpopular that in some later versions of the Bible the verse was changed from "no interest" to "excessive interest." Of course, while "no" is clear, "excessive" is in the eye of the beholder. What might seem like excessive interest to the person paying it could seem perfectly reasonable to the person receiving payment.

Treatment Of Aliens

Although chapter four of *Deuteronomy* gets a lot of attention, since it contains the ten most quoted commandments, nobody fights to have chapter ten posted in public buildings or claims it was part of the bedrock on which the nation was founded: [God] "defends the cause of the fatherless and the widow, and loves the alien, giving him food and clothing. And you are to love those who are aliens, for you yourselves were aliens in Egypt" (10:18-19). The authors of the Old Testament weren't referring to extraterrestrial visitors, rather they were reporting that God wanted them to be kind and generous to those from outside their country as well as those not of their religion.

Treatment Of Employees

I've never seen chapter twenty-four from *Deuteronomy* posted in a factory or other place of business: "Do not take advantage of a hired man who is poor and needy, whether he is a brother Israelite or an alien living in one of your towns... Otherwise he may cry to the LORD against you, and you will be guilty of sin" (24:14-15).

Tithing

Deuteronomy is chock full of God's commandments. In one chapter God directs people every three years to take a tenth of their income and give it away. This is referred to as tithing. Over the centuries the meaning of the word *tithe* has come to mean: "1. One tenth of somebody's income or produce paid voluntarily or as a tax for the support of a church or its clergy; 2. The obligation to pay a tithe to a church or its clergy."[278] In our time when tithing is mentioned it is usually in reference to the practice of giving ten percent of one's income to the church one attends. But that isn't how tithing is described in the Bible: "When you have finished setting aside a tenth of all your produce in the third year, the year of the tithe, you shall give it to the Levite, the alien, the fatherless and the widow, so that they may eat in your towns and be satisfied (*Deuteronomy* 26:12). A Levite was an assistant to the priests in the temple, so it is easy to see how the practice ought to include financial support for clergy. Notice God didn't specifically state one support had to go to the synagogue (churches didn't yet exist) one attended. Therefore it would be perfectly appropriate for one to tithe to a house of worship other than one's own, particularly if one's own place of worship were financially well off and secure. But clergy make up only a fourth of the commandment, what about the remaining seventy-five percent, the alien, the fatherless and the widow? Whatever became of their portion?

Helping The Needy

> "He that feeds the hungry feeds God also."
>
> *Talmud* (Rabbinical writings 100-600 A.D.)

Job's description of himself would have pleased Jesus, and serves as a model for us all: "Whoever heard me spoke well of me, and those who saw me commended me, because I rescued the poor who cried for help, and the fatherless who had none to assist him. The man who was dying blessed me; I made the widow's heart sing. I put on righteousness as my clothing; justice was my robe and my turban. I was eyes to the blind and feet to the lame. I was a father to the needy; I took up the case of the stranger" (*Job* 29:11-17). Certainly if Jesus showed up at our door as thirsty and hungry we would gladly invite him in and happily provide him with food and drink until he had his fill. But it seems very unlikely that Jesus will ring our doorbells any time soon; does that mean we are off the hook? Not according to Jesus when he described truly righteous people:

> "Come, you who are blessed by my Father; take your inheritance, the kingdom prepared for you since the creation of the world. For I was hungry and you gave me something to eat, I was thirsty and you gave me something to drink, I was a stranger and you invited me in, I needed clothes and you clothed me, I was sick and you looked after me, I was in prison and you came to visit me." Then the righteous will answer him, "Lord, when did we see you hungry and feed you, or thirsty and give you something to drink? When did we see you a stranger and invite you in, or needing clothes and clothe you? When did

> we see you sick or in prison and go to visit you?'" The King will reply, "I tell you the truth, whatever you did for one of the least of these brothers of mine, you did for me" (*Matthew* 25:34-40).

The Holy Grail

Medieval tales are full of knights risking their lives on quests to find the cup which Jesus was supposed to have used at his last supper with his disciples known as the Holy Grail. In many paintings the Holy Grail is usually portrayed as an ornate golden cup. For centuries the official papal chalice, which some believe to be the Holy Grail, has been a vessel made of alabaster, gold, and gemstones. Knowing what we know about the style of life led by Jesus it seems very unlikely that he had access to a cup made of gold. In all likelihood, as was the custom of the day, he would have used a simple wooden or clay bowl from which to drink. Despite this, many churches insist on using an expensive chalice during Holy Communion. In 2008 the archdiocese of Minneapolis demanded that the priests at Saint Stephen's church get rid of the simple ceramic vessels they had been using for years to serve communion and replace them with containers made of precious metals as required by the rules in the *General Instructions of the Roman Missal.* Since Saint Stephen's was an inner city church attended mostly by poor people the priests and members thought there were better uses for their funds than purchasing expensive cups. When the archdiocese demanded the rules be followed the clergy and the congregation chose to leave their 119 year-old church and began holding mass in the gym of a school.[279]

Image of the Last Supper on the ceiling of a French church (Photo by Mic Hunter)

How Would A Christian Nation Behave?

What If America Were a Christian Nation Again?
Book title by D. James Kennedy & Jerry Newcombe

For a country that many people claim is a "Christian nation" America certainly doesn't always act in accordance with the teachings of Jesus.

"You have lived on earth in luxury and self-indulgence" (James 5:5)

According to the Self Storage Association in 2009 one in ten homes rented a storage unit and the United States had 2.3 billion square feet of self-storage space-more than seven square feet of space for every person in the country. They claimed it would be, "physically possible that every American could stand-all at the same time-under the canopy of self-storage roofing." Ten percent of households had so much stuff that wasn't necessary for daily living it didn't all fit in their homes and they would rather pay to keep it in a warehouse than to give it to the poor.

Journalist David Villano summarized the American lifestyle:

> While accounting for just 5 percent of the world's population, the U.S. burns nearly 25 percent of the world's energy and is the No. 1 user of virtually all traded commodities like corn, copper, and rubber. Americans consume, on average, three times more meat than the rest of the world. The U.S. uses about one-third of the world's paper. In the end, the U.S. produces 30 percent of the world's waste (including 25 percent of global carbon dioxide emissions) and throws out a staggering 96 billion pounds of edible food each year. By one estimation, if all 6.7 billion people on Earth raised their living standard so they consumed like Americans, the present population would feel like 72 billion...If China and India consumed as much per capita as the United States, by 2030, those two countries

alone would require one additional planet Earth to meet their needs.[280]

"If anyone has material possessions and sees his brother in need but has no pity on him, how can the love of God be in him?" (1st John 3:17)

When polled Americans consistently overestimated the amount of their tax dollars devoted to foreign aid by a factor of approximately fourteen. That meant they thought for every dollar we were actually spending they mistakenly imagined we were spending fourteen. Even when told the actual level of foreign assistance 13% still considered it excessive.[281]

Even when it comes to our own citizens, Americans are more willing to let their people live in poverty. A child is more likely to live in poverty in America than a child in twenty-three other developed countries. Here is a list of the percentages of children in households that earn less than fifty percent of a country's median income:[33] It shows that an American child is nearly eight times more likely to live in poverty than a Danish child. All of these countries have democratic governments and some form of capitalism. How is it that these countries manage to treat their children with more concern than America?

33 Not average income, where the amount of all incomes are added together and then divided by the number of households, but the income level where the same number of households make more as the number of households that make less.

Percentage Of A Country's Children Who Live In Families With Less Than Half Of The Median Income

Denmark	2.4%
Finland	3.4%
Norway	3.6%
Sweden	3.6%
Belgium	6.7%
Czech Republic	7.2%
France	7.3%
Netherlands	9.0%
Germany	12.4%
Austria	13.3%
Canada	13.6%
Japan	14.3%
Poland	14.5%
New Zealand	14.6%
Portugal	15.6%
Spain	15.6%
Ireland	15.7%
Italy	15.7%
United Kingdom	16.2%
United States Of America	21.7%[282]

Poverty means more than merely not having the newest video game; the single best predictor of child abuse is poverty. Although child abuse occurs in families at every economic level, a child raised in a family that has an annual income of less than $15,000 is twenty-two times more likely to be abused than children from families with more income. In 2010 one in five American children lived in poverty-a total of fourteen million children. Every year the Department of Health and Human Services notes that there are three million reports of child abuse and neglect in America.[283] How many children's abuse is never reported?

The authors of Bible directed; "Withhold not correction from a child: for if thou strike him with the rod, he shall not die. Thou shalt beat him with the rod, and deliver his soul from hell." (*Proverbs* 23:13-14). Unfortunately, they were mistaken; children do die at the hands of their parents. Child abuse is more than harsh treatment; parents kill each year at least two thousand American children. America leads the world's richest nations in the rate of child abuse fatalities. The rate of death from child abuse and neglect in America is three times higher than Canada's and eleven times greater than Italy's. Even those children who come to the attention of child protection services don't get much help; in Texas fifty percent of the children who end up being killed by their parents came from families that had previously been investigated but meaningful intervention didn't occur.[284] But all of this is nothing more than facts and figures; let's get personal.

Jacquelyn Williams, 31, wasn't satisfied with her six-year-old son's performance at school. So just like numerous times in the past, she had her boyfriend, Troy Clay, 37, take the child into their basement, tie his hands around a post, and whip him with an extension cord. Two days later when school officials questioned him about his wounds the boy claimed a dog had attacked him. Dr. Rich Kaplan, a physician who specialized in child abuse cases was asked to examine the boy. He reported in addition to internal injuries there were bruises and abrasion that left, "virtually no skin on the back without evidence of trauma." He added, "It was marks overlapping each other…crossways, boom, boom, boom." The boy's ten year-old brother reported he had also been, "whooped."[285] Numerous scars covered his back, arms, and legs. His most recent beating had been for failing to take out the trash. Child protection workers noted that the boys' mother had a previous child who died while suffering from eleven bruises, four internal injuries, and nine broken bones.[286]

Jaden Smith was eight months old when he was found in his crib blue and cold. Hours before when his mother left him in the care of his father, Jesse Hummel, age thirty, he had been alive and healthy. The medical examiner who completed an autopsy of baby Jaden determined had died as a result of, "complex homicidal violence." In every day language what this meant was the baby's body was covered in bruises, there was trauma to the back of his head and broken blood vessels in his brain indicating, "violent shaking." His lower lip had puncture wounds that lined up with two teeth indicating his mouth had been forced shut. This was not the first time Mr. Smith had come to the attention of law enforcement personnel; seven years previously he had been convicted of "malicious punishment of a child" for shaking another of his sons who was three months old. He had also been convicted of domestic assault for strangling his girlfriend.[287]

Byrant and Pamela Mendenhall took their eighteen day old son to an emergency room because he wasn't eating and had a high fever. On examination the cause of these symptoms became clear; he had a fractured elbow, numerous skull fractures, and bleeding in his brain. Although he was expected to live he would have permanent brain damage. The cause of the injuries was the baby's father, who was angry after an argument with the baby's mother. Therefore, he "squeezed the baby's head with such force that he heard an audible popping sound and felt the skull bone squish in his hands."[288]

These three cases came from articles in one Minneapolis newspaper on <u>a single day</u>. If you find them disturbing, and well you should, imagine how disturbing it was for the victims.

Like many others before her pediatric physician Seema Jilani in her article, "America Fails Abused Kids," referred to adults who abuse children as, "monsters." Describing people who abuse children as monsters makes it easier to us to assure ourselves that since we, and those we love, aren't monsters, we, and those we love, could never abuse a child. But as reassuring as is this idea, a consequence of it is that many people overlook signs of abuse in their families because they can't bring themselves to believe a loved one is a monster. Labeling those who abuse children as monsters dehumanizes them and makes it easier to withhold funding for prevention and treatment programs, because monsters don't deserve compassion and assistance, they only deserve distain and punishment. How is it that in 2003 Americans found $1.6 million dollars to spend on thong underwear for tweens (ages 7-12), but can't find money to properly fund child abuse prevention or the treatment of victims or offenders?[289]

"Love your enemies and pray for those who persecute you""(Matthew 5:44)

The entire State Department budget plus all the foreign aid to other countries totaled less than less than 1.5% of the federal budget ($40 billion).[290] Contrast this with the $160 billion <u>yearly</u> expense for the war in Iraq. Every time our military fired a Tomahawk missile it cost the American taxpayers $500,000, an amount of money that could build twenty schools in Iraq or Afghanistan.[291] More than half (54%) of the entire federal budget goes to military spending. America's military is not only the most expensive in the world, but it costs more than the total outlay of the other nine most expensive militaries <u>combined!</u>[292]

Based on our spending it appeared we would rather kill people than provide non-violent assistance to them. In 2005 the U.S. government sold or gave foreign governments $12 billion worth of weapons, small arms, tanks, fighter jets, helicopters, and warships. By 2008 the figure had more than doubled to $32 billion. One may argue this was the price we must pay to defend ourselves, but at the same time we were spending our tax dollars on weapons for other countries American businesses were selling another $92 billion worth of weapons throughout the world.[293] In 2008 America sold more weapons than any other nation on the planet.[294]

"Look! The wages you failed to pay the workmen who mowed your fields are crying out against you. The cries of the harvesters have reached the ears of the Lord Almighty" (James 4)

In 2008 the median income in America fell to its lowest point in twelve years, and the percentage of Americans who lived in poverty jumped to over thirteen percent, the highest rate in eleven years. That same year the wealthiest ten percent of Americans-those who made more than $138,000 each year-earned nearly eleven and half times more money than those who lived near or below the poverty line ($12,000).[295] According to *Forbes* in 2009 the combined wealth of the ten richest Americans was $245,900,000,000. There were only thirty-six countries whose entire gross national product was more than that.[34] The richest man on the list, Bill Gates, was worth fifty billion dollars, even after he lost seven billion dollars due to his Microsoft stock losing value over the previous year. The owners of Wal-mart, placed fourth through seventh on the list, and had a combined wealth of $79,400,000,000. The average take home pay for a Wal-Mart employee was under two hundred and fifty dollars a week, therefore the majority of its employees with children lived below the poverty line. Despite the fact that Wal-Mart employed

---

34 The gross national product-the total value of all goods and services produced within a country in a year, including net income from investments in other countries." *Encarta World Dictionary*, 1999.

more people than any other company in America, other than the Federal government, one-third of Wal-mart's employees were limited to less than 28 hours of work per week, and therefore were not eligible for benefits.[296] If the members of the family that owns Wal-mart were to give each of their one and a half million employees a thousand dollars they would still have $79,400,000 to live on.

All These Taxes Are Cramping My Style

In 2008 Denver lawyer Gabriel Nathan Schwartz came to Saint Paul for the Republican National Convention because he wanted, "less taxes and more war." While he looked for a candidate whose platform he could support, he made the mistake of taking a woman he had just met at a bar back to his hotel room for sex and more drinks. Unfortunately, when the woman mixed a drink for him she added some drug other than alcohol that caused him to become unconscious. When he awoke from his stupor he found the woman had not had sex with him as promised, and worse yet, had robbed him. She walked off with his $1,000 belt, $5,000 necklace, $20,000 ring, $30,000 wristwatch, and $64,000 in cash.[297]

Brother, Can You Spare A Penny?

The migrant farm workers in South Florida who harvest tomatoes by hand work ten to twelve hours a day. During a typical day each worker picks, carries, and unloads two tons of tomatoes. For their efforts they are paid at the rate of about forty-five cents for every thirty-two pound bucket they fill. But American corporations insisted they were paying too much for the tomatoes to put on our hamburgers and in our tacos and salads. In 2005 Taco Bell ended a consumer boycott by agreeing to pay an extra penny per pound for its tomatoes, with the extra cent going directly to the farm workers. This was the workers' first significant pay raise since the late 1970s. In 2007 McDonald's agreed to increase the wages of its tomato pickers to about seventy-seven cents per bucket (an increase of twenty-two cents). But when Burger King refused to pay the extra penny tomato growers canceled the deals already made with Taco Bell and McDonald's. Then the Florida Tomato Growers Exchange announced it was forbidding any of its members to collect the extra penny for farm workers. Then just to make sure no grower would violate the ban the Growers Exchange threatened a fine of $100,000 for any grower who accepted an extra penny per pound for migrant wages. The executive vice president of the group, Reggie Brown, described the penny surcharge for the workers as, "pretty much near un-American." Un-American or not, if Burger King had been willing to pay an extra penny for tomatoes it would cost approximately $250,000 a year.[298] That may sound like a lot of money, but then Lloyd Blankfein, the Chief Executive of Goldman Sachs Capital Partners, one of the major stockholders of Burger King was paid the largest annual bonus in Wall Street history-$67.9 million.[299] Nor was he the only one getting rich off the efforts of the tomato pickers; in 2006, the bonuses of the top twelve Goldman Sachs executives came to over $200 million; which happened to be more than twice as much money as the combined incomes of every one of the 10,000 tomato pickers in southern Florida that year.[300]

"I was in prison and you came to visit me." (*Matthew* 25:36)

Research by the International Centre for Prison Studies at King's College in London found more people are behind bars in the United States than in any other country. China ranks second with 1.5 million prisoners, followed by Russia with 870,000. Not only are we number one in terms of the actual number of people we have behind bars, we have the highest rate of incarceration of any country. The U.S. incarceration rate of 737 per 100,000 people is the highest, followed by 611 in Russia. We incarcerate our citizens at a rate five to eight times higher than Canada and European countries. The incarceration rates in many Western industrial nations range around 100 per 100,000 people.[301]

> "It should be a scandal that California spends $216,000 on each child in the juvenile justice system, and only $8,000 on each child in the Oakland public schools."
>
> Nicholas D. Kristof[302]

While American prisons focus on containment and punishment prisons in some other nations, such as Norway, concentrate on education and rehabilitation. How well do these two philosophies succeed? While over half of prisoners who are released in America will be caught re-offending, the recidivism rate for criminals in Norway is only twenty percent.[303] Ninety-five percent of American inmates will be released at some point. Fifteen percent of them are released with under-treated or untreated mental illnesses.[304] Many more suffer from the lasting effects of enduring repeated physical and sexual assault while incarcerated.

In addition to having the highest number of prisoners, America is consistently is ranked among the nations that execute prisoners. Each year Amnesty International releases a report on the number of executions carried out throughout the world. In 2009 ninety-five percent of all known executions were carried out in only six countries: China, Iran, Saudi Arabia, the United States, Pakistan, and Iraq.[305] It is interesting to note that approximately ninety percent of the executions that were carried out in America since the death penalty was reinstated were in the States that made up the former Confederate States Of America during the Civil War, which are also the States that make up the so-called Bible belt.[306]

Countries with the Most Confirmed Executions

2005
China-1,770
Iran-94
Saudi Arabia-86
United States-60
Pakistan-31
Yemen-24

2006
China-1,010
Iran-177
Pakistan-82
Iraq-65
Sudan-65
United States-53

2007
China-470
Iran-317
Saudi Arabia-143
Pakistan-135
United States-42[35]

2008
China-1,718
Iran-346
Saudi Arabia-102
United States-37[36]
Pakistan-36
Iraq –34

---

35 Sixty percent took place in Texas.
36 Almost half of these were in Texas.

2009[307]
China-470
Iran-317
Saudi Arabia-143
Pakistan-135
Democratic Republic of the Congo-100
<u>United States</u>-52
Egypt-48

179 countries had no executions in 2009[308]

But what does it matter that America consistently makes the list of countries that legally put people to death? The fifty-two executions in America may seem like an insignificant number, particularly given that in that same year China executed nine times more people. Insignificant, of course, unless if one of those fifty-two executions involved you, or someone you loved, in which case it was extremely significant. Again, what does it matter that a relatively small number of people who are guilty of horrible crimes are put to death? Well, for one thing, some of the people on death row are innocent of the crime for which they have been wrongfully convicted.

If a person is convicted doesn't that mean he or she is guilty? Maybe, and maybe not; from 1992 to 2009 the Innocence Project has shown through the use of DNA testing that two-hundred-fifty-four people on death row were wrongly convicted.[309] How is that possible? Well, one common reason is sub-standard services from attorneys. If you were charged with a crime, much less one that could lead to your death, wouldn't you want your attorney to be awake during the trial? I know I would. Calvin Burdine wasn't so lucky; his court-appointed attorney, Joe Cannon, repeatedly slept for prolonged periods during the trial, thereby failing to intervene at significant moments during the proceedings. During the prosecutor's cross-examination of Mr. Burdine, which was eighty-two pages long when transcribed, his attorney said absolutely nothing because he was fast asleep. After being convicted and sentenced to death Mr. Burdine, with the help of a new attorney, appealed his case to a three-judge panel of the Fifth Circuit Court in Texas. During the appeal the attorneys representing the State of Texas conceded the fact that Mr. Burdine's lawyer had slept through much of the trial, but argued that the conviction and death sentence should be upheld because a sleeping lawyer is no different from a lawyer who is intoxicated, under the influence of drugs, suffering from Alzheimer's disease or having a psychotic break. (Which, although true, doesn't really address the issue of being represented by a competent attorney, but merely gives examples of more ways lawyers can be incapacitated.) The Court ruled (two to one) that Mr. Burdine wasn't entitled to a new trial because the official record didn't show that Mr. Cannon slept through "crucial" parts of the trial and because Mr. Burdine didn't think to make a written record of times when his attorney slept.[310]

"I was sick and you looked after me." (*Matthew* 25:36)

According to the U.S. Census Bureau's annual report, as of September 2009 over forty-six million, or fifteen out of every one hundred, American citizens had no health insurance. How does this situation compare with the rest of the world? One gauge would be to compare the U.S. with its fellow members of the so called G-20,[37] which according to its website was, "established in 1999 to bring together systemically important industrialized and developing economies to discuss key issues in the global economy."[311]

---

37 The Group of Twenty Finance Ministers and Central Bank Governors.

The G-20 is basically the twenty most prosperous economies in the world and consists of: Argentina, Australia, Brazil, Canada, China, France, Germany, India, Indonesia, Italy, Japan, Mexico, Russia, Saudi Arabia, South Africa, South Korea, Turkey, United Kingdom, the European Union, and the United States of America[38] Except for the U.S., all of the other countries have universal health care. Another measure would be to compare our country to the top thirty-two developed nations and the year they obtained health care for all their citizens:

Israel-1995
Switzerland-1994
Hong Kong-1993
Singapore-1993
Iceland-1990
South Korea-1988
Spain-1986
Greece-1983
Cyprus-1980
Portugal-1979
Italy-1978
Ireland-1977
Australia-1975
France-1974
Denmark-1973
Luxembourg-1973
Finland-1972
Slovenia-1972
United Arab Emirates-1971
Austria-1967
Canada-1966
Netherlands-1966

---

38 The European Union and the European Central Bank, is the 20th member of the G-20.

Brunei-1958
Bahrain-1957
Sweden-1955
Kuwait-1950
United Kingdom-1948
Belgium-1945
Germany-1941
Japan-1938
New Zealand-1938
Norway-1912

When discussing America's unwillingness to see to it that all of its citizens have access to health care some Americans claim that America's health care system is the best in the world and the envy of every other country. Is that boast accurate? I guess it depends on who is asked. In June 2008, a Financial Times/Harris Poll found that 59% of British adults and 70% of French adults believed their countries' health care systems were "the envy of the world." But what do a bunch of overseas foreigners know about the American health care system? What do other North Americans think? In 2009 a Harris/Decima poll in Canada that found seventy percent of those Canadians polled thought their system was "performing well," and fifty-five percent favored an expansion of government-run health care over private sector health care. Furthermore, nine out of ten Canadians reported in their opinion their system was "superior" to the U.S. system.[312] So what? Just because Canadians think they have a better system doesn't make it so. What do real Americans think? In 2008 a Harris Poll in the United States, conducted with the Harvard School of Public Health found that only forty-five percent of Americans believed that we had, "the best health care system in the world." Only twelve percent of Americans thought that, "the system works pretty well, and thirty-three percent of Americans believed there was, "so much wrong with the health care system, we need to completely rebuild it." [313] But all that is merely public opinion, what do the facts tell us? It is true that America spends more on health care as a percentage of our Gross Domestic Product than other counties:

United States	13.4%
Canada	10.0%
Finland	9.1%
Sweden	8.6%
Germany	8.4%
Netherlands	8.4%
Norway	7.6%
Japan	6.8%
United Kingdom	6.6%
Denmark	6.5%

Does our expensive health care system keep us alive longer? No. More of our babies die at birth, and our life expectancy is shorter than the citizens of many other developed nations.

Infant Deaths Per 1,000 Live Births	
United States	10.4
United Kingdom	9.4
Germany	8.5
Denmark	8.1
Canada	7.9
Norway	7.9
Netherlands	7.8
Switzerland	6.8
Finland	5.9
Sweden	5.9
Japan	5.0

Life Expectancy in Years

	Men	Women
Japan	76	82
France	72	81
Switzerland	74	81
Netherlands	73	80
Sweden	74	80
Canada	73	80
Norway	73	79
Germany	72	79
Finland	70	78
UnitedStates	71	78

The American health system is run primarily, not by physicians or the government, but by business people, so making money for stockholders is high on the list of priorities. In 2009 the CEO of United Health, Stephen Hemsley, received a pay package worth $101.96 million dollars. That was six times the amount paid to the next highest CEO in Minnesota where United Health was located. Stock options given to him by the board of directors accounted for $98.6 million of his income.[314] How does a company insure that stockholders get paid? It makes a profit, of course. How does a health care company make a profit? By reducing costs, and one way to reduce costs is to reduce the medical procedures available to patients.

The necessity to make a profit can lead to life threatening situations such as the time I found one of my patients sitting in my waiting room even though he didn't have an appointment. I assumed he was merely confused about the date of our next scheduled meeting, so I was shocked when he handed me a piece of paper explaining, "I just wanted to thank you for all you have done for me and to say goodbye." The piece of paper he had given me was a suicide note. I immediately lead him into my office where I could watch him while I called a hospital emergency room to get him admitted. A nurse informed me that according to the requirements of his medical insurance she couldn't admit him unless he as, "at immediate risk of killing himself." I told her he was curled up sobbing and had written a suicide note, but was informed that unless he had immediate access to a method of killing himself he was not, "sufficiently suicidal."

Paging Dr. Jesus

I wonder how Jesus would measure a health care system. Would Jesus say, "Strive to have the most expensive, high-tech health care system in the world, even if it doesn't come to the aid of millions of your fellow citizens?" I don't think so. I believe it be more in line with his principles to see to it that everyone got at least some health care regardless of their income or social status.

Questions To Help In Personal Reflection Or Group Discussion

Do you think one of God's primary goals is to see to it that we obtain material wealth in this life?

What do you think Jesus believed about material wealth?

Describe a time you experienced greed.

What would change in America if we moved from the competitive type of capitalism to the more cooperative form?

How do you feel knowing the amount of the Earth's resources America uses?

Were Jesus here today, would he be found in the company of child abusers? If so, how would he treat them?

What percentage, if any, of your taxes would you like to see spent on aid to poor countries?

How do you think the world would be changed if we spent over half of our national budget on helping the poor of the world rather than buying weapons?

Would you pay $1.01 instead of $1.00 for your Whopper Jr. on the value menu at Burger King if that penny went to the tomato pickers? If you would, are you willing to write the head of Burger King and say you won't eat at their restaurant until they agreed to pay the picker a better wage? If not, what are your reasons?

If he were here today, how much of his income would Jesus spend on lingerie for children and what percent on seeing to it that victims and offenders received services that would change the course of their lives?

What kind of a health care system do you think Jesus would endorse?

The Treatment Of Homosexuals

Pop Quiz-What Did Jesus Say About Homosexuals?

Check All That Apply

__. "Yay verily, they are an abomination, and shall burn in Hell for all eternity."

__. "Let those who have ears hear this; these are among the most damned and shall never know the Kingdom of God."

__. "Their sin is great, they shalt be stoned unto death on the steps of the temple by those who love God."

__. "Pity those who burn with unholy desires, be grateful to God for not being one of these, but suffer not their company, lest one become tempted."

__. "Pray for them for they can repent their sins, be made clean by the power of God and forgiven. Never again to sin in this way."

Answer(s) to be found later in the text

Which Would Jesus Hate More, Wars or "Fags"?

In 2007 despite being court ordered to pay eleven million dollars in damages, members of the Westboro

Baptist Church vowed to continue standing up for God's alleged hatred of homosexuals. The award was the result of a lawsuit for invasion of privacy and intent to inflict emotional distress brought against the church by Albert Snyder. He objected to church members coming to his son's funeral with signs that said; "Thank God for dead soldiers," "Soldiers Die, God Laughs," and, "God hates fags." Although Marine Lance Corporal Matthew Snyder wasn't a homosexual he was killed while stationed in Iraq. The church members protested at his, and other military, funerals because they believed that U.S. deaths in the Iraq war were punishment for the America's tolerance of homosexuality. At another of their protests Reverend Fred Phelps held a sign emblazoned with, "God is your enemy," as his daughter stood on an American flag while she held a sign that proclaimed, "God hates fag enablers." Meanwhile other members of the group sang, "God Hates America," to the tune of "God Bless America." [315] According to the Westboro Baptist Church website (GodHatesFags.com) from 1991 to the middle of 2009 the churches members had conducted, "41,226 peaceful demonstrations opposing the fag lifestyle of soul-damning, nation-destroying filth."

How Does This Hatred Of Homosexuals Affect Our Ability To Be A Follower Of Jesus?

Nobody can deny that openly expressed hatred affects at least one group of people, namely homosexuals. Who wouldn't be bothered by constant references in the print and broadcast media, as well as from the pulpit, that one is damned to hell? It puts homosexuals in a bind where they believe they must choose between the religious tradition of their childhoods and being true to themselves and their loved ones, including their biological families. One might say, "Well so what? They deserve to be unhappy!" But then they aren't the only group of people who are negatively affected; the parents, siblings, and other family members of homosexuals are also in the predicament where they have to choose between following the teachings of their religion and their loved ones. I have seen family relationships destroyed when members are told they have to choose one or the other, but they can't have both. Some say, "Hate the sin, love the sinner." That sounds good, but how does one accomplish it? What is accomplished when a parent says, "I love you son, but I hate the fact that you love another man, so you can't bring him to our house for Christmas dinner?" It does nothing but put the son in the situation where he has to decide whether to spend the holiday with his family of origin or his family of choice. Again, one might exclaim, "So some people get hurt, that is the price we must pay to be loyal to the teaching of the Bible!" But as we shall soon see the teachings of the Bible are not as clear on this subject as many people have been led to believe, and it is not only a few people who get hurt by this hatred. In addition to homosexuals and their loved ones, <u>everyone</u> who seeks to be a follower of Jesus is harmed by this hatred. As soon as we permit any group of people to be hated in the name of God we have started to stray from the teachings of Jesus. We have begun the inevitable descent down the slippery slope to hating other groups and individuals, and thereby further ignoring the principles taught by Jesus. Even those who aren't homosexuals, have no loved ones who are, or aren't interested in living according to the teachings of Jesus are put at greater risk of harm in a country with an irrational hatred of homosexuals:[39]

> The U.S. Air Force has spent an estimated $25 million training combat pilot Lt. Col. Victor Fehrenbach but is about to discharge

---

39 In a chapter in my book *Honor Betrayed: Sexual Abuse In America's Military* I go into detail on how homophobia damages the readiness and effectiveness of our military.

> him involuntarily because he is gay. Born of military-officer parents, Fehrenbach has earned 30 awards and decorations, with tours flying F-15Es in Kosovo, Afghanistan and Iraq. He was one of the elite fighters called on to patrol the airspace over Washington, D.C., on Sept. 11, 2001. Also about to be discharged solely for being gay is Army infantry officer Daniel Choi, a West Point graduate and Arabic speaker, who would be (based on a 2005 Government Accounting Office report) at least the 56th gay Arabic linguist to be dismissed from the U.S. military since the first terrorist attack on the World Trade Center in 1993.[316]

An example of how the hatred of the stereotype of gay men affects one's view of larger issues is Seattle minister Mark Driscoll. He complains that mainstream churches have distorted Jesus from the macho man he really was into, "a Richard Simmons, hippie, queer Christ...a neutered and limp-wristed popular Sky Fairy of pop culture."[317] In order to insure that Jesus isn't thought of that way Mr. Driscoll and others focus on Jesus as a tough guy who was much more focused on sin and punishment, including Hell, than on love and forgiveness. Once Jesus is perceived in this way it becomes much easier to think of him as someone who would support violence against gays and holy war against non-Christians.[40] Instead of the prince of peace they want a Jesus who was an action hero, ready at a moment's notice to judge harshly and punish without mercy. They want to believe Jesus was swift to damn and smite, not quick to forgive and love.

---

40 I use the term *non-Christians* rather than *non-believers* since most people who aren't Christians still have their own cherished spiritual beliefs.

If It's Forbidden In The Bible That's All I Need To Know

The word *homosexual* has only been in existence for about one hundred years; therefore it was impossible for it to appear in any of the early translations of the Bible.[318] In fact the entire concept of homosexuality as a sexual orientation did not exist in Biblical times, so the Bible only addressed sexual acts between those of the same sex, but not homosexuality as a sexual identity.

When It Comes To Homos, Consult The King James Bible, But Not King James Himself

The King James Version Of The Bible was first published in 1611 A.C.E. Most copies now are based on the 1769 edition, with updated spelling. The American Bible Organization claimed, "so many people have used the KJV over the centuries that it has become the single most important book in shaping the modern English language."[319] I would go even further and say it is it the single most important book in shaping modern Western civilization. It is still the most widely owned English translation of the Bible in America.[320] It is titled *The King James* because British King James I commanded that, "there should be one more exact Translation of the Holy Scriptures into the English tongue."[321] I find it ironic that the version of the Bible that is so commonly cited as evidence of God's hatred of same-sex sexual behavior is named after a man who, not only was known to engage in sex with other men, but also fell in love with several of them. In 1607 even as *The King James Version* was being translated the forty-one-year-old King began a sexual/romantic relationship with a then penniless seventeen-year-old Robert Carr. For the first seven years things went well for young Mr. Carr; he became wealthy, was made an earl, and married a woman. Then things took a turn for the worst, the King sentenced Mr. Carr and his wife to death. But then the King decided to be merciful and imprisoned them in the Tower of London for six years.[322]

The Teachings Of The Old Testament

The Ten Commandments

There are actually several places in the Bible to which people can turn for information on commandments. The section most people think of as containing

THE TEN COMMANDMENTS

is *Exodus* 34 mostly because in chapter 28 the authors used that exact phrase:

> Then the LORD said to Moses, "Write down these words, for in accordance with these words I have made a covenant with you and with Israel." Moses was there with the LORD forty days and forty nights without eating bread or drinking water. And he wrote on the tablets the words of the covenant—the Ten Commandments (*Exodus* 34:27-28).

However most people don't realize this was the second time Moses had taken dictation from God and carved commandments in stone:

> The LORD said to Moses, "Chisel out two stone tablets like the first ones, and I will write on them the words that were on the first tablets, which you broke" (*Exodus* 34:1).

The second version that appears in *Exodus* 34 dropped all but two of the commandments that appeared in *Exodus* 20 (no false idols and keeping the Sabbath) and added several new commandments (observe Passover, never appear before God empty-handed, first fruit to the tabernacle, and no boiling a kid in it's mother's milk). So which commandments are we supposed to follow:

A) The first version-because these were the first ones given by God.
B) The second version-because God's priorities must have changed from the first version to the second.
C) All of them-because God meant us to combine the two lists.
D) God expected us, as individuals or as a group, to pick the ones that are relevant to us.

Regardless of your answer it is relevant to the topic of homosexuality because same-sex sexual behavior wasn't mentioned in either list of commandments. According to the scriptures it was these commandments that constituted the covenant (sacred contract) between God and the people, and furthermore that they came directly from God, actually spoken to Moses.

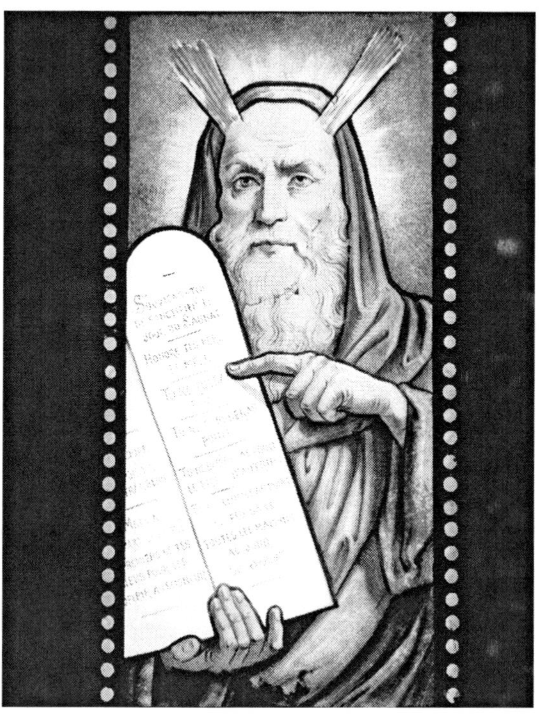

Moses and the Ten Commandments from a window in a French mausoleum (Photo by Mic Hunter).

Whatever Happened To The Fourth Commandment?

Since we are examining the Old Testament for direction on how to treat people who are homosexuals, let's take a moment to look at how well one of the Ten Commandments is being followed in modern day America. According to *Exodus* 20:8 God commanded us to, "'Remember the Sabbath day, to keep it holy." That seems simple enough; God apparently thought we would know exactly what was meant by, "keep it holy." But just to be sure Americans passed laws to make sure that the Sabbath, at least the Christian Sabbath, was kept holy.[41] These laws came to be known as blue laws: "A blue law is a type of law, typically found in the United States, designed to enforce religious standards, particularly the observance of Sunday as a day of worship or rest, and a restriction on Sunday shopping."[323] Years ago in some States all stores had to be closed on Sundays. But over time people found this inconvenient so little by little the restrictions eroded until now in many places Sunday is just another day for business as usual. There are some token actions, such as buying vehicles and liquor, that are still restricted, but exceptions are made even for these. Basically, we have gotten to the point where most people's idea of keeping the Sabbath holy is to wait till Monday to buy their new car, and to hold off on buying booze until after church.

Christian Bookstores

It would seem that whether or not secular law permitted retail stores to be open on Sundays the one type of store that would voluntarily remain closed in observation of the Sabbath would be Christian bookstores, thereby setting a good example for others and making sure that their employees could keep the Sabbath holy. However, this is not the case, at least not in Minneapolis and Saint

41 For Jews, from Friday at sundown and Saturday is the Sabbath.

Paul. I know this because one Sunday I sat down with a phone book and called the numerous stores listed under "Christian Bookstores" and to my surprise found all but a couple of them were open. I then asked the employees who answered if they considered being at work on the Sabbath a violation of the Commandment. Most of them had no idea what I was talking about. Then I asked to speak to the manager and inquired if he or she thought requiring employees to work on the Sabbath was appropriate. Every one of them hung up on me.

My point is, that Americans who have no trouble basically ignoring the forth Commandment suddenly become rigid followers of Biblical teaching when it comes to the subject of homosexuality. If they were as steadfast in their commitment to keeping the fourth Commandment as they are to being against homosexuality they would not only refuse to work on the Sabbath but would boycott any businesses that were open on Sundays.

Other Verses From The Old Testament

There are two portions of the Old Testament that people cite to support their stand against same-sex sexual behavior. The first is the story of Lot that appears in *Genesi*s 19:1-13). It is worth quoting in its entirety because the context of the story is vital if one is to understand the message of the story.

> The two angels came to Sodom in the evening; and Lot was sitting in the gate of Sodom. When Lot saw them, he rose to meet them, and bowed himself with his face to the earth, and said, "My lords, turn aside, I pray you, to your servant's house and spend the night and wash your feet; then you may rise up early and go on your way." They said, "No; we will spend the night in the street." But he urged

them strongly; so they turned aside to him and entered his house; and he made them a feast, and baked unleavened bread, and they ate. But before they lay down, the men of the city, the men of Sodom, both young and old, all the people to the last man, surrounded the house; and they called to Lot, "Where are the men who came to you tonight? Bring them out to us, that we may know them.[42] Lot went out of the door to the men, shut the door after him, and said, "I beg you, my brothers, do not act so wickedly. Behold, I have two daughters who have not known men; let me bring them out to you, and do to them as you please;[43] only do nothing to these men, for they have come under the shelter of my roof." But they said, "Stand back!" And they said, "This fellow came to sojourn, and he would play the judge![44] Now we will deal worse with you than with them." Then they pressed hard against the man Lot, and drew near to break the door. But the men put forth their hands and brought Lot into the house to them and shut the door. And they struck with blindness the men both small and great, so that they wearied themselves groping for the door. Then the men said to Lot, "Have you any one else here? Sons-in-law, sons, daughters, or any one you have in the city, bring them out of the place, for we are about to destroy

---

42 "**know**, 8. to engage in sexual intercourse with somebody." *Encarta Dictionary*, 1999.

43 Even though Lot offered his virgin daughters to be raped by the crowd, ("Do to them as you please") he was saved by God from the destruction of the town of Sodom.

44 "Sojourn, a short stay at a place." *Encarta Dictionary,* 1999.

> this place, because the outcry against its people has become great before the Lord, and the Lord has sent us to destroy it."

The authors of the Old Testament stressed the importance welcoming and caring for strangers: "When a stranger sojourns (stays) with you in your land, you shall not do him wrong. The stranger who sojourns with you shall be to you as the native among you, and you shall love him as yourself" (*Leviticus* 19: 33-34). Hospitality was an important custom because in the harsh conditions of the Holy Land, whether one was able to obtain shelter, food and water when traveling was a matter of life or death. Understanding the context of the story shows, "the sin of Sodom", wasn't homosexuality as an orientation, or even consensual same-sex behavior, but was a violation of a religiously based hospitality code combined with an attempted gang rape. Bishop John Shelby Spong agreed that this is the actual meaning of the story of Lot:

> It is a story about gang rape, which cannot ever be anything but evil. It is a narrative that expresses violent malevolence toward women that few people today, even among the fundamentalists, would be eager to condone. In the biblical world of male values, the humiliation of a male was best achieved by making the males act like a woman in the sex act. To act like a woman, to be the passive participant in coitus, was thought to be insulting to the dignity of the male. This, far more than homosexuality, was the underlying theme of the Sodom story.[324]

Further evidence to support this interpretation can be found in *Ezekiel* where God listed the sins of Sodom as (depending on the which translation is used); pride, complacency, condescending arrogance, overindulgence in food, barbarity, and prosperousness without aiding the poor and needy, but same-sex behavior wasn't listed (16: 49-50). A similar, but rarely quoted, story was depicted in *Judges* (19:22-29):

> Now as they were making their hearts merry, behold, the men of the city, certain sons of Belial, beset the house round about, and beat at the door, and spoke to the master of the house, the old man, saying, "Bring forth the man that came into thine house, that we may know him." And the man, the master of the house, went out unto them, and said unto them, "Nay, my brethren, nay, I pray you, do not so wickedly; seeing that this man is come into mine house, do not this folly. Behold, here is my daughter a maiden, and his concubine; them I will bring out now, and humble ye them, and do with them what seemeth good unto you: but unto this man do not so vile a thing." But the men would not hearken to him: so the man took his concubine, and brought her forth unto them; and they knew her, and abused her all the night until the morning: and when the day began to spring, they let her go. Then came the woman in the dawning of the day, and fell down at the door of the man's house where her lord was, till it was light. And her lord rose up in the morning, and opened the doors of the house, and went out to go his way: and, behold, the woman his concubine was fallen down at the door of the house, and her hands were upon the threshold. And he said unto her, "Up, and let us be going."

> But none answered. Then the man took her up upon an ass, and the man rose up, and gat him unto his place. And when he was come into his house, he took a knife, and laid hold on his concubine, and divided her, together with her bones, into twelve pieces, and sent her into all the coasts of Israel.

In this story a stranger came to town and was given shelter as directed by Jewish law and tradition. A crowd of men came to the house demanded that the stranger be given to them so they could sexually assault him. The host protected the stranger by offering to provide his daughter to be raped. The stranger provided the crowd with his concubine (a woman with whom he was in a sexual relationship, but to whom he was not married) and they gang raped her. In the morning the stranger found the woman on the doorstep unconscious after her ordeal. When she wasn't immediately able to continue on their journey he took a knife, killed her, and chopped her up into twelve chunks. This story is even more gruesome than the story of Sodom because in the end, the victim of this heterosexual gang rape was murdered because she was too injured to continue traveling on the man's schedule. So what do these either of these stories of heterosexual gang rape and murder have to do with two consenting adults of the same sex engaging lovemaking? Nothing. Let me say that again-nothing. Despite this fact, the story in *Leviticus* continues to be cited as an indication that God is against homosexuality. However, almost nobody ever mentions chapters one through four of *Leviticus* that are entirely about how to ritually kill and butcher cattle, sheep, goats, and birds as sacrifices to God. When was the last time you went to church and the clergy person was sprinkling the blood of a freshly killed animal upon the altar as directed by God in *Leviticus*? Never I'll wager. Why is it that all these verses are complete ignored?

Jesus made mention of the story of Sodom in *Luke* (10: 10-13). To him it was a cautionary tale concerning the violation of the Jewish law and virtue of hospitality to strangers. He was quoted as saying, "When you enter a town and they do not make you welcome...I tell you, it will be more bearable for Sodom on that great day than for that town." Nowhere was it written he ever said, "When you enter a town watch out for gays," or "If you are a man, when you enter a town, be careful not to fall in love with another man."

The other section of the Old Testament related to same-sex sexual behavior is the Holiness Code found in *Leviticus*. Among others things the Code denounced sexual acts between men: "You shall not lie with a male as with a woman," (18:22) and "If a man lies with a male as with a woman, both of them have committed an abomination; they shall be put to death, their blood is upon them" (20:13).[325] As with the story of Lot knowing the historical/cultural context of these passages is essential to understanding what the authors meant. The purpose of the Code was to contrast, "God's chosen people," with the surrounding tribes that engaged in idolatry and the use of both male and female temple prostitutes.[326] Other than the two verses just quoted the remainder of the Holiness Code is infrequently cited, mostly because it includes acts in which most modern Americans, Christian or not, engage. So if the justification for keeping known homosexuals from being members of a church is because same-sex sexual contact is forbidden in the Bible where is the outrage at these other forbidden behaviors (Behaviors Forbidden By The Holy Code From *Leviticus*)? Why are clean-shaven men permitted in churches? When will we see footage of Christians being arrested because they were blocking the entrances to tattoo parlors in an attempt to prevent the sin of tattooing?

Behaviors Forbidden By The Holy Code From *Leviticus*

Sins For Which The Punishment Is Banishment	**Secular View**
Sex With A Woman Who Is Having Her "Uncleanness" (Menstrual period)	Not a crime
Marrying A Harlot (Prostitute)	Not a crime
Marrying A Woman Who Has Been Defiled (Not a virgin)	Not a crime
Marrying A Who Woman Has Been Divorced	Not a crime
Breeding Cattle Of Different Varieties Together	Not a crime
Wearing A Garment Of Cloth Made Of Two Different Fabrics	Not a crime
Eating Flesh With Blood In It (a.k.a. "rare")	Not a crime
Eating Shellfish (e.g. lobster & shrimp)	Not a crime
Cutting The Hair On One's Temples	Not a crime
Cutting One's Beard	Not a crime
Marking One's Skin By Cutting	Not a crime
Marking One's Skin By Tattooing	Legal for those of the age of consent

Another of the many teachings of *Leviticus* that is completely ignored by modern day people is chapter twenty-one that described those forbidden to be priests (Job Opening For Priest). I went to numerous websites to look at the requirements for clergy training and didn't find a single one that mentioned denying admission to students who have the characteristics found in chapter twenty-one.

Again, how do people justify ignoring these directives while insisting that 18:22 and 20:13 are still relevant enough to justify keeping people out of churches and telling them they are hated by God and are doomed to Hell?

Job Opening For Priests

Job opening: Organization, based on the Old Testament, seeks qualified personnel to be clergy. Applicant CANNOT be blind, hunchbacked, or a dwarf. In terms of legs-one leg can't be longer than the other (therefore two legs are required), nor can an applicant have even one broken leg. Those with scurvy, scars from boils, or crushed testes need not apply.

I Guess Not All Abominations Are Equally Abominable

Most people believe the word *abomination* is used to describe some behavior that is inherently evil. But in Biblical times an abomination meant an act that was ritually unclean. For example, "If a soul touch any unclean thing, whether it be a carcass of an unclean beast, or a carcass of unclean cattle, or the carcass of unclean creeping things, and if it be hidden from him; he also shall be unclean, and guilty" (*Leviticus* 5: 2); "And that ye may put difference between holy and unholy, and between unclean and clean" (*Leviticus* 5:10.) What behaviors were described in *Leviticus* as being abominations? There are of course the two some many people love to quote:

"You shall not lie with a male as with a woman; it is an abomination (18:22).

"If a man also lie with mankind, as he lieth with a woman, both of them have committed an abomination:

they shall surely be put to death; their blood shall be upon them" (20:13).

Then there are the lesser-know abominations. Most Americans are happy to comply with the dietary restrictions that forbid the eating of eagles, osprey, vultures, kites, owls, hawks, owls, cormorants, swans, and the pelicans, storks, herons, and bats (11:13-19). Likewise, most Americans are happy to comply with not eating creepy crawly things:

> And every creeping thing that creepeth upon the earth shall be an abomination; it shall not be eaten. Whatsoever goeth upon the belly, and whatsoever goeth upon all four, or whatsoever hath more feet among all creeping things that creep upon the earth, them ye shall not eat; for they are an **abomination**. Ye shall not make yourselves abominable with any creeping thing that creepeth, neither shall ye make yourselves unclean with them, that ye should be defiled thereby (11: 41-43).

There is also the abomination concerning the maximum amount of time it is safe to leave sacrificial food before it spoils:

> And if ye offer a sacrifice of peace offerings unto the LORD, ye shall offer it at your own will. It shall be eaten the same day ye offer it, and on the morrow: and if it remains until the third day, it shall be burnt in the fire. And if it be eaten at all on the third day, it is **abominable**; it shall not be accepted" (19:5-7).

That abomination doesn't get mentioned much anymore because hardly anyone makes burnt offering to God, not to mention that most Americans wouldn't eat a piece of meat that has been sitting out in the open unrefrigerated for two days.

Finally, one never hears sermons about the abomination of eating shellfish like lobster and crab:

> And all that have not fins and scales in the seas, and in the rivers, of all that move in the waters, and of any living thing which is in the waters, they shall be an **abomination** unto you: They shall be even an **abomination** unto you; ye shall not eat of their flesh, but ye shall have their carcasses in **abomination**. Whatsoever hath no fins nor scales in the waters, that shall be an **abomination** unto you (11: 10-20).

Although all of these behaviors are described as abominations the only time most Americans hear anything described as abominable is when discussing homosexuals and the Yeti (also known as the abominable snowman).

How Do The People Of The Old Testament Currently Deal With Homosexuality?

One would think that if anyone would be able to understand and apply the messages of the "Old Testament" it would be the Jews since they have been studying the first books of the Bible, (Dare I say it?) religiously for thousands of years even before Jesus was born. In 2006 the highest legal body in Conservative Judaism voted to allow the ordination of openly gay rabbis and the celebration of same-sex commitment ceremonies within temples. More than ten years before that the more liberal Reform and

Reconstructionist movements had already accepted gay rabbis, leaving only the more traditional Orthodox form of Judaism still rejecting gay rabbis and refusing to bless same-sex unions. This is not to say that there weren't detractors. Some members of the committee resigned after the vote, but Judaism is a religion that has long accepted there is nothing on which all members will agree. Therefore each group and individual must come to terms with their differences according to their own understanding of God's will.[327]

The Teaching Of The New Testament

It is fascinating to me that so many Christians are obsessed with homosexuals based the prohibition of same-sex sexual behavior in the Old Testament, while nowhere in the New Testament did Jesus utter a single word on the topic. Therefore the correct answer to the pop quiz at the beginning of this section is-none of the above. References to same sex behavior in the New Testament can be found in three sections:

Timothy 1:8-11

> Now we know that the law is good, if any one used it lawfully, understanding this, that the law is not laid down for the just but for the lawless and disobedient, for the ungodly and sinners, for the unholy, and profane, for murderers of fathers and murderers of mothers, for manslayers, immoral persons, sodomites, kidnappers, liars, perjurers, and whatever else is contrary to sound doctrine in accordance with the glorious gospel of the blessed God with which I have been entrusted.

Romans 1:24-32

> Therefore God gave them up in the lusts of their hearts to impurity, to the dishonoring of their bodies among themselves, because they exchanged the truth about God for a lie and worshipped and served the creature rather than the Creator, who is blessed forever. Amen. For this reason God gave them up to dishonorable passions. Their women exchanged natural relations for unnatural, and the men likewise gave up natural relations with women and were consumed with passion for one another, men committing shameless acts with men and receiving in their own persons the due penalty for their error. And since they did not see fit to acknowledge God, God gave them up to a base mind and to improper conduct. They were filled with all manner of wickedness, evil, covetousness, malice. Full of envy, murder, strife, deceit, malignity,[45] they are gossips, slanderers, haters of god, insolent, haughty, boastful, inventors of evil, disobedient to parents, foolish, faithless, heartless, ruthless. Though they know God's decree that those who do such things deserve to die, they not only do them but approve those who practice them."

1st Corinthians 6:9-10

"Know ye not that the unrighteous shall not inherit the kingdom of God? Be not deceived; neither fornicators,

---

45 ma·lig·ni·ty n 1. intense hatred and a strong desire to harm others 2. an intentionally harmful or evil act." *Encarta World Dictionary*

nor idolaters, nor adulterers, nor effeminate, nor abusers of themselves with mankind, nor thieves, nor covetous, nor drunkards, nor revilers, nor extortionists, shall inherit the kingdom of God."

Romans 1:24-32

In *Romans* Paul wrote of, "women exchanging natural relations for unnatural," and, "men committing shameless acts with men," and was clear on the appropriate punishment- "those who do such things deserve to die." After that verse he goes on: "They were filled with all manner of wickedness, evil, convetousness, malice. Full of envy, murder, strife, deceit, malignity, they are gossips, slanderers, haters of god, insolent, haughty, boastful, inventors of evil, disobedient to parents, foolish, faithless, heartless, ruthless." Exactly who is "they?" Was Paul focused only on a particular group of people or was he claiming that all women and men who engage in same-sex sexual acts have all the nasty characteristics listed? If he meant the latter then he was misinformed, grossly mistaken, or hung around the wrong people. I know plenty of homosexual women and men, who are honest, humble, faithful, and love God. Not once have I feared they would murder me.

Noted theologian James Nelson who has written extensively on Biblical teachings regarding sexual behavior interpreted all these writing as not intended to be, "directed toward all homosexual persons but rather to specific acts, namely exploitation, homosexual prostitution, and sexual use of boys by adult males."[328] He insisted Paul's writing in *Romans* is focused, not on homosexuality per se, but "specifically of same-sex acts that express idolatry and acts undertaken in lust (not tenderness or mutual respect) by heterosexuals who willfully act contrary to their own sexual natures."[329] The very wording found in the earliest known copies of Paul's writing support Dr. Nelson's claim; if Paul had been referring to consensual sexual behavior between two males of equal status he have used the Greek term, *paiderasste*.[330]

Whether one believes these explanations or not, several things ought to be taken into account when reading any of the verses attributed to Paul. In the gospels there are sometimes duplicate stories, some even using the same language, which offers some credence that events occurred, but there is no such repetition of Paul's claims. Secondly, Paul by his own admission never actually met Jesus before his crucifixion. Thirdly, Paul didn't actually claim his statements were based the teachings of Jesus. When Jesus was mentioned he was presented as a savior, but not as the originator of the material being presented. Paul's stance on these matters was nothing more than his personal opinion.

1st Corinthians 6:9-10

Ascertaining the correct meaning 1st *Corinthians* 6:9-10 is difficult because depending on which of the twenty-five English language versions of the Bible one is consulting the language used in the verses varies widely. Many of translations focus only on males, such as, "Men who practice homosexuality," and "Men who have sexual relations with other men." How is it that male-to-male sexual contact is considered an abomination but female-to-female sexual activity is not even mentioned? Also it is worth repeating that the word *homosexual* didn't exist at the time these verses were originally written so its use is completely an addition of modern translators.

There's a wide variety of other forbidden behaviors listed in verses nine and ten that almost never are thought of as being anywhere near as immoral as is same-sex sexual behavior. Perhaps the lack of attention to these other taboo behaviors is due to the fact that many people, both homosexuals and heterosexuals engage in these behaviors and hate to think they will prevent us from inheriting the Kingdom of Heaven. For example a majority of Americans who marry aren't virgins on the day of their wedding; including those who describe themselves as, "religious," and even those who had taken abstinence pledges.[331] Sex prior to marriage is fornication and is forbidden in *1st Corinthians*. Does that mean a majority of married couples won't inherit the Kingdom of Heaven? According to *1st Corinthians* 6:9-10 they won't. Then there is sodomy, a term usually associated only with homosexual men. Most people think the term sodomy only applies to same-sex sexual behavior, however both oral and anal sex even between consenting men and women has a long history of being criminal and referred to in statutes as sodomy. Legal or illegal a majority of American male and females couples, married and unmarried, engage in oral sex and eight to ten percent engage in anal sex. How about being unfaithful in marriage, being wasteful, greedy, selfish, lustful, or dishonest? Who among us can claim to never have engaged in any of these behaviors that are forbidden in the exact same chapter and verses that are cited by those who insist God hates homosexuals? [46]

In the chapter that precedes the chapter of *1st* Corinthians that we have been examining Paul reminded the reader; "I wrote to you not to associate with any so-called brother if he is an immoral person, or covetous, or an idolater, or a reviler, or a drunkard, or a swindler-- not even to eat with such a one" (*1st Corinthians* 5:11). Yet churches do not forbid drunkards from attending services and taking communion. In fact many churches permit Alcoholics Anonymous meetings to take place within their buildings. Nor are adulterers treated with the hatred and disgust that faces homosexuals. Those who have committed crimes such as extortion, robbery, and even murder are permitted in churches. Some churches even sponsor

46 Be careful before you answer; remember the Bible doesn't have any exception for so-called little white lies.

prison outreach programs where they seek out thieves, rapists, and murderers in order to convert them. What is the source of this obsession so many people have with *1st Corinthians* 6:9-10, *Timothy* 1:8-11, and *Romans* 1:24-32? Particularly when there are other passages that are much more clear, even within the same book: "Let us behave properly as in the day, not in carousing and drunkenness, not in sexual promiscuity and sensuality, not in strife and jealousy" (*Romans* 13:13) and "For this you know with certainty, that no immoral or impure person or covetous man, who is an idolater, has an inheritance in the kingdom of Christ and God" (*Ephesians* 5:5). These verses are clear as to their intent; be moral, as in knowing right from wrong, in all acts not just those of a sexual nature. It is good advice, yet these verses are rarely quoted.

Timothy 1:8-11

An examination of fourteen versions of the bible finds that the behaviors in *Timothy* 1:8-11 basically fall into four categories crimes against persons, dishonesty, inappropriate sexual behavior and anything else that is in violation of doctrine. The word in these verses from *Timothy* that gets the most attention is "sodomite." Three of the versions use this term. It recalls the story of the destruction of the city of Sodom that we earlier examined. The term *sodomy* has come to be used to refer to any non-vaginal intercourse, violent or not. In earlier times the word was used in reference to sexual assaults. When the editors of *The New International Version Of The Bible* used the translation, "homosexual offenders," a more accurate term would have been sex offender or rapist.

What can one learn from all this? Simply that, like the other verses previously examined, *Timothy* 1:8-11 contains bans on numerous types of behavior, only some of which are sexual, and a subset of those are specific to sex between people of the same sex. So once again the question has to be asked, what is it about heterosexual people that so much negative attention is directed towards the same-sex behavior and so little interest is paid towards the remaining banned behaviors?

Apparently Your Preaching Thoroughly Convinced Them

In 2009 in the African nation of Uganda a federal bill was proposed that required the death penalty for people who have previous convictions for same-sex sexual behavior, or were found to be HIV-positive, or engaged in same-sex acts with anyone less than 18 years of age. Prior this proposal the penalty for homosexuality was incarceration for up to fourteen years. The bill called for Ugandans who engaged in same-sex sexual relations outside of Uganda to be extradited back to Uganda for punishment. In addition, the bill required anyone who was aware of an offense, including individuals, private companies, and media organizations, to report the offender within twenty-four hours. Failure to do so could lead to imprisonment for up to three years. Furthermore, the bill included penalties for individuals, companies, media organizations, or non-governmental organizations that merely supported gay rights. What motivated the introduction of this legislation? It followed a two-day conference held in the capital of Uganda at which three American Christians preached that homosexuality was a direct threat to the integrity of African families. One of the three Americans who spoke was Scott Lively, who had written several books opposing homosexuality, including *Seven Steps To Recruit-proof Your Child: A Parent's Guide To Protecting Children And From Homosexuality And The "Gay" Movement*. Also speaking was Caleb Lee Brundidge, a self-professed former gay man who led workshops on how to heal homosexuality. During these workshops he compared homosexuality to child molestation and bestiality. He insisted that the African family was being threatened by homosexuals looking to recruit youth into their ranks. Also speaking was American Don Schmierer, a board member of Exodus International, an organization devoted to promoting, "freedom from homosexuality through the power of Jesus Christ".[332] The conference focused on "how to make gay people straight, how gay men often sodomize teenage boys, and how "the gay movement is an evil institution," whose goal was, "to defeat the marriage-based society and replace it with a culture of sexual promiscuity".[333] Those attending the conference were provided with <u>completely incorrect</u> statistics by an unlicensed conversion therapist named Richard A. Cohen including:

> Homosexuals are at least twelve times more likely to molest children than heterosexuals; homosexual teachers are at least seven times more likely to molest a pupil; homosexual teachers are estimated to have committed at least twenty-five percent of pupil molestation; forty percent of molestation assaults were made by those who engage in homosexuality.

What the attendees were not told was that these figures came from Dr. Paul Cameron who had been expelled from the American Psychological Association for refusing to cooperate with an ethics investigation brought on by a complaint made against him. Nor were they informed that the American Sociological Association and the Canadian Psychological Association had issued official statements that accused Dr. Cameron of misrepresenting social science research. Dr. Cameron later admitted that the statistics cited were wrong, and promised that when his book was reprinted they would be removed.[334]

During the conference it was announced that the Ugandan Parliament, "feels it is necessary to draft a new law that deals comprehensively with the issue of homosexuality and takes into account the international gay agenda... Right now there is a proposal that a new law be drafted."[335] Shortly thereafter the Ugandan Parliament passed a resolution allowing Member of Parliament David Bahati to submit a private member's bill to, "strengthening the nation's capacity to deal with emerging internal and external threats to the traditional heterosexual family", and to "protect the cherished culture of the people of Uganda, legal, religious, and traditional family values of the people of Uganda against the attempts of sexual rights activists seeking to impose their values of sexual promiscuity on the people of Uganda". Following the introduction of this bill a Ugandan newspaper began publishing articles on how to identify gays, and printing the names of suspected homosexuals.[336] Not long after that on a government-sponsored website it was declared that those who are homosexual have, "surrendered their right to human rights."[337]

Many religious leaders throughout the world were swift to condemn the bill. The Archbishop of Canterbury, Dr. Rowan Williams, publicly stated the bill was "shocking" and made, "pastoral care impossible" since it required pastors to become, "informers."[338] Even the right-wing evangelicals at Exodus International, the group that preached, "freedom from homosexuality," thought things had gotten a wee bit too extreme, so they sent a letter to Ugandan President Museveni stating, "The Christian church... must be permitted to extend the love and compassion of Christ to all. We believe that this legislation would make this mission a difficult if not impossible task to carry out."[339] I can't help but agree with them; it is nearly impossible to extend love and compassion to someone after you have put him to death.

It Was Adam & Eve, Not Adam & Steve

Some people are fanatically pro-marriage, unless of course two women or two men want to marry, in which case they are even more fanatical about insuring the sanctity of marriage is maintained by preventing two consenting adults, who happen to be of the same sex, from legally marrying. In 2008 California voters passed Proposition Eight, the Marriage Protection Act, which changed the State Constitution so as to eliminate the right of same-sex couples to marry in California. Furthermore, only marriages between a man and a woman would be valid or recognized in California, even if the marriage was legal in another State before the couple moved to California. Not long after it was passed a suit (Perry v. Schwarzenegger) was filed in Federal District Court complaining that Proposition Eight violated the Federal Constitution: because it constituted, "unequal treatment" by denying gays and lesbians of "the basic liberties and equal protection under the law that are guaranteed by the Fourteenth Amendment." During that trial one of the witnessed called in the defense of the Marriage Protection Act was David Blankenhorn, the founder of the Institute of American Values. Mr. Blankenhorn, who had no scholarly expertise on marriage, homosexuality, or law, was asked to cite any research conducted by him, his Institute, or any other organization, that supported his position that homosexual marriage would reduce heterosexual marriage, and wasn't able to come up with a single reference.

Christians haven't always been so concerned about the sanctity of marriage, in fact for longer than not it was viewed as quite un-holy. Tatian the Assyrian (120–180 A.C.E.), whose book combined the four gospels into one and was standard reading for Christians until the fifth century, wrote that marriage was a foul way of life and polluted those unfortunate enough to be involved in it. Under his leadership in the Syrian Church no man who had ever been married could be baptized, and only celibate men could become Christians. Tertullian, the first known person to write on the concept of the Trinity (Father, Son, & Holy Ghost), also had thoughts on marriage. He referred to it as a moral crime more dreadful than any punishment or even death.[340] Bishop Ambrose (340-397 A.C.E.), who was later sainted, claimed that marriage was a crime against God because it robbed men and women the state of virginity that God had granted them at birth, and it made prostitutes of women.[341] Although Augustine, the Bishop of Hippo (354-430 A,C.E.), titled his book *On The Good Marriage,* he didn't really seem to view marriage as good, but merely the lesser of two evils. He wrote, "Marriage is not good, but it is a good in comparison with fornication." The Council of Trent was a 16th-century Ecumenical Council of the Roman Catholic Church, and is widely considered to be one of the most significant gatherings of Christian leaders ever convened; therefore it is still studied by both Catholics and Protestant theological students. Among other things, they decreed that any person, who hinted that the state of matrimony was more blessed or even equal to celibacy, would be declared a heretic, excommunicated, and forever cursed.

It wasn't until the Middle Ages (1000-1300 A.C.E) that there was even an agreed upon definition of a valid marriage. Before that if a man and woman said they were husband and wife that was enough to make it so. The earliest Christian marriage ceremonies consisted of little more than blessing the couple outside of the church, because it was a violation of religious law to be wed in the church itself since that was considered an endorsement of a lustful lifestyle choice. It wasn't until 1215 A.C.E. when the Fourth Lateran Council met and formally sanctioned weddings within churches. Prior to that some rogue clergy had been secretly performing weddings within their churches for heterosexual couples, despite it being against church doctrine, just as some clergy are now performing weddings for same-sex couples.[342]

Sculpture Of A German Wedding (Photo by Mic Hunter)

Homosexuality & Divorce: Compare & Contrast

We have examined all the fuss that has resulted from just two verses in the Old Testament (*Leviticus* 18:22 & 20:13) and three verses in the New Testament (*Romans* 1:24-27; *Timothy* 1:10 & *1st Corinthians* 6:9), which noted that Jesus had nothing to say on the topic of homosexuals and that all the verses from the New Testament are from letters written by Paul. Now let's compare the commotion concerning homosexuals and the contemporary response to divorce. What does the Bible have to say about divorce? From the Old Testament in the book of *Genesis* man and woman came together as one, but whether there is anyway for them to separate wasn't addressed:

> And Jehovah God said, "It is not good that the man should be alone; I will make him a help meet for him" and the rib, which Jehovah God had taken from the man, made he a woman, and brought her unto the man.' And the man said, "This is now bone of my bones, and flesh of my flesh: she shall be called Woman, because she was taken out of Man. Therefore shall a man leave his father and his mother, and shall cleave unto his wife: and they shall be one flesh" (*Genesis* 2:18 & 22-24).

In the New Testament, Paul had a great deal to say about divorce and it appeared in the very same three letters in which he condemned other immoral acts:

> For the woman that hath a husband is bound by law to the husband while he liveth; but if the husband die, she is discharged from the law of the husband. So then if, while the husband liveth, she be joined to another man, she shall be called an adulteress: but if the husband

> die, she is free from the law, so that she is no adulteress, though she be joined to another man (*Romans* 7:2-3).

> But unto the married I give charge, yea not I, but the Lord, That the wife depart not from her husband (but should she depart, let her remain unmarried, or else be reconciled to her husband); and that the husband leave not his wife (*1st Corinthians* 7:10-11).

> If God does not join the two together when they conform to the rules of their community, then it is no marriage and the children that may be born are illegitimate. Paul makes the argument that if God does not sanction the marriage the children are unclean, but when God does approve the marriages, the children are holy (*1st Corinthians* 7:14).

> A wife is bound for so long time as her husband liveth; but if the husband be dead, she is free to be married to whom she will; only in the Lord (*1st Corinthians* 7:39).

Unlike the topic of homosexuality Jesus made numerous statements about divorce:

> "It was said also, whosoever shall put away his wife, let him give her a writing of divorcement: but I say unto you, that every one that putteth away his wife, saving for the cause of fornication, maketh her an adulteress: and whosoever shall marry her when she is put away committeth adultery" (*Matthew* 5:31-32).

And there came unto him Pharisees, trying him, and saying, "Is it lawful for a man to put away his wife for every cause?" And he answered and said, "Have ye not read, that he who made them from the beginning made them male and female, " and said, "For this cause shall a man leave his father and mother, and shall cleave to his wife; and the two shall become one flesh? So that they are no more two, but one flesh. What therefore God hath joined together, let not man put asunder." They say unto him, "Why then did Moses command to give a bill of divorcement, and to put her away?" He saith unto them, "Moses for your hardness of heart suffered you to put away your wives: but from the beginning it hath not been so. And I say unto you, Whosoever shall put away his wife, except for fornication, and shall marry another, committeth adultery: and he that marrieth her when she is put away committeth adultery" (*Matthew* 19:3-9).

And there came unto him Pharisees, and asked him, "Is it lawful for a man to put away his wife?" trying him. And he answered and said unto them, "What did Moses command you?" And they said, "Moses suffered to write a bill of divorcement, and to put her away." But Jesus said unto them, "For your hardness of heart he wrote you this commandment. But from the beginning of the creation, Male and female made he them. For this cause shall a man leave his father and mother, and shall cleave to his wife; and the two shall become one flesh: so that they are no more

> two, but one flesh. What therefore God hath joined together, let not man put asunder. And in the house the disciples asked him again of this matter. And he saith unto them, Whosoever shall put away his wife, and marry another, committeth adultery against her: and if she herself shall put away her husband, and marry another, she committeth adultery" (*Mark* 10:2-12).
>
> "Every one that putteth away his wife, and marrieth another, committeth adultery: and he that marrieth one that is put away from a husband committeth adultery" (*Luke* 16:18).

Jesus is quoted in eighteen verses on his stand against divorce, but not a single verse on same-sex behavior is attributed to him, yet divorce gets much less negative attention than the issue of homosexuals. What's more when the topic of divorce does come up it is never discussed in the hateful tones that are used when discussing gays. Jesus said, "Whoever divorces his wife, except for unchastity and marries another, commits adultery" (*Matthew* 19:9). There are still cultures that consider adultery to be a very serious offense. In 2009 Indonesian legislators passed a law requiring death by stoning for adultery. Adultery was considered worse than homosexuality, for which the punishment was whipping, as well as for rape or sex with children that called for public lashing.[343] Why then don't churches banish those who have divorced?

When surveyed Americans claim to value marriage more than those in most other countries, yet we have the highest rate of divorce of any country. A higher portion of American couples who live together with or without being married break up than do couples in New Zealand, Australia, Japan and Europe. A child born of married

American parents is much more likely to see their parents' relationship end than is a child born to unwed Swedish parents. The number of divorced people in America quadrupled from 1970 to 1998. By age thirty-five, ten percent of American women have lived with three or more husbands or domestic partners.[344] This revolving door pattern of relationships significantly affects children. In his book, *The Marriage-Go-Round*, Andrew Cherlin reported: "For each partner who entered or left a household of a single parent, the odds that the adolescent [who lived there] had stolen something, skipped school, gotten drunk, or done something similar rose by twelve percent."

Being Normal Isn't Always A Positive Thing

A major study, conducted by the Barna Research Group of adults from the forty-eight contiguous States found eleven percent of the adult population was currently divorced, and twenty-five percent of all adults had divorced at least once.[345] Data from the 2002 Census Bureau found that approximately half of the marriages in America end in divorce. In California the divorce rate was a staggering sixty to seventy percent.[346] When half to three quarters of the population is doing something then that is the very definition of normal; therefore in America divorce is normal and life-long marriages are abnormal. Which of these violates the sanctity of marriage more-gays who want to marry or half of all marriages ending in divorce?

We Could Replace, "Till Death Do Us Part" With, "For The Foreseeable Future"

How about heterosexuals that repeatedly divorce? Actress Joan Collins married five different men. Actress Elizabeth Taylor was divorced eight times. Will people protest at their funerals with signs that say, "God hates divorcees?" What about Mickey Rooney and Zsa Zsa Gabor?

They both had nine spouses. Are they desecrating the sanctity of marriage? Then there was Linda Wolfe who had twenty-three ex-husbands. Were the first dozen marriages sacred? Which number marriage crossed the line and violated the sanctity of marriage? Should she have been permitted to have twenty-three church weddings? She admitted the twenty-third one was a publicity stunt. Was that marriage sacred?[347] Is a heterosexual marriage instantly sacred? How sacred was the marriage between pop singer Britney Spears and Jason Alexander that lasted fifty hours before it was annulled? Three days after her divorce from her first husband (Sonny Bono) singer Cher married musician Gregg Allman; was the second marriage as sacred as the first? Was the sacredness of it in any way affected by the fact that she filed for her second divorce after only nine days of wedlock?

Does The Family That Prays Together Stay Together?

What about Christian marriages? Common sense tells us that the more religious the couple the more successful their marriage. But that is not the case; the divorce rate among the most conservative Christians is significantly higher than the divorce rate for less strict faith groups:

Evangelical Christian-34%
Baptists -29%
Mainline Protestants -25%
Mormons-24%
Catholics-21%
Lutherans-21%

Furthermore, the divorce rate for both agnostics (those who believe it is impossible to prove or disprove the existence of God) and atheists (those who don't believe in God) was the same as the lowest rates for Christian marriages (21%).[348]

Tom W. Smith conducted a full probability sample of the adult U.S. population titled Adult Sexual Behavior in 1989: Numbers of Partners, Frequency and Risk, in which he reported that "Overall... less than 1% [of the study population] has been exclusively homosexual." Statistically speaking homosexuality is very uncommon; on the other hand divorce is quite common. With these high rates of divorce, what motivates some Christians to spend so much of their time, energy and money trying to prevent the one percent of the population that is gay from marrying while twenty-one to thirty-four percent of Christians are going against the teachings of Jesus by divorcing?

Save The Children

Besides claiming that permitting same-sex couples to marry would destroy the sanity of marriage the other major justification given is the fear that gay couples will want to raise children; which of course, some gay couples want to do, and for the same reasons as heterosexual couples desire children in their lives. Opponents of same-sex marriage warn that the children of these unions will be emotionally, psychologically, and spirituality damaged. How realistic are these fears? Research on families headed by same-sex couples has consistently found that the children raised in these homes are as well adjusted as those raised in families with a woman and a man. Award winning researcher, Dr. Charlotte Patterson of the University of Virginia wrote:

> Psychological research cannot resolve disagreements over basic values. Psychologists are, however, well placed to address many questions that have arisen in the context of debates surrounding the family lives of lesbian and gay citizens...More than 25 years of research on the offspring of nonheterosexual

> parents has yielded results of remarkable clarity. Regardless of whether researchers have studied the offspring of divorced lesbian and gay parents[47] or those born to lesbian or gay parents, their findings have been similar. Regardless of whether researchers have studied children or adolescents, they have reported similar results. Regardless of whether researchers have examined sexual identity, self-esteem, adjustment, or qualities of social relationships, the results have been remarkably consistent. In study after study, the offspring of lesbian and gay parents have been found to be at least as well adjusted overall as those of other parents.[349]

Gay? We Can Fix That!

In 2009 a twenty-minute video was posted on the YouTube that showed adult members of the Manifested Glory Ministries in Bridgeport, Connecticut performing an exorcism on a sixteen-year-old boy. Their goal was to cast out a, "homosexual demon," from the boy's body. The video that was made by church members and posted on the church's website showed a boy thrashing and vomiting as various adults yelled: "You homosexual spirit, we call you out right now! Come out of his belly. It's in the belly — push. Come on, you homosexual demon! Rip it from his throat! You homosexual spirit, we call you out right now! Loose your grip, Lucifer!" This was the third time the church members had attempted to change the boy's sexual orientation by casting out demons.[350] This video received much attention, although most people who attempt to change other people's sexual orientation use far less dra-

47 People who were in heterosexual marriages, but then divorced when they determined they were homosexual, and went on to parent with a person of the same sex.

matic methods. The Christian organization Focus on the Family has sponsored a web site and conference called, "Love Wins Out," where they insisted that homosexuality needed to be "healed" and "overcome." They believed that men turn to homosexual behavior because of the types of families in which they were raised. Similarly, female homosexuality was presented as resulting from "relational deficits" and "the effects of abuse." They claimed, "The heart of lesbianism" was "emotional dependency." Since they believed homosexuality was the result of psychological and spiritual problems they encouraged people to get treatment, thinking that once the underlying issues were resolved the attraction to people of the same sex would disappear. At their conference they offered workshops with titles such as "Hope for Those Who Struggle:"

> Choosing to leave homosexuality is a difficult process. However, tens of thousands of men and women have successfully done just that. This breakout session is specifically for those battling unwanted same-sex attractions who are looking for practical tools and resources, a place to ask questions and find some encouragement while on the journey.[351]

For decades all types of treatments have been tried get people to change their sexual orientation. Do these treatments work? Like any complex issue the results of the research on this topic aren't clear-cut. I noted earlier that people tend to notice the sections of the Bible that confirm their beliefs and ignore the rest. So it is with research results; people point to the results that support their position and minimize contradictory conclusions. That being said, Dr. Marshall Forstein summarized the attempts that have been made:

> Efforts to change homosexual orientation to heterosexual have been made with every conceivable technology or psychological theory. Attempts have included electroshock therapy after viewing graphic homoerotic pictures, convulsive therapy, nausea inducing drugs, testicular implants, behavior therapy and psychoanalysis. Biological attempts to change sexual orientation have included attempts to manipulate the sex hormones with the assumption that both men and women have homoerotic interests because they lack the appropriate hormone levels.[352]

How effective are these treatments? The answer depends on how one defines "healed." In most cases even with highly motivated patients who voluntarily sought treatment a successful outcome means the patient is capable of refraining from acting on same-sex urges, but the desire to do so remains. In other words, the behavior is changed, not the orientation. The American Psychiatric[48] Association publicly stated that, "there is no published scientific evidence supporting the efficacy of 'reparative therapy' as a treatment to change one's sexual orientation."[353] In 2009 the American Psychological[49] Association issued a resolution that "insufficient evidence" exists to claim such treatments are effective. Furthermore, it advised members; "Instead of telling clients that they can change [their sexual orientation], therapists should help them find ways to become more comfortable with their sexual orientation." In addition parents were counseled to, "avoid treatment that portrays homosexuality as

48 A psychiatrist is a physician who has had specialized training in mental disorders.

49 A psychologist has a doctoral degree in psychology.

a mental illness or developmental disorder."[354] The Association took this stand based on the findings of its Task Force on Appropriate Therapeutic Responses to Sexual Orientations, which examined the results of the published scientific research. They found the studies that claimed positive results with changing sexual orientation had "numerous" problems in their design that called into question the validity of the results. Dr. Judith Glassgold summarized the findings; "There really is no evidence that orientation can change who you're attracted to or who you fall in love with."[355]

But what do supporters of conversion or reparative therapy say? A advocate of conversion therapy proudly reported overall 38% of his patients achieved "solid heterosexual shifts." However he also noted:

> Most, if not all, people who have been homosexual continue to have some homosexual feelings, fantasies and interests. More often than not, they also have occasional, or more than occasional, homosexual outlets, even while being "happily married."[356]

How happy are the spouses of these patients when they learn about the, "more than occasional homosexual outlets," (meaning sexual encounters)? I know most of the male and female couples for which I provide therapy wouldn't consider themselves to be "happily married" while one of them still "occasionally" had sex with one or more people.

Yeah, But They Have A Choice

In 2009 Julian Bond, the chairman of the National Association for the Advancement of Colored People (NAACP), in a speech on same-sex marriage insisted, "Black people, of all people, should not oppose equality."[357] But African-Americans Christians have been particularly slow to accept homosexuals. That same year a Pew Research Center poll found that sixty-six percent of black Protestants opposed same-sex marriage.[358] In 2008 citizens of California voted on whether to change the State Constitution to eliminate the right of same-sex couples to marry in California, and that only marriages between a man and a woman would be valid or recognized in California even if same-sex marriage was legal in another State and the couple later moved to California. Seventy percent of the black voters cast their ballots in favor of the ban.[359] Many African-Americans balk at the suggestion that the struggle for civil rights currently engaged in by homosexuals is similar in any way to the discrimination blacks endure. They claim that unlike race, which is something outside of one's control, sexual orientation is a choice. This belief, combined with the conviction that God sees homosexuality as abomination, makes it easy for them not only to avoid helping, but even actively resisting, gays in the quest for equal rights. It was these attitudes that led Marion Barry to be the only member of the Washington, D.C. city council to vote against a bill to recognize same-sex legal marriages from other States even though he claimed to be in favor of civil rights for gays. The four time divorced council member explained his position: "What you've got to understand is 98 percent of my constituents are black and we don't have but a handful of openly gay residents, Secondly, at least seventy percent of those who express themselves to me about this are opposed to anything dealing with this issue. The ministers think it is a sin, and I have to be sensitive to that." He went on to warn that in the event that the council took any further action to accept same-sex marriage: "All hell is going to break lose. We may have a civil war. The black community is just adamant against this."[360]

Mr. Barry was a man with impressive civil rights experience; he was the first president of the Student Nonviolent Coordinating Committee (SNCC) which was one of the principal organizations of the American Civil Rights Movement in the 1960s. The group played a major role in organizing Southern voter registration drives, the 1963 March on Washington, and sit-ins to protest racial segregation. Mr. Barry and his fellow SNCC members put themselves at great risk of harm, even death, in their efforts to see to it that African-Americans were permitted to fully exercise their civil rights as Americans. Women's participation in SNCC and other civil rights organizations essentially created the beginnings of second-wave feminism which focused on changing social inequalities as opposed first-wave feminism that focused on legal issues such as the right to vote. The influence of the Civil Rights movement also introduced mass protests and awareness campaigns as the main methods to obtain sexual equality. At a time when few African-Americans held high office, Mr. Barry went on to be elected the mayor of Washington, D.C. serving several terms. He then became a member of the city council. Mr. Barry's past demonstrated that he was passionate about civil rights for African-Americans, at least heterosexual African-Americans. But when it came to gays, black or white, he wasn't so ready to fight for equality. He had been willing to violate the law of the land in order to stand up to corrupt election officials, furious white voters, aggressive armed law-enforcement officers, homicidal members of the Ku Klux Klan, and enraged white clergy, all of whom stubbornly stood in the way of African-American exercising their basic rights as citizens. But he wasn't willing to risk the wrath of black clergy members by supporting the civil rights of gay Americans.

As it turned out not all blacks or clergy members were against same-sex marriage. Among the first couples to be legally married in Washington, D.C. under the new Religious Freedom and Civil Marriage Equality Amendment Act of 2009 were Darlene Garner and Candy Holmes, both of whom were African-American as well as Christian clergy. The pastor who performed their marriage ceremony was also an African-American woman.[361]

For years white Christians in America forbade Christians of African descent to worship with them, and cited Bible verses to justify their discrimination such as when Noah cursed his grandson Ham (a.k.a. Canaan) turning his skin black and relegating him to eternally serve both of his brothers and their descendants through the end of all time (*Genesis* 9:21-27).[362] Now in many areas of the country European-Americans and African-Americans worship together in comfort as a part of racially integrated churches. How many years will pass before straight and openly gay Christians will comfortably worship together?[50]

What If God Made Them That Way?

Is homosexuality a preference, meaning a choice, or is it an orientation, meaning it is something with which one is basically born? In other words, is homosexuality a choice made by a willful human, or is it something given by God? If it is merely a preference, as many Christians believe, then it follows that a person can choose to stop being gay. This viewpoint never fully explains why otherwise rational people would freely choose to engage in a "lifestyle" that exposes them to contempt, discrimination, and violence, subjects them to discharge from the military, and being ostracized from their religious community. In any case it is the belief that homosexuality is merely a sinful choice that led Archbishop John Nienstedt to write:

---

50 I say "openly gay" because all places of worship have always had gay members, they just weren't open about it for fear of how they would be abused.

> Those who actively encourage or promote homosexual acts or such activity within a homosexual lifestyle formally cooperate in a grave evil and, if they do so knowingly and willingly, are guilty of mortal sin. They have broken communion with the church and are prohibited from receiving Holy Communion until they have had a conversion of heart, expressed sorrow for their action and received sacramental absolution from a priest.[363]

However, if a person's orientation is a result of genetic factors then it isn't a choice because it is the way God created that person. In that case, who are we to judge those whom God created? In recent years more Americans have come to believe sexual orientation, both homosexual and heterosexual, is something that "a person is born with." In 1977 only thirteen percent of respondents thought genetics played any role in determining orientation, but by 2001 more than half of those asked (56%) reported that genetics play a role.[364] Research on twins has found evidence that genetics plays a role in one's sexual orientation. One study found in male identical twins if one twin was homosexual the other twin had a 52% chance of also being homosexual. In non-identical twins the chance was less than half that (22%), and with non-twin biological brothers the chance went down to only 9.2%.[365] In other words the more genes the gay sibling had in common with the other sibling the higher the chances of the other sibling also being homosexual. Another study of female twins found a similar pattern. In identical twins if one twin was homosexual than her twin sister had a 48% chance of also being lesbian, and when non-identical twins were studied the chance was only 16%.[366]

"It is blasphemy to condemn God
for creating people according to the divine wisdom,
rather than pinched human prejudges."

Maggie Ross[367]

Yes, but...On the other hand...Yet, still

On Halloween Day of 1986 the Vatican released *Letter to the Bishops of the Catholic Church on the Pastoral Care of Homosexual Persons*. It was signed by two members of the Congregation for the Doctrine of the Faith, one of whom was Joseph Ratzinger who would go on to become Pope Benedict XVI in 2005. The text showed the struggle the Catholic Church, like many other Christian churches, has long had with how to deal with those who are in love with a person of the same sex. The authors attempted to separate the sin from the sinner by indicating the sexual <u>orientation</u> of homosexuality wasn't the main problem rather their primary objection was to the sexual <u>acts</u> between persons of the same sex, going to far as to call these act, "an intrinsic moral evil."

> In the discussion which followed the publication of the *Declaration on Certain Questions Concerning Sexual Ethics* (12/29/1975), however, an overly benign interpretation was given to the homosexual condition itself, some going so far as to call it neutral, or even good. Although the particular inclination of the homosexual person is not a sin, it is a more or less strong tendency ordered toward an intrinsic moral evil; and thus the inclination itself must be seen as an objective disorder.
>
> It is only in the marital relationship that the use of the sexual faculty can be morally good.

> A person engaging in homosexual behavior therefore acts immorally.

While continuing to contend that sexual acts between consenting adults of the same sex were taboo, a here-to never before loophole appeared in this document.

> It has been argued that the homosexual orientation in certain cases is not the result of deliberate choice; and so the homosexual person would then have no choice but to behave in a homosexual fashion. Lacking this freedom, such a person, even if engaged in homosexual activity, would not be culpable.

Or more simply, there may be cases in which homosexuality isn't a choice, and in such instances these people shouldn't be blamed or punished.

Despite their condemnation of same-sex sexual acts, the authors insisted that gay and lesbian people shouldn't be discriminated against or otherwise mistreated.

> The human person, made in the image and likeness of God, can hardly be adequately described by a reductionist [sic] reference to his or her sexual orientation. Every one living on the face of the earth has personal problems and difficulties, but challenges to growth, strengths, talents and gifts as well. Today, the Church provides a badly needed context for the care of the human person when she refuses to consider the person as a "heterosexual" or a "homosexual" and insists that every person has a fundamental identity: the creature of God, and by grace, his child and heir to eternal life.

> It is deplorable that homosexual persons have been and are the object of violent malice in speech or in action. Such treatment deserves condemnation from the Church's pastors wherever it occurs. It reveals a kind of disregard for others which endangers the most fundamental principles of a healthy society. The intrinsic dignity of each person must always be respected in word, in action and law.

As supportive as were these passages, the authors immediately followed them with a long worded statement that essentially meant, "But if they are going to demand equal civil rights they can expect to get beaten up."

> But the proper reaction to crimes committed against homosexual persons should not be to claim that the homosexual condition is not disordered. When such a claim is made and when homosexual activity is consequently condoned, or when civil legislation is introduced to protect behavior to which no one has any conceivable right, neither the Church nor society at large should be surprised when other distorted notions and practices gain ground, and irrational and violent reactions increase.

Even though the authors insisted that gays and lesbians shouldn't be discriminated against early in the document, by the end they made it clear that Church officials weren't to provide any support to organizations such as Dignity, an organization that promotes education, support, fellowship and worship within the Catholic tradition, and whose members are primarily gay and lesbian Catholics. As a result of this section of the document, Dignity masses were ended in dioceses throughout America.[368]

> All support should be withdrawn from any organizations which seek to undermine the teaching of the Church, which are ambiguous about it, or which neglect it entirely. Such support, or even the semblance of such support, can be gravely misinterpreted. Special attention should be given to the practice of scheduling religious services and to the use of Church buildings by these groups, including the facilities of Catholic schools and colleges. To some, such permission to use Church property may seem only just and charitable; but in reality it is contradictory to the purpose for which these institutions were founded, it is misleading and often scandalous.

A Tolerance Continuum

The Ontario Consultants on Religious Tolerance identified six common viewpoints on homosexuality:[369]

Viewpoint	Description or main emphasis
Abomination	Homosexuality is profoundly immoral in any circumstances.
Change is expected	Homosexuals can and should change their sexual orientation.
Celibacy is expected	If homosexuals can't change their orientation they should be celibate.

Marginally accepted	Since homosexuals seem unable to change their orientation then they should only be sexual in committed homosexual relationships.
Affirmation	Homosexuality is morally neutral, therefore homosexuals should have the same rights as heterosexuals.
Liberation	Homophobia, not being gay, is sinful.

These viewpoints can be held by individuals as well as being part of a religion's teaching. In the next segment we will utilize some of the principles Jesus' taught to try to determine which viewpoint he might hold.

The Teachings Of Jesus

Unfortunately nowhere in the Bible is there any mention of Jesus' stand on same-sex sexual acts. Of course this makes it impossible to know for sure what he believed, and extremely easy for each of us to project our own beliefs on him and be confident that he would wholeheartedly agree with our position. Those who are convinced that all same-sex sexual behavior is against the will of God can easily dismiss my claims that the historical and cultural mindset of the Biblical authors is important to understanding what was written, and insist that although there is no written record on Jesus' stand he no doubt was against it. Those who believe the primary message of Jesus was, "Love thy neighbor," can just as easily point to those sections of the Bible that describe how Jesus frequently violated the laws and customs of his time:

He dismissed the dietary laws of the Old Testament (*Mark* 7:18-23);
He violated the Holiness Code by discouraging a crowd from stoning an adulteress (*John* 7:53-8:11);
He violated social custom by speaking openly with a woman who was not a member of his family (*John* 4:1-42);
He interacted with social outcasts, including the "unclean" (*Mark* 1:40-45);
He taught and healed on the Sabbath in violation of Old Testament law (*Luke* 6:6-11, 13:10-16, 14:1-7).

Given that Jesus blatantly violated the laws of his religion and customs of his society that he considered rigid, overly strict, and not based on a spirit of love, one could easily claim that had he taken a stand on the issue of consensual sex behavior between two adults who love each other he wouldn't rely solely on the words of the Old Testament to make up his mind. All of us have only the general teachings of Jesus to apply when addressing the question of how he would respond to the present day controversy surrounding homosexuality.

Focus On Your Behavior Rather Than On The Behavior Of Others

Regardless of whether Jesus viewed same-sex behavior as an abomination or not, based on this principle he would likely recommend to others who think same-sex sexual behavior is wrong not to engage in it, but also to stop harassing other people about their sexual behavior.

Treat Others The Way You Want God To Treat You

No matter what his viewpoint on homosexuality Jesus would likely suggest to others that whatever their viewpoint on the matter they ought to keep in mind how they want God to treat them when deciding how they are going to treat homosexuals.

The Wellbeing Of Others Is More Important Than Following Rules

If Jesus were a member of a church whose dogma included the belief that homosexuality is an abomination and therefore homosexual men and women should be hated and ostracized he likely would ignore this rule, interact with homosexuals, and do what he could to improve their well-being.

Focus On A Person's Humanity Rather Than Rank Or Status

In contemporary American society homosexual men and women are considered second-class citizens. Merely being homosexual can get them discharged from the military. They are forbidden to marry. Some denominations refuse to permit them to be ordained as clergy. As a group they are regularly told they are unworthy and not loved by God. Even though heterosexual couples engage in some of the same sexual behaviors as homosexuals (oral and anal sex), when gay men and women engage in these behaviors they are told it is disgusting, sick, and perverse. Despite all the hostility, even hatred, which is directed towards homosexual men and women in America, Jesus certainly would focus on each person's worth.

Treat Others As You Want To Be Treated

No matter which view Jesus held he would clearly expect that his followers would treat homosexuals the way they would want to be treated by other people.

God Is Good

The God that Jesus worshipped was kind, generous, and loving, therefore Jesus would expect God to treat his homosexual children in that way. Jesus wouldn't approve of people waving signs that say things like, "God hates fags."

Be Compassionate

Jesus stated, "It is not those who are well who need a physician, but those who are sick" (*Luke* 5:31). Therefore if Jesus thought homosexuality was an illness he would offer compassion to people afflicted with that illness. If he believed homosexuality was a sinful lifestyle choice he would offer compassion to those people as well.

Serve Others

Whatever viewpoint Jesus would have on homosexuality he would deem it appropriate to serve homosexual men and women because he would not see himself as superior to them.

There Are No People Unworthy Of Our Loving Attention

In Biblical times Jesus freely interacted with those who were outcasts regardless of the reason they were ostracized. If he were here today he likely would be ministering to those suffering from A.I.D.S. no matter how they became infected.

We Are All One People

Since Jesus considered all people to be members of God's family he would be willing to attend worship services with homosexual women and men.

Forgive Others

If Jesus viewed homosexuality as a sinful lifestyle he would continue to forgive people who engaged in same-sex behavior regardless of how many times they engaged in it.

Act On Your Beliefs, Faith Alone Isn't Sufficient

Jesus wouldn't settle for his disciples ignoring or merely tolerating homosexuals. He would expect that we actively engage with them, and demonstrate the love of God by the way we treat them.

Use Non-Violent Resistance To Fight Injustice

Even if Jesus viewed homosexuality as an abomination, he wouldn't approve of, "fag bashing," or other forms of violence towards homosexual men and women. He would have mourned when Matthew Shepard was beaten to death for being gay.

Be Loving And Love Your Enemy

Even in the unlikely event that Jesus thought there was, "a homosexual agenda," intent on the destruction of the family and violating the sanctity of marriage he would preach that homosexuals and those who support them still ought to be loved.

Summary

Interpretations of Biblical verse have continued to change over time to the point that some are considered obsolete. In *Ephesians* (96:5) Paul wrote, "Slaves, be obedient to those who are your earthly masters, with fear and trembling, in singleness of heart, as to Christ." For years this one verse was used to justify slavery in America. It wasn't until 1865, eighty-nine years after the country was founded that the Thirteenth Amendment made slavery illegal. In current day America if anyone insisted that slavery was consistent with the teaching of Jesus he or she would be ridiculed regardless of which passages from the Bible were quoted as proof. From the time of Jesus up to now, there have been all sorts of things that were considered immoral at one time, but over the years have become accepted by the general public and Christians; for example autopsies, vaccinations, blood transfusions, organ transplants, artificial insemination, and in vitro fertilization. History suggests that at some point in the near future homosexuality will join this list.[370] As early as 1987, thirty-four percent of Catholics polled by the *Los Angeles Times* stated they believed that homosexuality wasn't a sin.[371] In 2007 The Pew Global Attitudes Project asked the citizens of various countries a simple question; "Should homosexuality be accepted by society?" Nearly half of the Americas polled reported they accepted homosexuality. As high as this number may seem, of the countries polled fourteen were more accepting than America.[372]

"Should Homosexuality Be Accepted By Society?[51]

	Yes	No
North America		
Canada*	70%	21%
United States	**49%**	**41%**
Western Europe		
Sweden*	86%	9%
France*	83%	17%
Spain*	82%	9%
Britain*	71%	21%
Italy*	65%	23%
Central Europe		
Czech Republic*	83%	16%
Germany*	81%	17%
Slovakia*	66%	29%
Poland	45%	41%
Latin America		
Argentina*	71%	21%
Brazil*	65%	30%
Chile*	64%	31%
Mexico*	60%	31%
Peru*	51%	43%
Venezuela	47%	50%
Bolivia	44%	49%
Eastern Europe		
Russia	20%	64%
Ukraine	19%	69%

51 Percentages do not add up to 100%.

<u>Southern Europe</u>		
Bulgaria	39%	38%
Turkey	14%	57%
<u>Middle East</u>		
Israel	38%	50%
Lebanon	18%	79%
Palestinian Territory	9%	58%
Kuwait	6%	85%
Jordan	6%	85%
Egypt	1%	95%

* Has a higher percentage of accepting citizens than does the USA

Questions To Help In Personal Reflection Or Group Discussion

Regent University is advertised as a "Christ-centered institution" that is, "committed to an evangelical interpretation and application of the Christian faith." Students are required to agree to a "Standard of Personal Conduct" that forbids the use of pornography, tobacco, alcohol, and illegal narcotics. The school's Nondiscriminatory Policy states: "Regent University's policies governing the admission of students relate to its mission statement, but are not applied to preclude a diverse student body in terms of disability, race, color, gender, religion or national or ethnic origin." Sexual orientation is not mentioned. If homosexuals are not accepted should the policy clearly state that they aren't welcome to apply?

In your view which of God's commandments are we supposed to follow;

A) The first version, because these must be of primary importance,
B) The second version, because God's priorities must have changed from the first version to the second,
C) All of them,
D) Only the ones I think are relevant.

Explain your answer.
If you answered D which ones do you think are relevant?

In which of the behaviors forbidden by The Holiness Code From *Leviticus* have you engaged?

Do you think these behaviors in which you engaged, or continue to engage, are as bad as having sex with another person of the same sex? If not, what are the criteria you use to determine which of the behaviors forbidden in the Old Testament are now acceptable and which ought to continue to be considered sinful?

Do you consider male-to-male sexual contact to be worse in God's eyes than female-to-female sexual contact? If so, explain your thinking.

In which of the behaviors found in *1st Corinthians* 6:9-11 have you engaged?

Have you ever eaten a lobster, shrimp, or crab? If you have, did you know at the time that this act was an abomination? If you didn't know, does that mean you are still abominable?

Now that you know that eating shellfish is an abomination will you ever eat them again? Is so, how do you justify engaging in a behavior that according to the Bible is forbidden by God? How do you feel knowing that, according to Paul, you are in the same category in God's eyes as cheaters, drunkards, evil-doers, extortionists, lechers, male prostitutes, men who have sex with boys, robbers, swindlers, thieves, and idol worshippers?

Do you consider a person's sexual orientation to be a matter of choice? If so, at what age did you choose your sexual orientation?

How and when did you decide whether to be heterosexual or homosexual?

How can it be sinful if a person's sexual orientation is the product of their genetic makeup rather than a matter of choice?

Which of these responses best describe your stand on homosexuality?

> Homosexuality is an abomination and profoundly immoral at all times.
> With effort homosexuals can, and should, change their sexual orientation.
> Homosexuals must either change their orientation or be celibate.
> Committed homosexual relationships are the least awful option.
> Homosexuality is morally neutral, therefore gays should have the same rights as everyone else.
> Being homosexual isn't sinful, but mistreating homosexuals is sinful.

Which of the six responses do you think best describes Jesus' stand on homosexuality?

How do you think Jesus would behave toward homosexual men and women?

How does that fit with the way you believe he would treat others who had violated The Holiness Code?

What did you think of the author's application of the principles Jesus taught to the issue of homosexuality?

Being A Follower Of Jesus

Throughout the ages many people have claimed to admire the teachings of Jesus, but most didn't actually want to follow his advice. In 1913 theologian Albert Schweitzer decided that Jesus had expected the world to end either during his lifetime or shortly thereafter, therefore his teachings were meant only to be an, "interim ethic," meaning that it was a fine way to live if Judgment Day was imminent, but it was an impractical way to live otherwise. Once he decided the teachings of Jesus were irrelevant to him he resigned his position as a theologian, went to Africa and worked in a hospital. I disagree with Dr. Schweitzer; I believe the teachings of Jesus are still relevant. I also think these principles are very demanding, so much so that most people refuse to follow them.

Seeking Authentic Followers Of Jesus

Wanted: Highly motivated persons for difficult but rewarding position. Need not necessarily leave current employment (unless one is a war lord, cruel dictator, etc.). Must be available, as needed, on a 24 hour, seven days a week, 365 days a year basis. No material payment for services. No paid vacation days or holidays. Co-workers may or may not be cooperative, or even friendly. Must be able to tolerate hostility. Humility required. Ability to forgive a must. Class, race, sex, age, physical ability, sexual orientation, and religion not a factor. Interested persons can begin immediately.

Recognizing An Authentic Follower Of Jesus

How would one recognize an authentic follower of Jesus? Look for a person that is behaving as if we are all one people, and that no one has more or less status in the eyes of God. This person behaves in a way that indicates she knows she isn't is superior to anyone else because of their age, income, education, ethnic background, physical appearance, intelligence, sexual orientation, stage of faith, or religion. Likewise she accepts that she isn't inferior to anyone. She has stopped comparing herself to others and instead focuses on relating to them by looking for similarities rather than differences. Since she believes she isn't superior to others she doesn't think it is her place to judge them. Instead she respects their right to choose, even when their choices don't agree with her choices. She is busy doing good, and isn't wasting her time attempting to prove to others that she is right. As a result of living this way she is serene and grateful.

"The Christian ideal has not been tried and found wanting.
It has been found difficult, and left untried."
Gilbert Keith Chesterton, 1910 A.C.E.

Questions To Help In Personal Reflection Or Group Discussion

Is there anyone, or any group of people, that you believe are superior to you in the eyes of God? If so, what makes them superior to you?

Is there anyone, or any group of people, that you believe are inferior to you in the eyes of God? If so, what makes them less than you?

To whom are you entitled to tell how to live his or her life?

Is, "What Would Jesus Do," The Wrong Question?

"The problem today is that Churches preach about Jesus
and very little about what Jesus taught.
This makes it easy to love Jesus,
but not follow his message."

Father John Clay

In the 1990s "What would Jesus do?" (Abbreviated to WWJD) became a popular slogan. At first it appeared on homemade bracelets, but soon it was commercially available on tee shirts, coffee mugs, and bumper stickers. Many people didn't know that the phrase had previously been popular one hundred years ago as the result Charles Sheldon's novel *In His Steps: What Would Jesus Do?* The book was based on a series of sermons he delivered in his Congregationalist church in Topeka, Kansas in which Jesus was held up as a moral example of how to live rather than as a savior. Today, as a hundred years ago, WWJD is supposed to serve as a reminder to people to consider before taking action what Jesus might do, or not do, in the same situation.

If one believes that Jesus performed miracles such as bringing eyesight to the blind or raising the dead then Jesus had many more options at his disposal than the rest of us. Yet Jesus didn't perform a miracle everyday of his life; most of his days were spent teaching and being of service to others in very human ways. Whether you believe Jesus performed miracles or not, he didn't preach <u>we</u> should raise the dead or perform other miracles. Therefore, rather than asking, "WWJD," a more fitting question is, "What would Jesus have me do?" Hopefully this book has already helped you answer that question. Now you are faced with the most important question of all; "Will you do it?" Let's live so we can sincerely pray; Our father, who art in Heaven, holy be your name. Your kingdom is coming as your will is being done on Earth as it is in heaven. Prior to taking any action Julia Butterfly Hill, who writes about spiritual-directed ecology, asks herself: "How is my life contributing to healing or to hurting? How is my life contributing to restoration or destruction? Is my life an example of the world I want to live in or an example of the world I don't want to live in?"[373] She believes if we don't ask ourselves these questions then we are part of the problem, rather than part of the solution.

Questions To Help In Personal Reflection Or Group Discussion

How would you answer Julia Butterfly Hill's questions?

How is my life contributing to healing or to hurting?
How is my life contributing to restoration or destruction?
Is my life an example of the world I want to live in or an example of the world I don't want to live in?
Is the way I live my life primarily part of the problem or part of the solution?

In what ways, if any, have your views of Jesus and his place in your life been changed by reading this book?

In what ways have your views of Jesus and his place in your life remained unchanged?

What do you think you will do differently after having read this book to have your life choices be more in line with the teachings of Jesus?

Final Thoughts

I have made my living for the previous thirty years in the business of psychotherapy. I can attest to the fact that people who once were filled with self-loathing and rage, who engaged in behaviors destructive to them and to others can, and do, change. When a client and I meet for the first time it is my custom to ask, "Do you have any spiritual resources that you might be able to utilize to help you deal with the problems you have been describing to me?" Fortunately, for them, and me, most people indicate they do have some form of spirituality that is important to them. It is fortunate for them because a practical spirituality applied to most any problem makes it easier to resolve or cope with. I am happy most of my clients want to employ spiritual principles in their lives because it makes my job so much easier. It has been my experience that regardless of whether my clients consider themselves Christian, most of them agree that practicing the principles taught by Jesus makes for a better life. Even after all these years I am amazed at how these principles will lead the most shattered person to become someone who is loving, compassionate, generous, forgiving, and kind. I wrote this book with deep respect for Jesus and his teachings; I hope that admiration was apparent, even in the sections in which you and I have differing beliefs. Regardless of the relationship you had with Jesus when you started this book it is my hope that reading it increased your understanding of the wisdom of Jesus. Likewise I hope reading it has made you more able, and willing, to apply these principles in all interactions each and every day. If more of us lived in the manner Jesus taught his early followers, the world would be a very different place. I have no doubt we would experience on Earth, the Kingdom of God.

Bibliography

A.A. World Services (1976). *Alcoholic Anonymous*. 3rd Ed. New York: New York.

A.A. World Services (1984). *Pass It On*. New York: New York.

Abanes, R. (1998). *End-Time Visions*. New York: Four Walls Eight Windows.

Acocella, Joan. (2006). The Saintly Sinner. *The New Yorker,* Feb. 13, pp. 140-149.

Allen, J.L., JR. (2004). Vatican Document recommends cultivation of 'feminine values.' *National Catholic Reporter,* August 13.

Aviram Oshri. (2005). Where was Jesus Born? *Archaeology,* Nov./Dec. pp. 42-45.

Ayo, N. (1992). *The Lord's Prayer.* Notre Dame: University of Notre Dame Press.

Bailey, J. M. and Benishay, D.S. (1993), "Familial Aggregation of Female Sexual Orientation," *American Journal of Psychiatry* 150(2): 272-277.

Bailey, J.M. and R.C. Pillard, R.C. (1991)., "A genetic study of male sexual orientation," *Archives of General Psychiatry*, vol. 48:1089-1096, Dec.

Barclay, W. (1950). *The Gospel of Matthew.* Philadelphia: Westminster Press, pp. 223-224.

Bauer, P. J., & Dow, G.A. (1994). Episodic memory in sixteen-and-twenty-month-old children: Specifics are generalized but not forgotten. *Developmental Psychology,* 30, 403-417.

Bayles, D., & Orland, T. (1993). *Art & Fear*. Santa Cruz, CA: Image Continuum.

Begley, S. (2007). Why Money Doesn't Buy Happiness. *Newsweek.com*. 10/15.

Bick, J. (2005). "The Microsoft Millionaires Come of Age", *The New York Times*. 5/29.

Bishop, T. (2004). "The rest of the motto", Todd Bishop's Microsoft Blog, *Seattle Post-Intelligencer*. Sept. 23.

Blanton, D. (2004). FOX Poll: Most Americans Pray (and Floss) Frequently. Dec. 19.
http://www.foxnews.com/story/0,2933,141885,00.html.

Bouldrey, B. (2001). *Monster: Adventures In American Machismo*. San Francisco: Council Oak Books.

Brown, C. (2010). For Monks, No Peace. *Star Tribune, 5/30, pp. B1 & 7.*

Brunswick, M. (2010). Aching for a chance to say thanks. *Star Tribune*, April 2, pp. A1 & A7.

Bryson, B. (2006). *The Life and Times of the Thunderbolt Kid*. New York: Broadway Books.

Campbell, J. (1949). *The Hero With A Thousand Faces*. New York: Pantheon Books.

Chapman, S. (2008). Do Americans want an angry president? *The New York Times*, Oct. 17, p. A23.

Chamberlin, J. (2009). Crime and Punishment. *Monitor On Psychology*, pp. 52-54.

Chandler, R. (1987). The *Times* Poll: Americans Like Pope but Challenge Doctrine. *Los Angeles Times,* August 23, p. 20.

Chapple, Christopher K. (1993). *Nonviolence to Animals, Earth, and Self in Asian Traditions*. New York: State University of New York Press.

Coen, Paolo. (1994). *Le Sette Chiese*, Rome: Newton Compton.

Cohen, D. (1999). *Prophets of Doom.* Brookfield CT: The Millbrook Press, Inc.

Coleman, A. (2007). Five Lottery Winner Tales: Money Doesn't Always Buy Happiness, 02/01, www.associatedcontent.com.

Coleman, N. (2008). The push for conformity shoves away parishioners. *Star Tribune, Mar*. 1.

Cromie, W.J. (2004). One-third of Americans pray for their health. But does it make a difference? Harvard News Office. http://www.news.harvard.edu/gazette/2004/05.13/01-prayer.html.

Crossan, J.D. (1998). *The Birth Of Christianity: Discovering What Happened In The Years Immediately After The Execution Of Jesus*. San Francisco: Harper.

Dias, E. (2010). Interfaith U. *Time*, September 6, p. 51.

Dionne, E. J., Jr. (2009). Christianity finds new life in struggle. *Star Tribune*, April 12, OP3.

Dixon, J. (1971). *The Call to Glory*. New York: Bantam Books.

Douglas-Klotz, N. (1990). *Prayers of the Cosmos.* San Francisco: Harper.

Douglas-Klotz, N. (1999). *The Hidden Gospel.* Wheaton, IL: Quest Books.

Dominguez, A. (2007). Funeral Protests Cost Church $11 Million. Nov. 1, http://news.aol.com/story/nc/_a/funeral-protests-cost-church-11-million/2007.

Ehrman, Bart. (2003). *Lost Christians: The Battle for Scripture and the Faith We Never Knew*. New York: Oxford University Press.

Ely, S. (2006). No Growing Pains for *Left Behind. USA Weekend.* June 2-4, p. 18.

Erwin, M. (2010). Catholics get a direct line to the Lord. *Metro*, March 3, p. 27.

Farquar, Michael. (2005). *A Treasury Of Deception.* New York: Penguin Books.

Fowler, J.W. (1981). *Stages Of Faith.* San Francisco: Harper.

Fox, E. (1934). *The Sermon On The Mount.* San Francisco: Harper.

Fuchs, M. (2006). Recreating Biblical Meals for the modern Kitchen. *The New York Times,* Nov. 4, A13.

Funk, R.W., & The Jesus Seminar. (1999). *The Gospel Of Jesus.* Santa Rosa, CA: Polebridge Press.

Gerson, M. (2008), Compassionate conservatism: A theological checkup, *Star Tribune,* June 1, OP5.

Gibbs, N. (2009). The Happiness Paradox. *Newsweek,* 11/23, p. 116.

Gleick, J. (2008). Keeping It Real. *The New York Times Magazine,* January 6, pp. 13-14.

Goodstein, L. (2006). Conservative Jews allow Gay Rabbis and Unions. *The New York Times,* Dec. 7, A24.

Goodstein, L. (2009b). For an Episcopal Parish, a Path to Catholicism, *The New York Times,* Oct. 25, p. 12.

Goodstein, L. (2009). Even in Recession, Believers Invest in the Gospel of Getting Rich, *The New York Times,* Aug. 16, p. 1.

Gould, S. J., (1997). *Questioning the Millennium.* New York: Harmony Books.

Grossman, C.L. (2008). Good Friday prayer revisions spark debate. *USA Today,* Feb. 7, 21A.

Green, J, & Shellenberger, R. (2000). The subtle energy of love. *Subtle Energies,* 4 (1) pp. 31-55.

Grosso, M. (1995). *Millennium Myth: Love and Death at the End of Time.* Wheaton, IL: Quest Books.

Grouzet, F.M.E., Kasser, T., Ahuvia, A., Dols, J.M.F., Kim, Y., Lau, S., Ryan, R., Saunders, S., Schmuck, P., & Sheldon, K. (2005). The structure of goal contents across 15 cultures. *Journal of Personality and Social Psychology*, 89, 800-816.

Hartley, Cecil. (1818). *Principles of Punctuation or the Art of Pointing.*

Hawley, c. (2007). Fox forgoes flattery in new book. *USA Today*, October 5, 8A.

Hellwig, M. (1976). *The Eucharist and the Hunger of the World.* New York: Paulist Press.

Herper, M. (2004). Money Won't Buy You Happiness. 09.21, Forbes.com.

Herman, A.L. (1999). *Community, Violence, & Peace*. New York: State University of New York.

Hill, D. (2006). Psychologies of religious fundamentalists. *The National Psychologist*, March/April, pp. 6-7.

Hochschild, A. (2009). Families, Class and Culture. *The New York Times Book Review*, Oct. 19, p. 27.

Householder, M., & Williams, C. (2010). Personal theology led to militia. *Star Tribune*, Mar. 31, p. A8.

Huxley, A. (1939). *Brave New World.* NY: Harper.

Jacobs, T. (2009). Morals Authority. *Miller-McCune*, May-June, pp. 46-55.

Jilani, S. (2010). America Fails Abused Kids. *Star Tribune*, May 29, p. A15.

Jost, J.T. (2007). Coda-After "The End of the End of Ideology." *American Psychologist,* Dec. 1077-1079.

Katie, B., & Mitchell, S. (2003). *Loving What Is: Four Questions That Can Change Your Life.* NY, NY: Harmony.

Kalb, C. (2009). No rest for an AIDS Veteran. *Newsweek,* April 6, p. 13.

Kasser, T., Cohn, S., Kanner, A, & Ryan, R. (2007). Some costs of American corporate capitalism: A psychological exploration of value and goal conflicts. *Psychological Inquiry,* 18, 1-22.

Keillor, G. (2010). Check in any time you'd like, but you can't stay. *Star Tribune*, Jan. 3, p. PO3.

Kidder, D.S., & Oppenheim, N. D. (2007). *The Intellectual Devotional.* New York, NW: Modern Times.

Kittel, G. (Ed. (1964). *Theological Dictionary of the New Testament,* volume 2. Grand Rapids, Michigan: Eerdmans.

Kopp, L. (1988). A Problem of Manipulated Data. In J. Gramick & P. Furey (Eds.). *The Vatican and Homosexuality,* New York: Crossroad. pp. 40-47.

Kramer, J. (2010). A Canterbury Tale. *The New Yorker*, April 26, pp. 40-50.

Kristof, N. D. (2008). It Takes A School, Not Missiles. *The New York Times*, July 13, p.14.

Kristof, N.D. (2010). Two Men And Two Paths. *The New York Times,* June 13, opinion page 12.

Kurtz, E. (19?). *Not-God, A History of Alcoholics Anonymous*. Center City, MN: Hazelden Educational Materials.

Kyle, R. (1998). *The Last Days are Here Again*. Grand Rapids, MI: Baker Books.

Largier, N. (2007). *In Praise Of The Whip*. G. Harman (trans.) Zone.

Lattin, D. (2003). Whose Commandments are we fighting over, anyway? *Star Tribune,* August 30, p. B5.

Lewis, C.S. (1952). *Mere Christianity*. San Francisco: Harper.

Lipton, E. (2008). With Push From White House U.S. Arms Sales Rise Sharply. *The New York Times*, Sept. 14, pp. 1 & 13.

Lonetree, A. (2010). Boy, 6, tied to post and beaten. *Star Tribune*, May 28, B1 & B4.

Lord, R. P. (1991). Personal perspective. *The Christian Century*, 108, 902-903.

Los Angeles Times. (2009). Cheating teens tend to become dishonest adults. *Star Tribune*, Oct. 29, p. A4.

Maccoby, Hyam. (1986). *The Mythmaker: Paul and the Invention of Christianity*. San Francisco: Barnes & Noble.

MacPherson, D. (1975). *The Incredible Cover-Up: The True Story of the Pre-Trib Rapture*, Plainfield, NJ: Logos International.

Manning, B. (2003). *A Glimpse of Jesus: The Stranger to Self-hatred*. San Francisco: Harper.

Marsh, C. (2006). Wayward Christian Soldiers, *The New York Times* Jan. 20.

Martinez, A. (2010). The Next American Century. *Time,* March 11, pp. 40-42.

Marty, Martin. (1962). *The Hidden Discipline.* Saint Louis: Concordia.

McIver, T. (1999). *The End of the World: An Annotated Bibliography.* Jefferson, NC: McFarlane & Co., Jefferson NC.

McKechnie, J. L. (Ed.) (1983). *Webster's New Universal Unabridged Dictionary,* New York, NY: 2nd ed. Dorset and Baber.

McKinney, M. (2010). Whipped Boy Had Brother Who Died. *Star Tribune*, May 29, p.B1 & B4

Meacham, J. (2006). Pilgrim's Progress. *Newsweek,* August 14, pp.37-43.

Miller, L. (2008). 4 Sale: Bones of the Saints. *Newsweek*, Feb. 11, p. 16.

Miller, L. (2009). A Graham Slam. *Newsweek,* pp. 18-19.

Miller, W. R. (1964). *Nonviolence: A Christian Interpretation.* London: Allen and Unwin.

Mirsky, S. (2007). *Anti Gravity.* Guilford, Connecticut: The Lyons Press.

Mooallem, J. (2009). The Self-storage Self. *The New York Times Magazine*, Sept. 6, pp.24-29.

Munsey, C. (2009). Insufficient evidence to support sexual orientation change efforts. *Monitor On Psychology,* Oct., pp. 29-30.

Murray, S. O. (2000). *Homosexualities,* University of Chicago.

Newman, A. (2007). A Chinese Orphan's Journey To A Jewish Rite Of Passage. *The New York Times,* March 8, p. A1 & A19.

Patterson, C.J. (2009). Children of Lesbian & Gay Parents: Psychology, Law, & Policy. *American Psychologist,* Nov., pp. 727-736.

Peck, M.S. (1978). *The Road Less Traveled.* New York, NY: Touchstone Books.

Peck, M.S. (1987). *The Different Drum.* New York, NY: Simon & Schuster.

Pheifer, P. (2010). Baby severely injured by father, charges say. *Star Tribune,* May 28, p. B4.

Phelps, D. (2010). Options fueled year's biggest pay package. *Star Tribune,* June 27, D1 & 3.

Pinker, S. (2008). The Moral Instinct. *The New York Times Magazine,* Jan. 13, pp. 33-56.

Pollan, M. (2007). Our Decrepit Food Factories. *The New York Times Magazine,* Dec. 16, pp. 25-27.

Porter, J. R. (2001). *The Lost Bible: Forgotten Scriptures Revealed.* The University of Chicago Press.

Powers, R. (2006). *The Playboy Interviews: Larger Than Life.* Milwaukee: M Press, pp. 217-252.

Randi, J. (1993). *The Mask of Nostradamus*. Amherst, NY: Prometheus Books.

Raub, J. J. (1993). *Who Told You That You Were Naked?* New York: Crossroad.

Reber, A.S. (1985). *Dictionary of Psychology*. New York, NY: Penguin Books.

Rendina, Claudio. (2000). *La grande Enciclopedia di Roma*, Rome: Netwon Compton.

Rosin, H. (2009). Did Christianity Cause the Crash? *The Atlantic* Dec. Vol. 304 No. 5, pp. 39-48.

Ross, M. (1989). *Pillars Of Flame: Power, Priesthood And Spiritual Maturity.* NY: Harper.

Salkin, A. (2008). If You Post It, They Will Pray. *The New York Times*, Nov. 30, p. 10.

Saqrfati, J. (1997). *Creation,* March, 19(2): 16–19.

Savage, D.G. 92009). Is a 'Human Sacrifice Channel' allowed by the First Amendment? *Star Tribune,* Oct. 7, p. A6.

Schlosser, E. (2007). Penny Foolish. *The New York Times.* November 29.

Schneiderman, R. M. (2010). Flock Is Now a Fight Team in Some Ministries. *The New York Times*, February, 1.

Schott, B. (2003). *Schott's Original Miscellany*. New York, NY: Bloomsbury.

Schwartz, H. (1996). *Century's End: An Orientation Manual Toward the Year 2000*. New York: Doubleday.

Schwartz, J. (2008). The Harder They Fall, the More I Smile. *The New Y3ork Times,* Oct. 12, Business Section, pp. 1 & 18.

Schwartz, S. (2007). Cultural and individual value correlates of capitalism: A comparative analysis. *Psychological Inquiry*, 18, 52-57.

Schwertley, B.M. (1999). Is the Pretribulation Rapture Biblical? http://www.reformedonline.com/view/reformedonline/rapture.htm

Segers. M.C. (1988). Morality and the Law: A Feminist Critque of the Vatican Letter. In J. Gramick & P. Furey (Eds.). *The Vatican and Homosexuality,* New York: Crossroad. pp. 81-89.

Shaw, E. (1995). *Eve of Destruction*. Los Angeles, CA: Lowell House.

Shepherd, C. (2009). News Of The Weird. *Star Tribune,* Oct. 17.

Shepherd, C. (2009b). News Of The Weird. *Star Tribune,* Oct. 24, p. E9.

Shepherd, C. (2009c). News Of The Weird. *Star Tribune,* April 3, p. E5.

Shepherd, C. (2010). Now, that's the life…in Norway prison. *Star Tribune,* June 19, p. E9.

Shepherd, C. (2010b). Get out the Segways: It's the Wox Cup, *Star Tribune*, July 10, 2010, p. E9.

Skinner, S. (1994). *Millennium Prophecies*. Stamford, CT: Longmeadow Press.

Smith, M. (2010). Haiti legend cited by Pat Robertson a 'fabrication,' scholar says. Jan. 14, CNN.com.

Spong, J.S. (1991). *Rescuing The Bible From Fundamentalism*. San Francisco: HarperSanFrancisco.

Stacy, M. (2008). Teen's dying wish brings hope for orphans. *Star Tribune*, Dec. 21: AA1-3.

Standley, F.L. (2004). Langston Hughes. Autobiography: I Wonder as I Wander, *African American Review*, Fall.

Stephens, J.R. (2006). *Weird History 101*. New York: Fall River Press.

Stone, J. (2008). Infinite Jest. *Smithsonian,* February, p. 108.

Strickler, J. (2009). A spiritual home for addicts. *Star Tribune*, May 30, pp. E1 & E3.

Strickler, J. (2010). A smorgasbord of spirituality. *Star Tribune*, April 3, pp. E1 & E2.

Strickler, J. (2010b). Catholic numbers increasing despite recent bad news. *Star Tribune*, April 3, p. E3.

Sullivan, A. (2010). Milestones, *Time*, September 20, p. 26.

Taylor, B. (2009). When Brryan Jackson was a baby... *Star Tribune*, June 6, p. A8.

Temoshok, L.R., & Chandra, P.S. (2000). The meaning of forgiveness in a specific situational and cultural context: Persons living with HIV/AIDS in India. In M. E. McCullough, K. I. Pargament, & C. E. Thoresen (Eds.) *Forgiveness: Theory, Research, And Practice*. New York, NY: The Guilford Press. pp 41-64.

Tevlin, E. (2008). Seeking records on pastor, IRS takes mega church to court. *Star Tribune*, August 22, pp. A1 & A10.

Thompson, M.R. (1995). *Mary of Magdala: Apostle & Leader.* New York: Paulist Press.

Thornburgh, N. (2010). Resumed Innocent. *Time,* May 31, pp. 24-31.

Toscani, O. (1999). *Cacas: The Encyclopedia of Poo*. Villa Minelli, Italy: Colors.

Truss, Lynee, (2003). *Eats, Shoots & Leaves: The Zero Tolerance Approach to Punctuation.* New York: Gotham Books.

Unger, R. K. (2007). Religious Ideology, a Neglected Variable. *American Psychologist,* Dec. pp. 1076-1077.

Villano, D. (2008). A Future Of Less. *Miller-McCune,* September, pp. 60-69.

Vowell, S.,(2009). A Plantation to Be Proud Of. *The New York Times*, July 5, p. 9.

Waldman, S., & Sheahen, L. (2006). Beliefwatch: Catch Hell. *Newsweek,* June 26, p. 8.

Weber, E. (1999). *Apocalypses*. Harvard University Press, Cambridge MA.

Webley, K. (2010). Book Burnings, *Time*, September 20, p. 25.

Weiner, E. (2008). *The Geography Of Bliss*, New York: Twelve.

Weiss, B. L. (1988). *Many Lives, Many Masters*. New York: Fireside Books.

Weiss, B. L. (1992). *Through Time Into Healing*. New York: Fireside.

Williams, G. (2009). Does His Business Have A Prayer? December 17, AOL Small Business, AOL.com.

Wolpert, S. (1991). *India*. Los Angeles: University of California Press.

Worth R. E. (2010). Crime (Sex) and Punishment (Stoning). *The New York Times*, August 22, 2010, p. 1& 4.

Worthen, M. (2009). Who Would Jesus Smack Down? *The New York Times Magazine*, Jan. 11, pp. 2023.

Yount, D. (2009). Poll: Few teens see clergy as role models. *Star Tribune*, April 4, p. A5.

Zoll, R. (2010). Pastor planning to burn Qur'ans follows his own path. *Star Tribune*, Sept. 9, p. A10.

About The Author

Mic Hunter, Psy.D. holds licenses as a Psychologist, and Marriage and Family Therapist. He has a psychotherapy practice for adults in Saint Paul, Minnesota, and four times a year he facilitates a couples' communication workshop at the Hazelden Foundation in Center City, Minnesota. For several decades he has been assisting people define and put into practice their personal relationship with the God of their understanding.

Dr. Hunter is the author, co-author, or editor of eight books including *Abused Boys: The Neglected Victims of Sexual Abuse*, *The Sexually Abused Male Volumes I & II*, *Child Victims & Perpetrators Of Sexual Abuse*, *Adult Survivors Of Sexual Abuse: Treatment Innovations*, *Honor Betrayed: Sexual Abuse In America's Military*, *The Ethical Use of Touch in Psychotherapy*, and *The American Barbershop: A Closer Look At A Disappearing Place*. He is currently working on three more books, *Emotions: The Lanquage Of Intimacy*, *The Next Right Thing: A Journey Through The Twelve Steps One Word At A Time*, and *Making Pearls: Creating The Relationship You've Always Wanted.*

He is a recipient of the Fay Honey Knopp Memorial Award, given by the National Organization on Male Sexual Victimization, "For recognition of his contributions to the field of male sexual victimization treatment and knowledge." In 2007 the Board of Directors of Male Survivor announced the creation of The Mic Hunter Award For Research Advances, and Dr. Hunter became the first recipient. It is given for, "ceaseless pursuit of knowledge about male sexual abuse in all its occurrences, of the eloquent dissemination of new knowledge in this area, and of the stimulation for further study and concern about revealing, treating and preventing male sexual abuse."

Mic has been sought out by the print and broadcast media for interviews over 100 times including *Oprah*, *CNN*, *The New York Times*, and *The Wall Street Journal*. He has presented throughout North America to professional audiences and the general public over 200 times. He has served as a reviewer for *The Journal of Child Sexual Abuse*, *The Journal of Men's Studies*, *The Journal of Interpersonal Violence*, *Sexual Addiction And Compulsivity*, and *Violence Against Women*.

End Notes

1 Fox, 1934, p. 118.
2 Miller, 2009.
3 Dionne, 2009.
4 Big Book, p. 9.
5 *Pass it On*, p. 147.
6 Bayles & Orland, 1993, p. 113.
7 Mirsky, 2007, p. 68-69.
8 *Sojourners*, August 1979.
9 Hellwig, 1976, p. 50.
10 Strickler, 2009.
11 Hoover, et al, 2002.
12 *Encarta World English Dictionary*, 1999 Microsoft Corporation.
13 *The Notebook of Elbert Hubbard*, 1926, p. 26.
14 *Mark Twain's Notebook*, edited by Albert Bigelow Paine, 1925.
15 *The Prophets*, 1962, p. 11.
16 *Get Right With God*, 2001.
17 *Time*, 3/22/10, p. 4.
18 "God Loves Everyone Is A Lie" on GodHatesFags.com.
19 Blanton, 2004.
20 Geoff, 2009.
21 Cromie, 2004.
22 Salkin, 2008.
23 Chapman, 2008.
24 http://www.independent.co.uk/sport/general/batting-for-jesus.
25 http://www.cbsnews.com/stories/2003/07/15/politics/main563247.shtml.
26 Shepherd, 2009.
27 Avo, 1992.
28 Douglas-Klotz, 1990, p. 19.

[29] Big Book, p. 87-88.
[30] Douglas-Klotz, 1990, p. 35.
[31] Readers' response. (1991). *The Christian Century*, November 20-27, 108, p. 34.
[32] Barclay, 1950.
[33] Federal Election Commission, 2004 Official Presidential Election Results, Feb. 11, 2005.
[34] http://web.utk.edu/~glenn/GopacMemo.html
[35] Powers, 2006, p. 245.
[36] Webley, 2010.
[37] Fox, 1934.
[38] Wills, 2006, p. 44.
[39] Fox, 1934, p. 19.
[40] Margonelli, 2008.
[41] Manning, 2003, p. 12.
[42] A.A., 1976.
[43] A.A., 1976.
[44] A.A., 1976, p. 58.
[45] Mirsky, 2007.
[46] Furst, 2006.
[47] Thenewcivilrightsmovement.com.
[48] http://thenewcivilrightsmovement.com/2012-presidential-candidate-newt-gingrich-on-gay-marriage-sarah-palin-and-religion/politics/2009/04/18/1827.
[49] http://thenewcivilrightsmovement.co.m/2012-presidential-candidate-newt-gingrich-on-gay-marriage-sarah-palin-and-religion/politics/2009/04/18/1827.
[50] *Encarta World English Dictionary*, 1999.
[51] Stevenson, 1962.
[52] *New Seeds of Contemplation,* 1961.
[53] A.A., 1953.
[54] *Time*, August 28, 2009.
[55] Evely, 1967, p. 113.
[56] Worth, 2010.
[57] Manning, 2003, p. 126.
[58] Frank, 2001, p. 421.

59 Manning, 2003, p. 129
60 Stephens, 2006, p. 113.
61 Saudi judge mulls paralyzing criminal, *Star Tribune*, 8/20/10, p. 2A.
62 Taylor, 2009.
63 A.A., 1976, p. 66.
64 A.A., 1976, pp. 66 & 67.
65 DouglasOKlotz, 1999.
66 *Beginnings Without End,* 1975, p. 7.
67 *The Professor at the Breakfast-Table,* 1860, p. 11.
68 Lewis, 1952, p. 3.
69 Kurtz.
70 A.A., 1976, p. 152-153.
71 *Encarta World English Dictionary*, 1999.
72 *Encarta World English Dictionary*, 1999.
73 A.A., 1976, page 60.
74 Douglas-Klotz, 1990, p. 62.
75 Douglas-Klotz, 1990, p. ix.
76 Raven heart Music/Bird Ave. Publishing, 1993.
77 A.A., 1953.
78 A.A., 1976, p. 67.
79 Stacy, 2008.
80 Ferrine, 1994, p. 47.
81 Evely, 1967, p. 146.
82 Neil Young, 2005, Silver Fiddle Music ASCAP (abridged).
83 "Jesus Christ: Milquetoast, Mealymouth, Namby-Pamby, Mollycodller, Hippie-Whimp Or Bold & Brave Preacher, King, Captain And Judge. GodHatesFags.com
84 *Civilization and Its Discontents*, 1930, p. 5.
85 *Star Tribune*, May, 7, 2009, A14.
86 Andrea Most, "'You've Got to Be Carefully Taught': The Politics of Race in Rodgers and Hammerstein's South Pacific" *Theater Journal* 52, no. 3 (October 2000), 306.
87 Douglas-Klotz, 1990, p. 48.
88 *Leo Rosten's Treasury of Jewish Quotations,* 1972, p. 375.
89 Briggs, 2006.

90 A.A., 1976, p. 95. Italics in original.
91 From a January 11, 1942 radio broadcast, cited in *Clive Lewis: A Dramatic Life*.
92 *The Notebook of Elbert Hubbard,* p. 194.
93 A.A., 1976, p. 58.
94 A.A., 1976, p. 60
95 http://www.swapmeetdave.com/Bible/JamesIntro.htm.
96 Redeeming Love Church, Maplewood, MN.
97 Stephens, 2006
98 Strickler, 2010, p. E1.
99 Spong, 1991, p. 242.
100 Douglas-Klotz, 1999, p. 129.
101 Ferrini, 1994.
102 Kidder & Oppenheim, 2007.
103 Brunswick, 2010.
104 Chapple, p. 10.
105 B. R. Nanda, http://www.mkgandhi.org/nonviolence/gandhi_and_non.htm.
106 Miller, p. 61.
107 Herman, 1999.
108 http://nytimes.com.
109 Kantor, 2008.
110 Perry, 1994.
111 Based on a much longer version written by Hyman S. Baras that first appeared on the Israel Baseball League web site, and reprinted in *Smithsonian*, June, 2008, p. 104.
112 Spong, 1991, p. 147.
113 Jacobs, 2009.
114 *Encarta World English Dictionary*.
115 Reber, 1985.
116 Gerson, 2008.
117 Manning, 2003, pp. 4-5.
118 Bouldrey, 2001, pp. 10-11.
119 Worthen, 2009, p. 22.
120 Kidder & Oppenheim, p. 38.

121 *Star Tribune*, 3/14/10, p. A4
122 http://worldinfozone.com/country.php?country=Haiti
123 http://www.politicsdaily.com/2010/01/21/haiti-and-the-pat-robertson-paradox.
124 Smith, 2010.
125 *Star Tribune*, Jan. 20, 2010, p. A8.
126 Can the pope be for life and against condoms? *Star Tribune*, 3/20/09, p. A19.
127 Kalb, 2009.
128 *Star Tribune*, 10/2/08, p. A8.
129 Pitts, 2006.
130 Pollan, 2007.
131 Manning, 2003, p. 7.
132 de Mello, 1978, pp. 114.
133 Peck, 1978, p. 15.
134 Stone, 2008.
135 *Encarta World Dictionary*.
136 http://www.talkingpix.co.uk/ReviewsPassionOfChrist.html.
137 www.ruthlessreviews.com/reviews.cfm/id/488/page/the_passion_of_the_christ.html.
138 GodHatesFags.com.
139 Strickler, 2010b.
140 Wypijewski, 1999, p. 68.
141 Feb. 6, 2010.
142 http://blogs.riverfronttimes.com/dailyrft/2009/04/church_ultimate_fighting_easter.
143 Schneiderman, 2010.
144 http://www.guardian.co.uk.
145 Shepherd, 2010c.
146 Stephens, 2006.
147 Largier, 2007.
148 Dailymail.co.uk, and *Star Tribune*, 12/26/09, p. E9.
149 Metcalf, 2007.
150 http://www.barna.org/FlexPage.aspx?Page=Topic&TopicID=8.

151 Douglas-Klotz, 1990, p. ix.

152 Vowell, 2009.

153 Bryson, 2006.

154 Brown, 2010, p. B7.

155 Quoted in Fowler, 1981, p. 154, but not cited.

156 Keillor, 2010.

157 Peck, 1987., p. 193.

158 Meacham, 2006.

159 Sullivan, 2010.

160 Dias, 2010.

161 Paul Ferrine, 1994, p. 11.

162 Peck, 1987.

163 Stephen, 2006, p. 75.

164 In North Carolina, Lawsuit Is Threatened Over Councilman's Lack of Belief in God. *The New York Times*, 12/13/09, p. 43. no author listed.

165 A cathedral, a gargoyl, a controversy. *Star Tribune*, Sept. 9, 2010, p. A12.

166 Zoll, 2010 & Preacher suspends Qur'an burning, *Star Tribune*, Sept. 10, 2010, pp. A1 & A4.

167 A.A., 1976, pp. 10-11.

168 A.A., 1976, p. 9.

169 A.A., 1976, p. 12.

170 A.A., 1976, 14.

171 A.A., 1976, p. 14.

172 A.A., 1976, 14.

173 Lewis, 1952, p. 35.

174 Peck, 1987, p. 246.

175 Theo, B. Hyslop, (1925). *The Great Abnormals,* p. 4.

176 *San Francisco Chronicle*.

177 Vonnegut, 2007, p. 22.

178 Sherpherd, 2010b.

179 Yaount, 2009.

180 *LA Times*, Oct. 29, 2009.

181 *Strength To Love*, 1963.

182 *Encarta World English Dictionary*, 1999.

183 Farquhar, 2005, p. 190.
184 Farquhar, 2005, p. 191.
185 Farquhar, 2005, p. 193.
186 Stephens, 2006.
187 *Encarta World English Dictionary*, 1999
188 Farquhar, 2005, p. 195.
189 Farquhar, 2005, p. 195.
190 Huxley, 1937.
191 Peck, 1987, p. 235.
192 Marsh, 2006.
193 Marsh, 2006.
194 Marsh, 2006.
195 Marsh, 2006.
196 Marsh, 2006.
197 abcnews.go.com/Blotter/military-year-fix-jesus-rifles/story.
198 Marsh, 2006.
199 Householder & Williams, 2010.
200 Brown, 2007.
201 http://thalesianfools.blogspot.com/2007/07/conscientious-objection-and-christs.html
202 Kopp, 1988, p. 45
203 Kopp, 1988, p. 45.
204 Kopp, 1988, p. 45.
205 Laundervill, 1996.
206 Kramer, 2010.
207 http://www.universalist.org/archives/000434jesus_and_the_woman_at_the_well.html
208 Thompson, 1995.
209 Thompson, 1995.
210 Thompson, 1995, p. 90.
211 Thompson, 1995, p. 89.
212 Thompson, 1995.
213 Stephens, 2006.
214 http://www.whatquote.com/quotes/Pat-Robertson/31211-Feminism-encourages-.htm.

215 Thompson, 1995.
216 Allen, 2004.
217 Accocella, 2006, p. 145.
218 Thompson, 1995.
219 *Time*, 1/25/10
220 http://religious-musings.blogspot.com/2006/11/mary-magdalene_13.html
221 Thompson, 1995.
222 *Encarta World English Dictionary.*
223 http://religious-musings.blogspot.com/2006/11/mary-magdalene_13.html.
224 Thompson, 1995.
225 Porter, 2001.
226 http://www.catholic.org/saints/saint.php?saint_id=83
227 Stephens, 2006.
228 Stephens, 2006.
229 Tabor, 2006.
230 Tabor, 2006.
231 Tabor, 2006.
232 Tabor, 2006.
233 Vets.solesource.com.
234 Kopp, 1988.
235 Bryson, 2006.
236 Goodstein, 2009b.
237 Savage, 2009.
238 Briggs, 2006.
239 washingtonpost.com, Vaccine for Sexually Transmitted Virus Is Urged for Both Sexes. Monday, July 31, 2006; A06.
240 Ramirez, 2007.
241 Bakalar, 2007.
242 http://www.catholic.com/library/Birth_Control.asp
243 Yardley, 2007.
244 Christ's Sexuality. No author listed. Time.com. Posted Friday, Apr. 09, 1965.
245 Christ's Sexuality. No author listed. Time.com. Posted Friday, Apr. 09, 1965.

[246] Lewis, 1952, 102-103.

[247] http://www.pbs.org/wgbh/amex/rockefellers/peopleevents/p_rock_jsr.html.

[248] Tevlin, 2008, p. A10.

[249] Shepherd, 2009.

[250] Jeff Strickler, *Star Tribune*, 1/16/09.

[251] Goodstein, 2009.

[252] Van Biema & Chu, 2006.

[253] http://geocities.com/Heartland/2964/homily-26sunday-c.html.

[254] Bryson, 2006.

[255] Evely, 1967, p. 14.

[256] The wife says $43 million simply won't cut it. *Star Tribune*, 3/19/09 D1 & 7.

[257] Income-distribution by Thomas Piketty and Emmanuel Saez, 2009.

[258] Begley, 2007.

[259] Begley, 2007.

[260] Begley, 2007.

[261] *Gaming Magazine*, http://www.gamingmagazine.com.

[262] Herper, 2004.

[263] University of California Regents, http://ucsfhr.ucsf.edu.

[264] Powerball.com.

[265] Certified Financial Planner Board of Standards, Inc. http://www.cfp-board.org/bulletin.html

[266] Coleman, 2007.

[267] Nettime, http://amsterdam.nettime.org.

[268] Weiner, 2008, p. 114.

[269] Weiner, 2008.

[270] *Time*, July 12, 2010, p. 24

[271] Gibbs, 2009.

[272] *The Conduct Of Life*, 1860.

[273] Stephens, 2006, p. 76.

[274] Bishop, 2004.

[275] Bick, 2005.

276 The Triumph of Capitalism, *Utne Reader*, September/ October 1999.

277 Kasser, Cohn, Kanner, & Ryan, 2007; Schwartz, 2007; Grouzet, et al, 2005.

278 *Encarta World English Dictionary,* 1999.

279 Coleman, 2008.

280 Villano, 2008, pp. 61& 65.

281 http://usforeignpolicy.about.com.

282 The UNICEF Research Center.

283 Jilani, 2010.

284 Jilani, 2010.

285 Lonetree, 2010.

286 McKinney, 2010.

287 Olson, 2010.

288 Pheifer, 2010.

289 *The New York Times Magazine,* 6/13/10.

290 http://usforeignpolicy.about.com.

291 Kristof, 2008.

292 Martinez, 2010.

293 Lipton, 2008.

294 *Star Tribune*, 12/27/08, p.1.

295 Gap between rich and poor widens in U.S. *Pioneer Press,* Sept. 29, p. 8A.

296 PBS.org.

297 Schwartz, 2008, p. 18.

298 Schlosser, 2007.

299 http://www.marketwatch.com/news/story/goldman-sachs-ceo.

300 Schlosser, 2007.

301 http://www.commondreams.org/headlines06/ 1209-01.htm.

302 Kristof, 2010.

303 Shepherd, 2010.

304 Chamberlin, 2009.

305 www.deathpenaltyinfo.org; www.nationmaster.com.

[306] http://www.pbs.org/wgbh/pages/frontline/shows/execution.

[307] http://www.nationmaster.com/graph/cri_exe-crime-executions.

[308] http://www.deathpenaltyinfo.org

[309] Thornburgh, 2010.

[310] http://www.thejusticeproject.org, Texas Death Row Defendant with Sleeping Lawyer Deserves New Trial, Rules Full Fifth Circuit Court, August 14, 2001.

[311] http://www.g20.org/

[312] http://www.news-medical.net/news/20090812/US-health-care-system.

[313] http://www.news-medical.net/news/20090812/US-health-care-system.

[314] Phelps, 2010, p. D3.

[315] Dominguez, 2007.

[316] Star Tribune 6/20/09 E9.

[317] Worthen, 2009, p. 22.

[318] Katz,

[319] www.americanbible.org/absport/news/item.php.

[320] www.americanbible.org/absport/news/item.php

[321] http://www.av1611.org/kjv/kjvhist.html

[322] Stephans, 2006.

[323] http://en.wikipedia.org/wiki/Blue_law.

[324] Spong, 1992, p. 7.

[325] *The Holy Bible,* 1962, Philadelphia: A.J. Holman Company, p. 112.

[326] Nelson, 1983.

[327] Goodstein, 2006.

[328] Nelson, 1983, p. 115.

[329] Nelson, 1983, p. 115

[330] Homosexuality in the Christian Scriptures. The "clobber passages."
http://www.religioustolerance.org/hom_bibc1.htm

[331] Briggs, 2006.

[332] Exodus International (2005). About Us.

333 Gettleman, J. (2010). Americans' Role Seen in Uganda Anti-Gay Push, *The New York Times,* January 3.

334 Rachel Maddow Shuts Down Gay-Cure Advocate, *New York,* December 9, 2009. Richard Cohen: Gay-To-Straight 'Therapist' Spars With Rachel Maddow (video), The Huffington Post, December 9, 2009. The Rachel Maddow Show, Interview with Richard Cohen, December 9, 2009.

335 Kaoma, K. (Winter 09/Spring 10). The U.S. Christian Right and the Attack on Gays in Africa, PublicEye.org.

336 BBC, (2009). Uganda MP urges death for gay sex, October 15.

337 Ankunda, P. (2010). Gays Bill: Uganda is being judged too harshly, Uganda Media Centre, January 11.

338 Schjonberg, M. F. (2009). Archbishop discusses Uganda's proposed anti-homosexuality law in newspaper interview, *Episcopal Life* online. December 14.

339 Right-wing evangelicals challenge Ugandan President over anti-gay bill, *Ekklesia*, November 19, 2009.

340 Kopp, 1988.

341 Kopp, 1988.

342 Kopp, 1988.

343 *Time, 9/29*, 2009, p. 14.

344 Hochschild, 2009.

345 "Christians are more likely to experience divorce than are non-Christians," Barna Research Group, 1999- DEC-21.

346 http://www.usattorneylegalservices.com/divorce-statistics.html.

347 Luscombe, B. (2010). Revoking the Marriage License, *Time,* May 3, p. 64.

348 "Christians are more likely to experience divorce than are non-Christians," Barna Research Group, 1999-DEC-21.

349 Patterson, 2009, pp. 727 & 732.

350 Church Creates Stir With Gay Exorcism, AP- http://news.aol.com/article/gay-exorcism-video.

351 http://www.lovewonout.com/conferences/sessions.cfm #breakout.
352 Forstein, 2001, p. 168.
353 *A.P.A. Fact Sheet on Homosexual and Bisexual Issues*, Drescher, 2001, p. 203.
354 Munsey, 2009, p. 29.
355 Munsey, 2009, p. 30.
356 Birk, 1980.
357 *Time*, 10/26/09, p. 17.
358 *Time*, 10/26/09.
359 *The New York Times*, 12/28/08, p. 8.
360 Tim Craig, May 5, 2009, Washington Post.com.
361 Same-sex couples get married in Washington, D.C., PioneerPress.com, 03/10/2010.
362 See David M. Goldberg's 2003 book, *The Curse of Ham Race and Slavery in Early Judaism, Christianity and Islam*.
363 Phillips, 2008.
364 June 4, 2001 Gallup Poll.
365 Bailey and Pillard, 1991.
366 Bailey and Pillard, 1993
367 Roth, 1989.
368 Segers, 1988.
369 Six views on homosexuality and bisexuality: Brief descriptions of the six belief systems, Ontario Consultants on Religious Tolerance. http://www.religioustolerance.org/hom6beli1.htm.
370 Pinker, 2008.
371 Chandler, 1987.
372 Murray, 2000.
373 Strickler, 2010, p. E2.

CPSIA information can be obtained at www.ICGtesting.com
228284LV00006B/26/P

9 781453 803